Barron's Regents Exams and Answers

Latin Level 3 (Comprehensive Latin)

KENNETH J. LARKIN
Chairman, Foreign Language Departments
Jericho High School and Middle School
Jericho, Long Island, New York

BARRON'S

Barron's Educational Series, Inc.

All inquiries should be addressed to:
Barron's Educational Series, Inc.
250 Wireless Boulevard
Hauppauge, New York 11788

ISBN 0-8120-3345-0

PRINTED IN THE UNITED STATES OF AMERICA

9 8 7 6 5 4 3 2 1

Contents

PREFACE

Forsan et haec ōlim meminisse juvābit.
(Vergil, *Aeneid*, I.203)

This book, organized into two sections, is intended as a practical resource to help students prepare for the Comprehensive Examination in Latin. The first section is a close look at each of the five parts of the examination. The second section contains the last eight Regents Examinations in their entirety, together with an answer sheet and the answer key for each exam.

In the first section, I will present suggestions and caveats to assist the student in each part of the exam. Many practical hints will alert the student as to what to look for and what to avoid. I will emphasize the guiding principle in taking this examination, and, for that matter, in taking any examination. That principle is to let the examination itself help you as much as possible. It won't be as obvious as the answer to the question: "What color was Julius Caesar's white horse?" Nevertheless, the examination itself can be very helpful. I will include many practice passages and questions, and I will guide the student in a step-by-step analysis of each section of the examination.

It is my hope that this book will prove practical and useful. The suggestions for each part are those that I have given to students for the past twenty-five years. I will present them in the same informal, personal manner that I would use in the classroom.

And perhaps, as Aeneas said to his weary comrades, it will prove beneficial and pleasing to remember some of these thoughts in the months and years to come.

Kenneth J. Larkin
Chairman, Foreign Language Departments
Jericho High School and Middle School
Jericho, L.I., N.Y.

Section One

Strategy and Techniques

PART I: Oral Reading (5 credits)

This oral reading test is prepared, administered, and graded by your teacher prior to the administration of the written test. The oral reading activity evaluates your attainment of the following proficiency for speaking at Checkpoint B in the New York State syllabus: "Reads familiar Latin aloud with accurate pronunciation, appropriate phrase grouping, voice inflection, and expression in classroom situations." Your teacher is instructed to use the following scale to determine your grade, *based on consistency with the proficiency statement:*

Performance	Score
Total consistent	5
Mostly consistent	4–3
Minimally consistent	2–1
Unsatisfactory	0

Make use of every opportunity to practice reading Latin aloud, both in the classroom and at home. Be as consistent as Latin is consistent in the pronunciation of the long and short vowels, especially **a** and **e**. The case of a first declension word, e.g. *nauta*, is nominative singular if the -a is short or ablative singular if the -a is long. Be careful in pronouncing infinitives of second conjugation verbs (e.g. **mo-NE-re**) where the 1st -e is long and the infinitives of third conjugation verbs (e.g. **MIT-te-re**, **CA-pe-re**) where the 1st -e is short. If you practice correct pronunciation, it will help you to keep such verbs in their proper conjugations. Be consistent in the proper pronunciation of **c**, **g**, **v**, **ch**, **th**, **ti** and the diphthongs **ae**, **au**, and **oe**. And finally, review the rules for correctly accenting Latin words. Your teacher will wince upon hearing **im-PE-ra-tor** as much as you would upon hearing **in-FOR-ma-tion**.

PART II: Dictation (5 credits)

Your teacher will read aloud a short passage in Latin. Listen carefully to this first reading. Then your teacher will read the passage in short phrases with a pause after each phrase. After each pause, write, in Latin, the phrase read by your teacher. Do not write a translation of the passage. There will be no penalty for improper use of macrons (i.e., a long mark over a vowel) or capitalization. After you have completed writing the passage in Latin, your teacher will read the entire passage one more time so that you may check your work. Your teacher will check 10 specific words and will award 1/2 credit for each correctly spelled word.

1

Remember two basic rules about Latin words. First, there are no silent syllables in Latin, and second, every Latin word will have as many syllables as there are vowels or diphthongs in the word. Since dictation is simply writing what you hear, the more practice you do in reading Latin aloud will pay dividends in the writing of Latin.

PART IIIA: Latin to English Translation

My first suggestion for all the parts of the examination is to read the directions carefully. The directions for Part IIIA state that you do not have to write a translation of the passage. However, I suggest that you do write a rough translation. Follow this procedure: as you translate each sentence, keep an eye on the questions asked about the underlined sentences or sentence parts. You can get a great deal of vocabulary assistance from the questions themselves.

When you begin to answer each question, focus on the word or expression that you are most certain about and use that to eliminate one, perhaps two, and sometimes even three of the choices given. In the margin of the test, write the numbers you have eliminated. Next focus on another word or expression that you feel fairly certain about. Then, as you did above, use that to eliminate one or more of the choices. Does your first choice of the best translation still stand up? Sometimes you can zero in on a third word or expression that can provide a triple-check. This procedure might seem time-consuming to you but be assured that you will have plenty of time to complete the examination in a careful manner. The whole point here in Part One is not to be satisfied with your first choice until you have put it to further double- and even triple-checking.

Let's put these suggestions into practice. Below is Part I of the 1974 Regents Examination, similar in form and difficulty to Part IIIA of the more recent examinations. Read the directions, follow the procedure I recommended, and see how well you do. Circle the number of the selection you think is the best translation. Remember, don't be satisfied with your first choice until you have done further checking. When you are finished, compare your answers with the answer key. I will analyze some of the questions and indicate how I arrived at the correct answer.

Practice Exercise

DIRECTIONS (1–15): *Do* not *write a translation of the following passages; read them through carefully several times to ascertain their meaning. Then in the spaces provided on the separate answer sheet, write the* number *of the alternative that best translates each of the underlined expressions* as it is used in the passage.   [15]

Duōs annōs Persēs, rēx Macedoniae, cum cōnsulibus tam variā
fortūnā pugnāverat ut plērumque superior esset magnamque partem
Graeciae ad sē perdūceret. Etiam Rhodiī, fīdissimī anteā Rōmānīs.
fortūnam rēgis spectantēs, nunc dubiā fidē vīsī sunt.

Tum senātus populusque Rōmānus creāvit cōnsulem L. Aemilium
Paulum, virum dignum summā laude propter virtūtem, quī et praetor
et cōnsul triumphāverat. Is Persam rēgem ingentī proeliō in
Macedoniā fugāvit et, castrīs cōpiīsque eius dēlētīs, destitūtum omnī
spē coēgit ē Macedoniā profugere. Patriā relictā. rēx fugam in īnsulā
Samothrāciā petīvit, crēdēns sē religiōnī templī supplicem. Ad eum
Cn. Octāvius praetor, quī classī praeerat, pervēnit et ratiōne magis
quam vī persuāsit ut sē Rōmānōrum fideī committeret. Ita Paulus,
maximum nōbilissimumque rēgem in triumphō dūcendō, multā
pecūniā aerāriō collātā, omnēs priōrēs victōrēs amplitūdine triumphī
vīcit..

—Paterculus, *Historiae Rōmānae* I, 9-10 (adapted)

1 cum cōnsulibus tam variā fortūnā pugnāverat
   1 had struggled differently with the consuls and with fortune
   2 when the consuls fought with him with such varied fortune
   3 fought for his fortune with a varied strategy
   4 had battled with the consuls with such varying fortune

2 magnamque partem Graeciae ad sē perdūceret
   1 and won a large portion of Greece over to his side
   2 conquered a large part of Greece by himself
   3 the Greeks brought him a greater share
   4 a large part surrendered to him in Greece

3 Etiam Rhodiī, fidissimī anteā Rōmānīs
   1 The Rhodians, too, were very loyal after the Romans came
   2 Even the Rhodians, formerly most loyal supporters of the Romans
   3 Also the Romans, in addition to the faithful Rhodians
   4 The Romans still were loyal to the Rhodians as in the past

4 Tum senātus populusque Rōmānus creāvit cōnsulem L.
  Aemilium Paulum
   1 At the same time the Roman senate honored the consul Lucius
     Aemilius Paulus
   2 When the consul Lucius Aemilius Paulus put his trust in the senate
     of the Roman people
   3 Then the senate and Roman people elected as consul Lucius
     Aemilius Paulus
   4 At that time the senate and Roman people created a plan for
     Lucius Aemilius Paulus

5 virum dignum summā laude propter virtūtem
   1 a man of dignity and courage, praised by all
   2 a man whose bravery was often praised to the skies
   3 an honorable man as well as courageous
   4 a man deserving of highest praise because of his valor

6 quī et praetor et cōnsul triumphāverat
   1 who had won victories both as praetor and as consul
   2 who had wanted to triumph over the praetor and consul alike
   3 to win a triumphant victory as praetor and consul
   4 over whom both the praetor and consul had been victorious

7 Is Persam rēgem ingentī proeliō in Macedoniā fugāvit
   1 This same Perses drove the king from Macedonia by waging war on
     him
   2 He put King Perses to flight in a tremendous battle in Macedonia
   3 This Persian king ran from a big battle into Macedonia
   4 He avoided a mighty battle with Perses, king of Macedonia

8 castrīs cōpiīsque eius dēlētīs
   1 restoring his depleted camp and forces
   2 with his camp and troops destroyed
   3 since his camp and troops were scattered
   4 having left his camp and supplies

9   destitūtum omnī spē coēgit ē Macedoniā profugere
   1   hopefully sought refuge in Macedonia
   2   drove him hopelessly to Macedonia in headlong flight
   3   gathered together the hopeless refugees from Macedonia
   4   forced him devoid of all hope to flee from Macedonia

10 Patriā relictā
   1   Deserted by his own people
   2   While remaining in his fatherland
   3   Upon abandoning his homeland
   4   With the resources left to him by his father

11 rēx fugam in īnsulā Samothrāciā petīvit
   1   the king sought refuge on the island of Samothrace
   2   the king in his flight attacked the island of Samothrace
   3   the king inquired who had fled to the island of Samothrace
   4   the king begged Samothrace to flee from the island

12 crēdēns sē religiōnī templī supplicem
   1   hoping that he would be protected by his religious beliefs
   2   confident that he would inflict punishment on the worshippers in the temple
   3   entrusting himself as a suppliant to the sanctity of the temple
   4   having little confidence in the temple as a place of worship

13 ratiōne magis quam vī persuāsit
   1   urged him to be more forceful in his reasoning
   2   persuaded him by reason rather than by force
   3   prevailed upon him to plan for even greater violence
   4   persuaded him quite easily by violent measures

14 ut sē Rōmānōrum fideī committeret
   1   as long as he trusted the loyalty of the Romans
   2   to entrust himself to the good faith of the Romans
   3   to join battle confidently with the Romans
   4   while pledging his loyalty to Rome

15 omnēs priōrēs victōrēs amplitūdine triumphī vīcit
   1   surpassed all previous conquerors in the splendor of his triumph
   2   was overcome by all the earlier contestants in great battles
   3   by his generosity overcame all the foremost champions
   4   won all his later victories with sufficient strategies

Procedure

This is a passage of moderate difficulty. Before looking at the answer key, let's examine some of the questions and practice the procedures that I recommended to you. In question 1, I focused on the word *pugnaverat*. Notice the pluperfect tense of that verb, which will be translated into English with the helping verb "had." If you know that, you can eliminate the second and third choices. Does the phrase *cum consulibus* help you in deciding between choices 1 and 4? The answer is no, because both choices correctly translate the phrase. It is time for a double check. What about the word *tam*? It can be translated by "so" or "such." If you know that, you can eliminate choice 1. Now for a triple check. Does the remaining choice, number 4, account for the word *varia*, which you can guess means "varying"? Yes, it does. Choice 4 must be the correct answer.

This procedure, at first sight, looks complicated and time-consuming. It really isn't, and as you practice it, it will become easier, quicker, and more mechanical. Go to question 3. The word *fidissimi* is a superlative, translated into English by "most" or "very." Knowing that enables you to throw out of consideration choices 3 and 4. Furthermore, since *antea* must be related to *ante*, "before," and not *post* you can eliminate choice 1 because of the word "after."

Sometimes one word can eliminate three of the choices immediately. Look at question 5. I am sure that you know the meaning of the common preposition *propter*, "on account of" or "because of." Knowing that, you are left with the correct translation found in choice 4.

The correct understanding of a common prepositional phrase can be the clue to focus upon. Look at question 7 and the phrase *in Macedoniā*. How many times have you heard that the preposition *in* followed by a word in the ablative case indicates the concept of "place where"? Does "from Macedonia" (choice 1) or "into Macedonia" (choice 3) or "of Macedonia" (choice 4) indicate the "place where" something is happening? Obviously not. Throw out choices 1, 3, and 4; number 2 must be the correct answer.

Sometimes the first word you focus upon does not help you at all. For example, the word *rex* in question 11 is in the nominative case and must be the subject of the sentence. But all four choices have "the king" as the subject. Look for something else that you are certain about. Look at the prepositional phrase *in insulā*, which must mean "on the island." On the basis of that alone, you eliminate choices 2, 3, and 4.

In question 14, *Romanorum* should clearly stand out as a genitive plural, probably expressing the concept of possession. That eliminates choices 3 and 4. The word *ut* with the verb *committeret* in the subjunctive mood frequently is a verbal construction expressing the concept of purpose.

English commonly expresses the idea of purpose by an infinitive phrase, as seen in choice 2, the correct choice.

Each translation could be analyzed in a similar manner. I think, however, that you are now familiar with the process that can insure a very good performance in Part IIIA:

- Take the time to write a rough translation of the passage.
- As you translate each sentence, get vocabulary assistance by looking below at the translations given for all underlined segments.
- When deciding on the best translation for each question, focus on a particular word or phrase and eliminate one or more of the choices given.
- Double-check with another word or phrase.
- If possible, triple-check.
- Don't worry, you will have plenty of time.

Answer Key

1. 4	4. 3	7. 2	10. 3	13. 2
2. 1	5. 4	8. 2	11. 1	14. 2
3. 2	6. 1	9. 4	12. 3	15. 1

PART IIIB: Comprehension (Questions in English)

Part IIIB of the examination requires you to comprehend the general meaning of a passage in Latin in order to answer, in English, questions based upon it. The questions are in English. The special instructions given to those who rate the answers are as follows: the answers do not have to be complete sentences—a phrase or a word may be sufficient for a completely correct answer; errors in English are not to be penalized; and finally, not all of the acceptable answers have been included in the answer key provided to the raters. With that in mind, let's go on to the procedure I would recommend for this part.

The directions again say not to write a translation of the passage. As in Part IIIA, I suggest that you do write a rought translation of the passage. Before translating, however, I want you to use your imagination. Look at the ten English questions that are asked about the passage. From the information given in the questions, try to reconstruct in English what the passage is all about. Many times, a very accurate and surprisingly complete understanding of the passage can be gained before you translate one sentence of the selection.

Base your answer solely upon the information given in the passage. Sometimes a name, or a place, or an event might be mentioned in the passage that you know about from other sources. Do not include that knowledge in your answer unless it was specially mentioned in the passage. And remember, a word or a phrase can sometimes be sufficient for a completely correct answer. Do not give more information than the question calls for.

Let's practice the recommended procedure on Part II of the 1975 "A" Regents Examination. (In two years, 1975 and 1978, two examinations were offered; these examinations are referred to as "A" or "B".)

Practice Exercise

DIRECTIONS (**16–25**): *Do not write a translation of the passage below; read it through carefully several times to ascertain its meaning. Then in the spaces provided on the separate answer sheet, write in English your answer to each question.* [10]

> Dum multī coniūratī perterritī dubitant, C. Cornēlius eques Rōmānus auxilium suum pollicitus, et cum eō L. Varguntēius senātor cōnstituērunt eā nocte cum armātīs hominibus īre quāsi ad Cicerōnem salūtandum ac subitō eum imparātum domī suae interficere. Curius ubi intellegit quantum perīculum cōnsulī impendeat, per Fulviam statim Cicerōnī dolum quī parābātur ēnūntiat. Ita illī iānuā prohibitī tantum maleficium frustrā suscēperant.
>
> —Sallustius, *Dē Catilīnae Coniūrātiōne*, XXVIII
> (adapted)

16 Before the plot, why did the conspirators hesitate?

17 Who is *one* of the would-be assassins?

18 To what class of society did C. Cornelius belong?

19 What did C. Cornelius offer?

20 What office did L. Vargunteius hold?

21 When was the plot drawn up?

22 Where did the conspirators expect to find Cicero?

23 What was the ultimate purpose of the plot?

24 How did Curius divulge the plot to Cicero?

25 What was *one* result of Cicero's forehand knowledge?

Procedure

Read carefully the ten English questions about this passage adapted from the description of the conspiracy of Catiline by the Roman author Sallust. Remember my warning: base your answer on the information given in the passage, not on any prior knowledge from other sources. You may be very familiar with the conspiracy of Catiline, and you may have information about the people whose names appear in the questions, but do not use any of that information unless it is specifically included in the passage given. With that caveat in mind, use your imagination.

How much of the selection from Sallust can you ascertain by reading the questions carefully? I believe you can learn a lot that will prove to be a great help in writing your rough translation of the passage. Questions 16, 21, 23, 24 mention the word "plot," which implies something sinister. In question 17 the word "assassins" is used, implying the intention of murder. The names of Cornelius and Vargunteius are given in questions 18, 19, and 20. Question 18 asks what class of society Cornelius belongs to: was he a member of the Optimates, or the Equites, or the Plebs? Question 20 asks what office Vargunteius held: was he a consul, a senator, a tribune or some other office that you are familiar with? Question 22 asks where the conspirators could expect to find Cicero, implying that the conspiracy or plot is aimed at Cicero. Question 23 asks about the ultimate purpose of the plot against Cicero; remember that the word "assassins" indicates that someone is planning murder. Question 24 mentions that a person named Curius divulged the plot to Cicero, which implies that Cicero knew about the plot ahead of time and probably would take steps to frustrate the planned actions against himself. A few other details are asked for: when was the plot drawn up? in the morning? at night? in the winter?

With all that information given to you in the questions, I am confident that you can write a rather accurate translation of the passage. And I am equally confident that you will "discover" that Cornelius and Vargunteius tried to assassinate Cicero but failed because he found out about the plot ahead of time from Curius. It makes translating so much easier when you know ahead of time what the story is all about.

After you have written your rough translation and have answered the ten questions, compare your answers with the ones I will give. I will include as many possible answers as possible and also indicate the precise source of the information.

Answer Key and Analysis

16. because of fear; they were afraid; because they were terrified
    In line 1, the word *peterriti* gives the reason why the conspirators (*coniurati*) were hesitating (*dubitant*).

17. either C. Cornelius or L. Vargunteius
    Only one would-be assassin is asked for, so give only one. Remember my caution: give only what they ask for. Do not attempt from prior knowledge to explain what the C. (*Gaius*) or the L. (*Lucius*) stand for. It is here that some students lose credit—they make errors regarding information that was not even required.

18. the Equities; the Equestrian Order; the Knights; a Knight
    In line 1, the word *eques* (*Romanus*) is put in apposition to the name C. Cornelius.

19. help; aid
    In line 1, Sallust says that Cornelius promised (*pollicitus*) his help or aid (*auxilium suum*).

20. a senator
    In line 2, the word *senator* is put in apposition to the name of L. Vargunteius.

21. in the nightime; at night; that night
    Line 2 mentions that they decided (*constituerunt*) that night (*ea nocte*) to go with armed men.

22. at home, in his own home
    At the end of line 3, the words *domi suae* indicate where the would-be assassins expected to find Cicero (*eum*) unprepared (*imparatum*) for the murder attempt.

23. the death of Cicero; to kill Cicero
    In line 4, the ultimate purpose of the plot is found in the word *interficere*, meaning "to kill."

24. through Fulvia; by telling Fulvia, who in turn told Cicero
    In lines 4 and 5, Sallust tells us that Curius, when he understood (*ubi intellegit*) how much danger the consul was in, immediately announced (*statim...enuntiat*) through Fulvia (*per Fulviam*) the planned deception (*dolum*) to Cicero (*Ciceroni*).

25. he stopped the conspirators at the door; he didn't let the conspirators into his house; he frustrated the assassination attempt, Cicero saved his life.
    Several acceptable answers are possible for this question. The key words are found in line 5, *ianuā prohibiti*, which tell us that because of Cicero's forehand knowledge, he was able to keep them from entering his home.

PART IIIC: Comprehension (Questions in Latin)

For many students, Part IIIC is the most difficult part of the examination because the passage, the questions based upon it, and the answer choices are all in Latin. I will give you five sample passages to practice with and the answer key for each.

The best suggestion I can give you in regard to this part of the examination is to repeat the guiding principle I gave you in the introduction: get as much help as you can from the examination itself. How can the examination help you in this section? By the relative simplicity of the Latin used in the questions and the choices given in the answers. For that reason, I suggest that you first translate the questions about each passage and then attempt a rough translation of the selection itself.

These are directions for Part IIIC:

DIRECTIONS: *Read the following passages carefully, but do not write a translation. Below each passage there are several questions or incomplete statements. For each, select the alternative that best answers the question or completes the statement* on the basis of the information given in the passage, *and write its* number *in the space provided on the separate answer sheet.*

Practice Exercise 1

The first practice selection was used in the 1977 Regents Examination. It is taken from *Ab Urbe Conditā* of the famous Roman historian Livy.

Cum cēterī, circumvenientēs victōrem Hannibalem, *congrātulārentur* persuadērentque, ut tantō bellō cōnfectō, daret quiētem *fessīs* mīlitibus illō diē nocteque sequente, Maharbal, praefectus equitum, inquit, "Immō, ut sciās quid actum sit hāc pugnā, quīntō diē victor in Capitōliō eris. Antecēdam Rōman cum equite. Sequere mē." Hannibal respondit sē Maharbalis cōnsilium laudāre sed tempus ad cōnsiderandum cōnsilium necesse esse. Maharbal inquit, "Hannibal, scīs quō modo vincās sed nēscīs quō modo utāris victōriā." Mora eius diēī firmiter crēditur fuisse salūtī urbī Rōmae atque imperiō.

—Livius, *Ab Urbe Conditā*, XXII, 51
(adapted)

congrātulārentur—deponent verb
fessīs—from *fessus, a, um,* tired

26 Proeliō factō, multī Hannibalem hortātī sunt
  1 ut quiescerent unā diē nocteque
  2 ut statim iter facerent
  3 nē mīlitibus praemia dōnāret
  4 nē hostēs circumdārent

27 Quis fuit Maharbal?
  1 Nāvibus praefuit.
  2 Centuriō fuit.
  3 Equitātum dūxit.
  4 Hostis Hannibalis fuit.

28 Sī Maharbalem audīvisset, quō tempore Hannibal Rōmae fuisset?
  1 duōbus diēbus
  2 quattuor mēnsibus
  3 quīnque diēbus
  4 sex hōrīs

29 Hannibal cōnsilium Maharbalis accept cum
  1 īrā
  2 gaudiō
  3 timōre
  4 laude

30 Salūs Rōmae facta est
  1 victōriā Carthāginiēnsium
  2 morā Hannibalis
  3 praesidiō Maharbalis
  4 potestāte cōpiārum Rōmānārum

Procedure

I think you would agree that the Latin contained in the statements and/or questions and in the various choices is basic both in structure and vocabulary. The five statements or questions can be translated:

26. After the battle had been ended, many urged Hannibal (that …)
27. Who was Maharbal?
28. If he had listened to Maharbal, at what time would Hannibal have been in Rome?
29. Hannibal accepted the advice of Maharbal with (…)
30. The safety of Rome was made (caused) (…)

Before you translate this passage, make your choices, and check them with the answer key, let me reinforce my guiding principle. In question 26, did you pay attention to the subjunctive forms of the verbs following *ut* (positive) and *ne* (negative)? Did you notice the use of the dative case (*militibus*) with a verb of "giving" (*donaret*)? In question 27, did you remember that the dative case (*navibus*) is used with verbs such as *praefuit*? Did you mentally review the locative case (*Romae*) in question 28? I could refer to other words and phrases; but my purpose is to remind you to use the test itself to obtain information that can help you in other sections of the examination, specifically, as you will see later, for Part IVA.

Practice Exercise 2

The next passage, from the *Noctēs Atticae* of Gellius, is taken from the 1978 "A" Regents Examination.

Hermippus scrīpsit Dēmosthenem, adulēscentem, in Acadēmiam venīre et Platōnem audīre velle. "Atque Dēmosthenēs," Hermippus inquit, "domō ēgressus, ut eius *mōs* erat, cum ad Platōnem prōcēderet et populōs concurrentēs vidēret, interrogāvit eius reī causam cognōscitque eōs currere ut Callistratum audiant." Hic Callistratus ōrātor Athēnīs fuit. "Dēmosthenēs vēnit," Hermippus inquit, "atque ita verbīs Callistratī mōtus et captus est ut Callistratum iam inde sequī coeperit et Acadēmiam Platōnemque relīquerit."
—A. Gellius, *Noctēs Atticae*, III. 13
(adapted)

mōs, mōris—custom

26 Fābula dē Dēmosthene nārrātur
    1 ā scrīptōre, Hermippō
    2 ab ōrātōre, Platōne
    3 ā scrīptōre, Vergiliō
    4 ab ōrātōre, Socrate

27 Dēmosthenēs ad Acadēmiam ībat ut
    1 Platōnem audīret
    2 Hermippum vidēret
    3 cum Platōne loquerētur
    4 ōrātiōnem faceret

28 Multī conveniunt ut
    1 domum Dēmosthenis videant
    2 Platōnem abdūcant
    3 ōrātōrēs laudent
    4 Callistratum audiant

29 Ōrātiō Callistratī Dēmosthenem dēlectat quod
   1 verba eum movent
   2 Callistratus Rōmānus erat
   3 verba aliēna erant
   4 Callistratus eum terret

30 Ōrātiōne Callistratī audītā, Dēmosthenēs
   1 domum revēnit
   2 Platōnem relīquit
   3 dīcere coepit
   4 eum interrogāvit

31 Quis est discipulus in hāc fabulā?
   1 Hermippus
   2 Dēmosthenēs
   3 Platō
   4 Callistratus

Procedure

The six statements or questions about this passage are:

26. A story is being told about Demosthenes (by…)
27. Demosthenes was going to the Academy to (…)
28. Many (people) are coming together to (…)
29. The oration of Callistratus delights Demosthenes because (…)
30. The oration of Callistratus having been heard, Demosthenes (…)
31. Who is the student in this story?

With that information in mind, translate the brief passage and then make your choice for each of the six statements or questions. Then check your choices with the answer key that follows the five practice exercises.

Practice Exercise 3

The third selection is also from the 1978 "A" Examination, and again is a passage from Gellius.

Quīntus Ennius dīcēbat sē habēre tria corda, quod loquī posset linguam Graecam et *Oscam* et Latīnam. Mithridātēs, autem, rēx Pontī, quī ā Cn. Pompeiō in bellō superātus est, scīvit quīnque et vignitī linguās gentium quās sub potestāte habuit, et numquam per interpretem locūtus est.

—A. Gellius, *Noctēs Atticae*, XVII. 17
(adapted)

Oscam—from *Osca, Oscan*, an ancient Italic dialect

32 Ennius vērē habuit
   1 servōs Graecōs
   2 duās linguās
   3 scientiam trium linguārum
   4 magnum imperium

33 Quid Pompeius ēgit?
   1 Mithridātem vīcit.
   2 Sapientiam mōnstrāvit.
   3 Linguam Graecam locūtus est.
   4 Cōpiās cōēgit.

34 Natiōnibus sub imperiō habitīs. Mithridātēs
   1 celeriter discessit
   2 male rēxit
   3 illōs populōs amāvit
   4 multās linguās scīvit

35 Nōn erat necesse Mithridātem habēre hominem quī
   1 aliēnīs loquerētur
   2 barbarōs sequerētur
   3 pācem peteret
   4 mīlitibus imperāret

Procedure

The four statements or questions about this passage are:

32. Ennius truly had (…)
33. What did Pompeius do?
34. Nations having been placed under his control, Mithridates (…)
35. It was not necessary for Mithridates to have a man who (…)

Use this information as an outline for your rough translation. Then see how you did after making your choices and checking them with the answer key.

Practice Exercise 4

The next selection is also from the *Noctes Atticae* of Gellius and was used in the 1978 "B" Regents Examination.

Prōcōnsul Crētae prōvinciae et eius pater Athēnās vēnerat ut philosophum, Taurum, visitarent et ex eō cognōscerent.

Taurus, discipulīs dīmissīs, in tablīnō sedēbat. Prōcōnsul prōvinciae et eius pater intrāvērunt; Taurus placidē *surrēxit* et post mūtuam salūtātiōnem resēdit. Una sella erat proxima. Haec sella prope Taurum posita est, dum alia afferēbātur. Taurus invītat patrem prōcōnsulis ut sedēret. Pater respondet: "Sedeat hic quī populī Rōmānī magistrātus est."

—A. Gellius, *Noctēs Atticae* II, 2
(adapted)

surrēxit—from *surgō*, stand up

26 Prōcōnsul Athēnās vēnit ut
   1 dē philosophō, Taurō, disceret
   2 pecūniam Taurō daret
   3 domī fratris manēret
   4 populōs Crētae dēfenderet

27 Quō tempore Taurus resēdit?
   1 prōcōnsule dīmissō
   2 patre pulsātō
   3 ianuā apertā
   4 salūtātiōnibus datīs

28 Pater prōcōnsulis dīcit suum fīlium dēbēre
   1 in sellā sedēre
   2 domum īre
   3 Taurum laudāre
   4 Rōmānōs amāre

29 Pater fīlium habet quī erat
   1 philosophus
   2 ōrātor
   3 mercātor
   4 magistrātus

Procedure

These four statements or questions are:

26. The Proconsul came to Athens to (...)
27. At what time did Taurus sit down again?
28. The father of the proconsul says that his own son ought (to...)
29. The father has a son who was (...)

Practice Exercise 5

The final selection, again from Gellius, was used in the 1978 "B" Regents Examination.

Bassus fuit vir genere et locō humilī; ā Strabōne, patre Pompeī Magnī, captus est cum suā mātre in Sociālī Bellō. Rōmānī contrā sociōs in Italiā pugnābant. Strabōne victōre, infans Bassus ā mātre ante currum imperātōris cum cēterīs captīvīs in triumphō portātus est.

Posteā, Bassus, adulēscēns, carrōs animāliaque *vēndidit* magistrātibus quī iter ad prōvinciās faciēbant. Apud hōs magistrātūs fuit C. Caesar quōcum Bassus in Galliam prōfectus est. In Galliā tam dīligenter labōrāvit et posteā in bellō cīvīlī tantam virtūtem dēmōnstrāvit ut nōn modo in amīcītiam Caesaris sed etiam in summum honōrem pervenīret. Mox tribūnus plēbis atque deinde praetor factus est. Tandem pontifex maximus ac cōnsul nōminātus est.

Tempore mortis Bassī populī Rōmānī *fūnus* pūblicum eī dedērunt.

—A. Gellius, *Noctēs Atticae*, XV, 4 (adapted)

cēndidit—from *vēndō*, sell
fūnus—funeral

30 Bassus nātus est
   1 in familiā nōn nōtā
   2 ē parente doctō
   3 ex senatōribus
   4 ex equitibus

31 Bassus ā Strabōne captīvus factur est, cum
   1 Bassus ex Italiā excēderet
   2 Pompeius mātrem eius in mātrimōnium dūceret
   3 Strabo, imperātor, proelium āmitteret
   4 Rōmānī in Sociālī Bellō pugnārent

32 Bassus infans cum alūs captīvīs ferēbātur, dum
   1 servus currum parat
   2 imperātor pugnat
   3 Strabo triumphat
   4 māter fugit

33 Quid prīmum fēcit Bassus adulēscēns?
   1 Cōnsul factur est.
   2 Contrā Caesarem pugnāvit.
   3 Agricola fuit.
   4 Mercātor animālium fuit.

34 Bassus tantam fortitūdinem mōnstrāvit ut
   1 amīcus Caesaris fieret
   2 in proeliō graviter vulnerātus esset
   3 dictātor fieret
   4 poenam magnā cum audāciā sustinēret

35 Post mortem Bassī, quid cīvēs Rōmānī ēgērunt?
   1 Honōrem eī mōnstrāvērunt.
   2 Templum prō eō nōmināvērunt.
   3 Arma cēpērunt.
   4 Inimīcōs Bassī interfēcērunt.

Procedure

The six statements or questions are:

30. Bassus was born (…)
31. Bassus was made a captive by Strabo when (…)
32. Bassus as an infant was being carried with other captives while (…)
33. What did Bassus first do as a young man?
34. Bassus demonstrated such great courage that (…)
35. After the death of Bassus, what did the Roman citizens do?

Exercise 1	Exercise 2	Exercise 3	Exercise 4	Exercise 5
26. 1	26. 1	32. 3	26. 1	30. 1
27. 3	27. 1	33. 1	27. 4	31. 4
28. 3	28. 4	34. 4	28. 1	32. 3
29. 4	29. 1	35. 1	29. 4	33. 4
30. 2	30. 2			34. 1
	31. 2			35. 1

PART IIID: Latin Potpourri

I refer to Part IIID of the Regents Examination as a potpourri because it has a little bit of many things: reading comprehension, grammar, vocabulary, word derivation, and so forth. It also happens to be the first part of the examination that allows you a choice; you answer ten of the twelve questions asked. Therefore, my first suggestion to you is to read the following directions carefully:

Read the following passage carefully, but do not write a translation. Below the passage you will find several questions or incomplete statements. Each question or statement is followed by four suggested answers numbered 1 through 4. Choose *ten* of these questions or statements, and in the space provided on the separate answer sheet, write the *number* of the word or expression that best answers the question or completes the statement *on the basis of what is stated or implied in the passage.*

The raters are instructed to consider only the required number of answers, in the order in which they appear on the student's answer paper. For example, if you were to answer eleven or twelve questions from this part, the teacher marking the test would rate only the first ten answers.

Again I suggest that you do work out a translation of the passage while keeping a close eye on the questions being asked. Although this part contains questions that can be answered with no reference to the passage, there are enough other questions to warrant a good understanding of the selection.

Practice Exercise 1

Let me illustrate what I mean about some questions that can be answered without seeing the passage itself. Answer the following fifteen questions that have appeared on previous exams.

1. Which English word is a derivative of *undīs*?
   1 undermine   3 undulate
   2 underwear   4 understand

2. A Latin word meaning the same as *celebrātus* is
   1 *doctus*   3 *obscūrus*
   2 *instrūctus*   4 *clārus*

3. The initial *T* stands for the Latin name
   1 Titus   3 Tibullus
   2 Tullius   4 Tiberius

4. Which English word is a derivative of *cupiēns*?
   1 cupidity   3 culprit
   2 cupola   4 cuspid

5. The imperative plural of *ferre* is
   1 *ferte*   3 *fertis*
   2 *fero*   4 *fers*

6. Which is a derivative of *cor*?
   1 correspond   3 cordial
   2 corporal   4 correct

7. A Latin word meaning the same as *quoque* is
   1 *etiam*   3 *statim*
   2 *sed*   4 *enim*

8. The Latin expression *Patrēs cōnscrīptī* means
   1 senators   3 kings
   2 ambassadors   4 enemies

9. The same rhetorical device is represented in *levāre lūctum, tū tālī*
   and *cōnsulārem, clārum*. It is called
   1 antithesis   3 anaphora
   2 alliteration   4 chiasmus

10. A Latin word meaning the opposite of *apertīs* is
    1 *clausīs*   3 *lātīs*
    2 *vīsīs*   4 *clāmātīs*

11. Which English word is a derivative of *cōnscrīpsērunt*?
    1 scribble   3 scrutiny
    2 consecration   4 contraction

12. The genitive plural of *virum* is
    1 *vīrium*   3 *virōrum*
    2 *vīribus*   4 *virī*

13. The Latin expression *negāre nōn* is an example of the rhetorical figure
    1 anaphora   3 litotes
    2 chiasmus   4 metaphor

14. A Latin word meaning the same as *locūtī sunt* is
    1 *dūxērunt*   3 *arbitrātī sunt*
    2 *lēgērunt*   4 *dīxērunt*

15. *Minimō* is a superlative form of
1 *parvus*
2 *magnus*
3 *multus*
4 *bonus*

Answer Key

1. 3	4. 1	7. 1	10. 1	13. 3
2. 4	5. 1	8. 1	11. 1	14. 4
3. 1	6. 3	9. 2	12. 3	15. 1

Analysis

Each one of the above questions could be answered without actually seeing lines referred to in the passage. A basic knowledge of Latin would be sufficient.

However, in an actual examination there are enough questions that require understanding of the passage to justify the time spent on writing a rough translation of the selection. Sometimes a question may be asked concerning the general tone of the entire passage or a good title for the selection. Such questions require you to know what the passage is actually saying.

Let's practice! Below is Part V of the 1977 Examination. Follow my suggestions, make your choices, and check your answers with the answer key that follows. Notice that the selection is from a letter of Cicero to his lifelong friend, Attius. Any first-person verb ending will refer to Cicero; any second-person ending will refer to Atticus.

Practice Exercise 2

Cicerō Atticō Sal.
Terentia tibi et saepe et maximās agit grātiās. Id est mihi grātissimum. Ego vīvō miserrimus et maximō dolōre cōnficior. Ad tē quid scrībam, nēsciō. Sī enim es Rōmae, iam mē *assequī* nōn potes, sīn es in viā, cum mē assecūtus eris, *cōram* agēmus quae erunt agenda. Tantum tē ōrō,
5 ut, quoniam mē ipsum semper amāstī, nunc, eōdem amōre sīs; ego enim īdem sum. Inimīcī meī mea mihi *adēmērunt* nōn mē ipsum *adēmērunt*. Cūrā ut valeās. Data a.d. IV Idūs Aprīlis.

—Cicerō, *Ad Atticum*, III, 5
(adapted)

assequī—from *assequor*, reach
cōram—face to face
adēmērunt—from *adimō*, to take away

46. Terentia, the person mentioned in line 1 of Cicero's letter, is Cicero's
    1 wife   3 daughter
    2 sister   4 mother

47. The Latin word *maximās* (line 1) is a superlative form of the Latin
    adjective
    1 *multus*   3 *magnus*
    2 *marīnus*   4 *bonus*

48. The Latin word *ego* (line 2) refers to
    1 Terentia   3 Cicero
    2 Atticus   4 an unidentified person

49. A Latin word meaning the opposite of *miserrimus* (line 2) is
    1 *pulcherrimus*   3 *gravissimus*
    2 *carissimus*   4 *laetissimus*

50. The Latin clause *quae erunt agenda* (line 4) is best translated as
    1 which must be done
    2 that have been discussed
    3 what they had planned
    4 who may finish

51. A Latin word meaning the same as *ōrō* (line 4) is
    1 *eō*   3 *ostendō*
    2 *petō*   4 *laudō*

52. *Mihi* (line 6) is best translated as
    1 with me
    2 because of me
    3 from me
    4 by me

53. The figure of speech represented in *meī mea mihi…mē* (line 6) is called
    1 personification   3 simile
    2 alliteration   4 metaphor

54. Which English word is not related by derivation to any of the Latin
    words (*Ego…cōnficior.*) in the third sentence?
    1 revive   3 condolence
    2 misery   4 fidelity

55. What expression is a modern day version of *Cūrā ut valeās* (line 7)?
   1 Take care of yourself.
   2 Very truly yours,
   3 Hope to see you soon.
   4 Write as soon as you can.

56. This letter was written on April
   (1) 10   (3) 17
   (2) 15   (4) 20

57. The dominant mood of this letter is one of
   1 happiness   3 anger
   2 sadness   4 indifference

Answer Key

46. 1	49. 4	52. 3	55. 1
47. 3	50. 1	53. 2	56. 1
48. 3	51. 2	54. 4	57. 2

Remember to leave out the two questions about which you feel least confident.

PART IVA: Grammar (10 credits)

We now come to the section of the examination that will test your knowledge of the basic structures of the Latin language. This section tests grammar. This book has been designed to help you successfully complete the Comprehensive Regents Examination in Latin. It is not a review book of the Latin language. Consequently, I will not review all the basic grammatical structures.

I will, however, give you a clue. Remember my guiding principle? Get as much out of the test as you can. Part IVA tests basic knowledge of grammar; Part IIIC uses in its statements, questions, and choices only basic Latin structure and vocabulary. As you do Part IIIC, keep an eye on Part IVA. One part can help the other. Let me give you some examples of what I mean from selection 3 of Part IIIC. Question 26 contains the word *Athenas*, which I translated "to Athens." Let this remind you that when Latin wants to express the place to *which* you are going, and that place happens to be the name of a town or city, or a small island, or the two special words *domus* and *rus*, no preposition is used. That can be helpful in Part IVA. Also in question 26, did you notice the forms of the verbs that completed the *ut* clause? *Discederet, daret, maneret,* and *defenderet* are all imperfect subjunctives. You will probably be tested on the use of the subjunctive to express purpose in Part IVA. In question 28, you see the word *dicit* followed by the accusative form of filius (*filium*) and the infinitive form of the verb *debere*. Let that remind you of the Latin grammatical structure needed to express indirect statements, which tend to be omnipresent and ubiquitous in Part IVA sections. Finally, did you notice in question 28 that the verb *debēre* was followed by four infinitive forms of the verbs in the four choices? Remember the rule: certain verbs like *debēre, posse,* etc. must be followed by complementary infinitives.

In the following practice exercise, I have assembled all of the Part IV questions that have appeared in the Regents Examinations from 1974, when the first Comprehensive Examination was given in its present format, to 1979, including the two examinations given in each of the years 1975 and 1978. I have then grouped these 80 questions into categories indicated by Roman numerals. I will provide an answer key for you at the end of this section. However, I am confident that, when you see what category I put each question into, you will easily be able to choose the correct word or expression that makes the sentence grammatically correct. The directions are simple: write the number of the word or expression which, when inserted in the blank, makes each sentence grammatically correct.

I also am confident you will readily notice the repetition of the same basic structures. Remember, the Regents Examination is not "out to get you"; rather, it is out to test fairly a student's basic knowledge of Latin. You will notice that there are *not* the same number of questions in each category. You can safely assume that the categories that have the most questions are the categories that are considered to be the most important. But *all* the categories are basic to the understanding of written Latin. One caveat: Do *not* presume that the following categories are the *only* ones that the examination is allowed to test. There is no particular order of the categories and there is no intention of indicating which category is more important than another.

Practice Exercise

I. The use of the dative case with certain verbs and adjectives:

1. Amīcus _____ persuādet.
   1 mihi   3 ego
   2 nōs   4 ā mē

2. Tribūnus _____ persuāsit ut imperāta facerent.
   1 mīlitēs   3 ā mīlitibus
   2 mīlitibus   4 mīlitem

3. Magister _____ praeerat.
   1 puerōs   3 puerum
   2 puerīs   4 puer

4. Haec fābula est grāta _____ .
   1 sorōrem   3 sorōris
   2 sorōrī   4 sorōre

5. Senātus dictātōrem _____ praefēcit.
   1 urbem   3 urbī
   2 urbs   4 dē urbe

II. The use of the ablative case to express the concept of time "when" or "within which," and the accusative case to express the concept of time "how long":

6. Quattuor _____ pācem facere cōnātī sumus.
   1 annum   3 annōs
   2 annōrum   4 annī

7. Gnaeus Pompeius _____ bellum cōnfēcit.
   1 mediā aestāte   3 mediae aestātī
   2 media aestās   4 mediam aestātem

8. Anna quīnque _____ iter fecit.
   1 hōra   3 hōrās
   2 hōrā   4 hōrae

9. _____ vēnit.
   1 Eō diē   3 Eī diēs
   2 Eius diēī   4 Eī diēī

10. _____ flōrēs pulchrae nōn sunt.
   1 Hiems   3 Hiemem
   2 Hiemī   4 Hieme

III. The dative case is used to express the indirect object, *id est*, the person to whom something is given or for whom something is done.

11. Magister _____ praemia saepe dabat.
    1 adulēscentēs   3 adulēscentibus
    2 ad adulēscentēs   4 adulēscentem

12. Praemium _____ datum est.
    1 lēgātum   3 lēgātōs
    2 lēgātus   4 lēgātō

13. Negōtium grave _____ datum erat.
    1 cōnsulem   3 cōnsule
    2 cōnsulī   4 cōnsul

14. Pater _____ pecūniam dedit.
    1 puer   3 puerum
    2 puerōs   4 puerō

IV. An adjective must agree with the noun or pronoun it modifies in gender, number and case.

15. Vir est _____ .
    1 optimus   3 optima
    2 optimum   4 optimam

16. Concilium _____ erat.
    1 brevis   3 breve
    2 brevem   4 brevī

17. Iter erat _____ .
    1 longa   3 longī
    2 longum   4 longō

V. A preposition must be followed by a noun or pronoun in the correct case for that preposition.

18. Mārcus in _____ īvit.
    1 urbem   3 urbs
    2 urbe   4 urbis

19. Hoc sine _____ nōn facere possum.
    1 auxiliōrum   3 auxilia
    2 auxilī   4 auxiliō

20. Contrā _____ bellum gessit.
    1 rēge   3 rēgis
    2 rēgī   4 rēgem

21. Ex _____ nāvigāmus.
    1 īnsulā   3 īnsulam
    2 īnsulae   4 īnsulārum

22. Montem cum _____ ascendit.
    1 amīcōs   3 amīcīs
    2 amīcī   4 amīcōrum

23. Sine _____ Caesar nāvigāvit.
    1 tempestātem   3 tempestāte
    2 tempestātis   4 tempestātī

VI. The ablative case is usually used to express the agent by which an action is performed. If the agent is personal, the preposition *ab* or *ā* is used; if the agent is nonpersonal, no preposition is used.

24. Gladiatōrēs _____ pugnābant.
    1 gladiīs   3 gladiōs
    2 gladiōrum   4 ā gladiīs

25. Tribūnus _____ dēfendēbātur.
    1 mīlite   3 mīlitī
    2 mīlitem   4 ā mīlite

26. Labor _____ factus est.
    1 ā fēminīs   3 fēminās
    2 fēmina   4 ad fēminās

27. Puer _____ servātus est.
    1 puellā   3 puellam
    2 ā puellā   4 puella

28. Multī in illo bellō _____ captī sunt.
    1 ab hostibus   3 hoste
    2 hostibus   4 hostem

29. Diāna _____ animal interfēcit.
    1 sagittam   3 sagittae
    2 sagittā   4 sagitta

30. Gladiātōrēs _____ victī sunt.
    1 Crassō   3 Crassus
    2 Crassum   4 ā Crassō

31. Signum _____ in proeliō āmissum erat.
    1 legiōnēs   3 legiōnis
    2 legiōnem   4 legiōne

32. Castra _____ semper mūniēbantur.
    1 ā mīlitibus   3 miles
    2 mīlitēs   4 mīlitem

VII. If a gerundive is involved, the dative case is used to express the agent by whom the action is performed.

33. Haec _____ facienda sunt.
    1 rēgēs   3 rēx
    2 rēgem   4 rēgibus

VIII. The locative case is used to express "place where" if it involves the name of a city, town, small island, or the words *domus* and *rus*.

34. Puer _____ habitat.
    1 Rōmā   3 ā Rōmā
    2 Rōmae   4 in Rōmam

IX. To express a comparison, either use *quam*, followed by the same case that was before the *quam*, or use the ablative case without the word *quam*.

35. Athlēta Graecus celerior est quam _____ .
   1 omnēs   3 omnium
   2 omnibus   4 omnī

X. The imperative/question combination with the vocative case. The imperative might be the negative construction of *noli(te)* and the infinitive.

36. Scrībe, _____ , epistulam ad frātrem tuum!
   1 Mārcus   3 Mārcō
   2 Mārcī   4 Mārce

37. Audī _____ verba patris tuī.
   1 fīlius   3 fīliō
   2 fīlium   4 fīlī

38. Nōlīte _____ !
   1 fugīte   3 fugiēns
   2 fugere   4 fugitis

39. Ubi curris, _____ ?
   1 amīcum   3 amīce
   2 amīcī   4 amīcō

40. _____ vīnum, hominēs!
   1 Bibēns   3 Bibite
   2 Bibere   4 Bibenda

41. Quam fortissimē, Mārce _____ !
   1 pugnāte   3 pugnārī
   2 pugnantēs   4 pugnā

42. Properā celeriter, _____ !
   1 Quīntus   3 Quīntī
   2 Quīnte   4 Quīntō

43. Nōlīte nostrōs sociōs _____ !
   1 relinque   3 relinquere
   2 relīquī   4 relictus es

XI. The concept of purpose is frequently expressed by the introductory words *ut* (if positive) or *ne* (if negative) and the subjunctive mood.

44. Scrībit ut nōs _____ .
    1 monēre   3 monēbat
    2 monuerat   4 moneat

45. Mīlitēs fortiter pugnant nē _____ .
    1 capere   3 capiantur
    2 cēpērunt   4 capī

46. Gallī vēnērunt ut oppidum _____ .
    1 capere   3 cēpērunt
    2 capiunt   4 caperent

47. Nūntius currit ut victōriam _____ .
    1 nūntiet   3 nūntiābat
    2 nūntiat   4 nūntiāverat

XII. To express the result of an action, the subjunctive is used introduced by *ut* (if positive) or *ut...non* (if negative). There is usually a "clue" word, such as *tam*, *tantus* etc.

48. Tanta erat auctōritās principis ut magna spēs pācis _____ .
    1 fuit   3 erat
    2 est   4 esset

49. Flūmen tam altum est ut trānsīre nōn _____ .
    1 potuisse   3 potuimus
    2 possīmus   4 posse

50. Rōmānī tam celeriter trādidērunt ut Gallī īnsidiās _____ .
    1 timuērunt   3 timērent
    2 timēre   4 timēbunt

51. Equus tam celeriter cucurrit ut nōn _____ .
    1 capiētur   3 capiēbātur
    2 caperētur   4 captus est

52. Tantus erat clāmor ut nōn ōrātor audīrī _____ .
    1 poterat   3 posse
    2 posset   4 potuisse

XIII.   An indirect question is expressed by the subjunctive introduced by
          an interrogative word, such as *quis, quid, ubi,* etc.

53. Puellae rogāvērunt quid puer _____ .
    1 dīxisset   3 dīcere
    2 dīcit   4 dīcēbat

54. Scīvit quid poēta _____ .
    1 scrībit   3 scrīpsisset
    2 scrīpsit   4 scrīpserat

55. Populus rogat quid _____ .
    1 vincat   3 vincēbat
    2 vincit   4 vincere

56. Magistra discipulōs rogāvit quis opus _____ .
    1 fēcit   3 facit
    2 fēcisset   4 fēcerat

57. Scīvī quid _____ .
    1 fēcerant   3 fēcissent
    2 fēcērunt   4 faciēbant

58. Quaesīvit quis dōna _____ .
    1 tulerat   3 tulī
    2 tulisset   4 tulit

59. Rogāvit ubi poēta _____ .
    1 esse   3 est
    2 esset   4 fuisse

60. Cicerō ē Catilīnā quaesīvit quid illā nocte _____ .
    1 fēcisset   3 fēcerat
    2 facit   4 fēcit

XIV.   With certain verbs, the present infinitive, active or passive, can be
         used either as a complementary infinitive or as an objective infinitive.

61. Cōnstituit iter _____ .
    1 fēcit   3 faciat
    2 faciō   4 facere

62. Portās scholae _____ volunt.
   1 claudere   3 claudēns
   2 clausī   4 clausūrum

63. Magister nōn cōgit puerōs puellāsque _____ librōs.
   1 trādunt   3 trādit
   2 trādidērunt   4 trādere

64. Tē hodiē _____ volumus.
   1 vidēmus   3 videāmus
   2 vidēre   4 vidēns

65. Diligenter _____ dēbēmus.
   1 labōrāre   3 labōrāmus
   2 labōrāns   4 labōrēmus

66. Legiōnēs hostium oppidum _____ nōn poterant.
   1 ut expugnārent   3 expugnāvisse
   2 expugnāre   4 ad expugnandum

67. Anna iussit filium celeriter _____ .
   1 ambulant   3 ambulāre
   2 ambulāvit   4 ambulantis

XV. The indirect statement requires the use of an infinitive form with the subject in the accusative case.

68. Dominus dīcit _____ pugnāre.
   1 servī   3 servōs
   2 servōrum   4 servus

69. Caesar sē mox in Ītaliam _____ dīxit.
   1 ventūrum esse   3 venit
   2 veniēbat   4 vēnisset

70. Dux dīcit _____ ventūrum esse.
   1 vir   3 virōs
   2 virum   4 virī

71. Explorātor cognōvit hostēs ad flumen castra _____ .
   1 pōnīte   3 pōnentēs
   2 posuērunt   4 posuisse

72. Putat magistrum iam _____ .
   1 pervēnit   3 perveniēbat
   2 pervenīre   4 pervēnisset

73. Iūlia scit _____ venīre.
   1 patrī   3 patre
   2 pater   4 patrem

74. Dīxit Graecōs dōna _____ .
   1 dare   3 dabant
   2 dent   4 dant

75. Audīvī Caesarem in Italiam _____ .
   1 revēniat   3 revēnit
   2 revēnērunt   4 revēnisse

XVI. The *si* clause, expressing conditions: The rules governing conditinal
     clauses are very complicated. It might prove helpful to follow an
     unscientific rule: choose like for like. In other words, if you see a
     present subjunctive in one clause, pick a present subjunctive for the
     other; if you see a pluperfect, choose a pluperfect. Like with like:
     unscientific, but helpful.

76. Tōtam Asiam āmīsissētis sī populus Rōmānus bellō Pompeium nōn

   _____ .
   1 praeposuiset   3 praepōnit
   2 praepōnēbat   4 praepōnet

77. Sī tē videam, laetus _____ .
   1 fueram   3 eram
   2 sim   4 erō

78. Sī rēx pugnāret, prōvinciam _____ .
   1 vincit   3 victūrōs esse
   2 vīcit   4 vinceret

79. Sī in oppidō _____ , te vīdissem.
   1 fuerās   3 fuissēs
   2 fueris   4 fuistī

XVII. The *cum* clause is used with the subjunctive, either circumstantial, causal, or concessive:

80. Cum perīculum _____ , amīcōs monuit.
    1 vīdisset   3 videt
    2 vidēbit   4 vidēre

Procedure

These seventeen categories represent basic Latin grammatical structures. As you complete the Part IV sections of the Regents Examinations prior to 1991 and the Part IVA sections of exams from 1991 on which make up the second part of this book, see how many of the categories of the 1970s examinations are represented. I am sure that you will see fulfilled the Latin dictum: *Repetitio mater scientiae est.*

Answer Key

1. 1	11. 3	21. 1	31. 4/3	41. 4	51. 2	61. 4	71. 4
2. 2	12. 4	22. 3	32. 1	42. 2	52. 2	62. 1	72. 2
3. 2	13. 2	23. 3	33. 4	43. 3	53. 1	63. 4	73. 4
4. 2	14. 4	24. 1	34. 2	44. 4	54. 3	64. 2	74. 1
5. 3	15. 1	25. 4	35. 1	45. 3	55. 1	65. 1	75. 4
6. 3	16. 3	26. 1	36. 4	46. 4	56. 2	66. 2	76. 1
7. 1	17. 2	27. 2	37. 4	47. 1	57. 3	67. 3	77. 2
8. 3	18. 1	28. 1	38. 2	48. 4	58. 2	68. 3	78. 4
9. 1	19. 4	29. 2	39. 3	49. 2	59. 2	69. 1	79. 3
10. 4	20. 4	30. 4	40. 3	50. 3	60. 4	70. 2	80. 1

PART IVB: English Derivatives (10 credits)

This section basically tests your knowledge of word derivation, the process by which literally thousands and thousands of English words have come from Latin words, directly or indirectly. Based upon your knowledge of Latin vocabulary, it also tests your understanding of those English words as found in a passage or passages from authentic materials in English. Look at the Part IVB sections in the exams since 1991 to familiarize yourself with the format of this section. Some questions require you to choose the meaning of the basic Latin root of the italicized English word.

One important caution here—look only for the meaning of the basic Latin root; do not look for a synonym for the italicized English word. Let's practice with the following fifteen sample questions, circle the number you think is the correct answer and then check with the answer key.

1. *claustrophobia*
   1 close
   2 climb
   3 secret
   4 work

2. *impetus*
   1 respect
   2 impress
   3 seek
   4 implore

3. *provision*
   1 law
   2 requirement
   3 buy
   4 see

4. *prevention*
   1 cure
   2 come
   3 wish
   4 sell

5. *projection*
   1 throw
   2 run
   3 call
   4 follow

6. *commute*
   1 establish
   2 shorten
   3 change
   4 end

7. *impulse*
   1 drive
   2 destroy
   3 prohibit
   4 retreat

8. *invincible*
   1 defeat
   2 come
   3 watch
   4 wound

9. *elucidate*
   1 law
   2 light
   3 play
   4 read

10. *tenacious*
    1 stretch
    2 hold
    3 fear
    4 roof

11. *dislocation*
    1 talk
    2 place
    3 depart
    4 island

12. *perfidious*
    1 faith
    2 make
    3 complete
    4 happy

13. *dormant*
    1 pain
    2 trick
    3 suffer
    4 sleep

14. *opposition*
    1 pull
    2 punish
    3 prepare
    4 put

15. *impending*
    1 think
    2 hang
    3 drag
    4 impress

Answer Key

1. 1	4. 2	7. 1	10. 2	13. 4
2. 3	5. 1	8. 1	11. 2	14. 4
3. 4	6. 3	9. 2	12. 1	15. 2

PART IVC: Latin Roots

This section tests your ability to "see into" English words to find the basic Latin word that is present and indicate the meaning of that Latin word.

You must do two things for each question: (1) write the Latin word with which the italicized English word is associated by derivation and (2) write the number of the word that best expresses the meaning of the italicized word. The raters are instructed to accept *any* correctly spelled form of the Latin word *except* prefixes and suffixes. Think of how many possibilities that can be! A few practical suggestions for the student who is up against the wall to write that "correctly spelled form" of the Latin noun, adjective, or verb from which the English word is derived:

1. If you are not sure what declension a noun or adjective is in but you are confident of the stem of the word, end the Latin word in *-is*. For example, I am confident that the Latin root of the word nominally is *nomin-* but beyond that I am not sure. Write *nominis*: you would be correct whether it were a first, second, or third declension noun. Try it with immortal: *mort-*, add *-is* = *mortis*.

2. All those words that end in *-ed* (e.g. collaborated), *-us* (e.g. consensus), *-or* (e.g. spectator), or *-ion* (audition) frequently are derived from the perfect participle stem (commonly the fourth principal part of many verbs), which can also end in *-is*. After you have eliminated the prefix and the suffix, add your *-is* to the Latin root that remains and you will have a "correctly spelled" form of the Latin word: *laboratis, sensis, spectatis, auditis*.

This system can help you when you are uncertain. Obviously, if you are immediately certain with which Latin word the English word is associated by derivation, by all means write that Latin word down in its most common form—the nominative case for nouns and adjectives and the first principal part of verbs: nominally - *nomen*; immortal - *mors*; collaborated - *laboro*; consensus - *sentio*; spectator - *specto*; audition - *audio*.

Let's practice. Below are twenty questions that have appeared on past Regents Examinations other than the ones that are contained in the second section of this book. In Column A, write the Latin word with which the italicized English word is associated by derivation. In Column B, write the number of the word that best expresses the meaning of the italicized word. I will provide an answer key at the end, but I will not attempt to provide all of the possible forms of the Latin word that would be correctly spelled forms.

                                             Column A   Column B

1. A *prudent* woman will have few regrets.
   | 1 happy | 3 brave |
   | 2 generous | 4 wise |

2. The army tried to *repel* the enemy.
   | 1 kill | 3 drive back |
   | 2 befriend | 4 encircle |

3. The investigator's task is to *certify* the information.
   | 1 confirm | 3 explain |
   | 2 obtain | 4 destroy |

	Column A	Column B

4. The ancient castle had many points of *egress*.
   1 weakness   3 exit
   2 attack   4 beauty

5. Fame is often *transitory*.
   1 frightening   3 unforgettable
   2 inspiring   4 fleeting

6. "Pomp and Circumstance" is the traditional
   music for the graduation *procession*.
   1 dance   3 banquet
   2 parade   4 capping

7. The student was given *latitude* in her choice
   of courses.
   1 wide range   3 advise
   2 encouragement 4 ample time

8. That country was *nominally* a democracy.
   1 by rule   3 by reputation
   2 by name   4 by law

9. There is *tangible* evidence of improvement
   in her work.
   1 concrete   3 unreliable
   2 much   4 slight

10. The politician demanded a *retraction* of
    the statement.
    1 withdrawal   3 reconsideration
    2 clarification 4 publication

11. The scientist studied the *retrograde*
    movement.
    1 slow   3 irregular
    2 accelerated   4 backward

12. He is trying to *impose* uniform standards
    in the office.
    1 strengthen   3 increase
    2 establish   4 display

Column A   Column B

13. The teacher told the pupils that they were too *credulous*.
    1 likely to be questioned 3 disloyal
    2 inclined to believe 4 misunderstood _____ _____

14. The woman was too *loquacious*.
    1 talkative 3 reserved
    2 temperamental 4 crazy _____ _____

15. The parent *concurred* with the results but for different reasons.
    1 found fault 3 struggled
    2 became alarmed 4 agreed _____ _____

16. The student had a *valid* reason for his action.
    1 strange 3 justifiable
    2 definite 4 inconsistent _____ _____

17. The work of the *itinerant* doctor was greatly praised.
    1 skillful 3 departing
    2 traveling 4 devoted _____ _____

18. There were unfortunate *connotations* in her speech.
    1 implications 3 concessions
    2 pronunciations 4 inflections _____ _____

19. Rome has made an *indelible* mark upon our heritage.
    1 imperceptible 3 indestructible
    2 insignificant 4 inexact _____ _____

20. High prices tend to *aggravate* inflation.
    1 influence 3 modify
    2 prophesy 4 worsen _____ _____

Answer Key

Column A	Column B	Column A	Column B
1. prudens	4	11. gradus, gradior	4
2. pello, repello	3	12. pono	2
3. verus, veritas	1	13. credo, credulus	2
4. gradior, egredior	3	14. loquor	1
5. eo, transeo	4	15. curro, concurro	4
6. procedo	2	16. valeo, validus	3
7. latus, latitudo	1	17. iter	2
8. nomen	2	18. noto, notus	1
9. tango	1	19. deleo	3
10. traho, retraho	1	20. gravis	4

PART IVD: Etymological Potpourri (5 credits)

This section varies in its format. It is testing your knowledge of the presence of Latin in everyday expressions, abbreviations, prefixes, and the like.

I will give you six sample sections for practice. The directions for each sample will be given and an answer key will immediately follow each sample.

Practice Exercise 1

DIRECTIONS: *For each italicized* English *derivative, write, in the space provided on the separate answer sheet, the number preceding the word or expression that best states the meaning of the prefix.* [5]

1. To *transmit* is to send _____ .
   1 away   3 across
   2 from   4 through

2. To *retrogress* is to go _____ .
   1 backward   3 down
   2 forward   4 around

3. To *permeate* is to spread _____ .
   1 steadily   3 lightly
   2 partially   4 thoroughly

4. To *antedate* is to occur _____ .
   1 after   3 simultaneously
   2 before   4 often

5. To *interrupt* is to break _____ .
   1 through   3 between
   2 down   4 out

Answer Key

1. 3
2. 1
3. 4
4. 2
5. 3

Practice Exercise 2

DIRECTIONS: *For each* English *translation, write the* letter *of the Latin expression,* chosen from the list below, *that most nearly has the same meaning.* [5]

English Translation	Latin Expression
1. in good faith	a op, cit.
2. for the time being	b ad infinitum
3. for example	c bona fide
4. something for something	d quid pro quo
5. endlessly	e pro tem
	f corpus deliciti
	g e.g.

Answer Key

1. c
2. e
3. g
4. d
5. b

Practice Exercise 3

DIRECTIONS: *For each italicized expression select the word or expression, chosen from the list below, which most accurately expresses the meaning of the Latin expression, and write its number in the space provided on the separate answer sheet.* [A number may be used more than once or not at all.] [5]

Possible Meanings
1 by the very fact
2 another self
3 the present state
4 without setting a day
5 before the war
6 in good faith
7 entirely

1. *sine die*
2. *ipso facto*
3. *bona fide*
4. *alter ego*
5. *status quo*

Answer Key

1. 4
2. 1
3. 6
4. 2
5. 3

Practice Exercise 4

DIRECTIONS: *Each of the following requires knowledge of the meaning of Latin phrases in English. For each, in the space provided on the separate answer sheet, write the* number *preceding the word or expression that best answers the question or completes the statement.* [5]

1. For privacy, famous people sometimes travel
   1 *consilio et armis*   3 *ex officio*
   2 *mare clausum*   4 *incognito*

2. Which phrase would most probably apply to a legal guardian?
   1 *pater patriae*   3 *in loco parentis*
   2 *ex post facto*   4 *in libris libertas*

3. Which Latin phrase might be found on a theater program?
   1 *in propria persona*   3 *Excelsior*
   2 *dramatis personae*   4 *ars longa; vita brevis*

4. Which abbreviation is used in footnotes to signify that two references are found in the same book?
   1 *ibid.*   3 *et al.*
   2 *etc.*   4 *i.e.*

5. Which expression means *legal*?
   1 *de facto*   3 *ad hoc*
   2 *ex post facto*   4 *de iure*

Answer Key

1. 4
2. 3
3. 2
4. 1
5. 4

Practice Exercise 5

DIRECTIONS: *For each italicized English derivative below, choose the word or expression which best states the meaning of the prefix.* [5]

1. to *circumvent* is to go
   1 near   3 under
   2 above   4 around

2. to *reread* is to read
   1 between   3 again
   2 into   4 soon

3. to *divert* is to turn
   1 towards   3 down
   2 away   4 through

4. to *juxtapose* is to place
   1 outside   3 far from
   2 inside   4 next to

5. to *preregister* is to sign up
   1 after   3 during
   2 before   4 on time

Answer Key

1. 4
2. 3
3. 2
4. 4
5. 2

Practice Exercise 6

DIRECTIONS: *For each abbreviation, select the word or expression, chosen from the list below, which most accurately expresses the meaning of that abbreviation, and write its* number *in the space provided on the separate answer sheet.* [A number may be used more than once or not at all.]   [5]

> *Possible Meanings*
> 1 noon
> 2 following
> 3 for example
> 4 after the birth of Christ
> 5 and others
> 6 before the birth of Christ
> 7 as much as you please

1. *e.g.*
2. *M.*
3. *etc.*
4. *et seq.*
5. *A.D.*

Answer Key

1. 3
2. 1
3. 5
4. 2
5. 4

PART V: Greco-Roman Culture

Part V of the examination will test your knowledge of mythology, history, political organization, literature, religion, social customs, geography, biographical details of famous people, and so forth. In short, it will test your knowledge of the Greco-Roman culture.

You are to answer only twenty of the thirty quesitons in Part V. The same instructions for raters given in Part IIID apply here; don't answer more than twenty questions.

In order to give you a good idea of the categories that could be tested, I will list for you *some* of the possible areas you should concentrate upon in your preparation for the Regents Examination. And to give you ample practice, I will give many sample questions that could either strictly or loosely, fit into the various categories. In this section, I can give only direction and focus; you must prepare yourself by wide reading. The categories are not in any order of importance or frequency. All the questions included have appeared on previous Regents Examinations and could appear again in other forms.

One further suggestion. As you examine each question, ask yourself questions about the other choices beyond that of the correct one for that question. Very often, the choice that is not the correct answer for this particular question might be the correct answer for another question. Practice phrasing questions that might make some or all of the choices given for each question the correct answer. For example, in the following question:

In the *Roman* name *Gaius Iulius Caesar*, *Gaius* is the

1 given name	3 nickname
2 clan name	4 family name

we know that the correct answer is choice 1, the given name. However, phrase a question that would make choice 3 the correct answer (cognomen), or choice 4 the correct answer (nomen). Such practice will positively expand your practice time.

Practice Exercise

I.   THE GRECO-ROMAN GODS AND GODDESSES
(Whenever you see the Greek name for a god or goddess, think of the Roman name for that god or goddess, and vice-versa.)

1. Which person was seized by Pluto and taken to the Underworld to remain there a few months of the year?

1 *Proserpina*	3 *Didō*
2 *Mēdēa*	4 *Pēnelopē*

2. Which English word is *not* a derivative of the name of a Roman deity?

1 cereal	3 volcano
2 diet	4 jovial

3. If a Roman boy had eaten a typical modern-day breakfast, to which goddess would he be grateful?
   1 *Diāna*   3 *Minerva*
   2 *Venus*   4 *Cerēs*

4. Which mythological character is correctly paired with the item for which he is remembered?
   1 Pluto—trident   3 Icarus—wings
   2 Theseus—seasons   4 Poloyphemus—lion

5. Where would ancient Greeks have gone to seek advice about the future?
   1 oracle of Apollo at Delphi
   2 home of the gods on Mount Olympus
   3 the nine Muses on Mount Parnassus
   4 Parthenon on the Acropolis

6. The neighbors of Baucis and Philemon were punished because they had violated the code of
   1 silence   3 justice
   2 humility   4 hospitality

7. Aeneas and Achilles, two heroes of the Trojan War, wore armor specially forged by
   1 *Mārs*   3 *Volcānus*
   2 *Daedalus*   4 *Neptūnus*

8. A demigod was a child of
   1 a mortal and a god   3 an animal and a god
   2 two gods   4 the king of the gods

9. The Roman counterpart of the Greek god Hermes was
   1 Apollo   3 Saturn
   2 Mercury   4 Mars

10. Which god was the son of Venus?
    1 Pan   3 Apollo
    2 Cupid   4 Mercury

11. *Geminī* refers to
    1 Pyramus and Thisbe
    2 Orpheus and Eurydice
    3 Daphne and Apollo
    4 Castor and Pollux

12. Neptune is usually associated with a
    1 caduceus   3 torch
    2 trident   4 forge

13. The Queen of the Roman gods was
    1 *Minerva*   3 *Iūnō*
    2 *Vesta*   4 *Proserpina*

14. Who did *not* live in the Underworld?
    1 *Cerberus*   3 *Plūto*
    2 *Charon*   4 *Aurōra*

15. Romulus is to Remus as Apollo is to
    1 Venus   3 Diana
    2 Juno   4 Minerva

II. **MYTHOLOGY**

16. Which hero is associated with a labyrinth?
    1 *Spartacus*   3 *Aenēās*
    2 *Regulus*   4 *Thēseus*

17. What did Jason have to do in order to obtain the Golden Fleece?
    1 clean the Augean Stables
    2 kill the Minotaur
    3 mount Pegasus
    4 sow the dragon's teeth

18. Food and water, just out of reach, were an eternal temptation to
    1 Tantalus   3 the Furies
    2 Ixion   4 the Danaides

19. Acording to mythology, fire was given to humans by
    1 Heracles   3 Prometheus
    2 Ceres   4 Pandora

20. Who led the Argonauts in the search for the Gold Fleece?
    1 Ulysses   3 Theseus
    2 Perseus   4 Jason

21. What was the name of the dangerous whirlpool that was off the coast of Sicily and opposite the six-headed monster, Scylla?
    1 Charybdis   3 Hydra
    2 Chimaera   4 Medusa

22. Which creatures could draw sailors to destruction by their singing?
    1 Sirens   3 Graces
    2 Gorgons   4 Satyrs

23. The tragic mother of seven sons and seven daughters who was turned into a column of stone from which tears continued to flow was
    1 Eurydice   3 Helen
    2 Hecuba   4 Niobe

24. The Minotaur lived in the labyrinth on the island of
    1 Rhodes   3 Crete
    2 Sicily   4 Corsica

III. THE EARLY LEGENDARY BEGINNINGS OF ROME

25. Early Rome's shortage of women was solved when the Romans
    1 imported Gallic women
    2 abducted Sabine women
    3 invited Etruscans to move to Rome
    4 "mail-ordered" brides from Greece

26. Which young Roman girl betrayed her city to the Sabines during the reign of Romulus?
    1 *Iūlia*   3 *Tarpeia*
    2 *Calpurnia*   4 *Cornēlia*

27. According to legend, Romulus and Remus were descendants of
    1 *Pyrrhus*   3 *Aenēās*
    2 *Hector*   4 *Paris*

28. The Carthaginian queen who fell hopelessly in love with Aeneas was
    1 Circe   3 Dido
    2 Penelope   4 Medea

29. The "Judgment of Paris" pleased the goddess
    1 Venus   3 Vesta
    2 Pales   4 Ceres

30. What was the name of the Roman hero who burned his right hand?
    1 *Rēgulus*   3 *Horātius*
    2 *Coriolānus*   4 *Scaevola*

IV.   ROMAN HISTORY

31. In the conflict between Carthage and Rome, both nations were deter-
    mined to establish a
    1 military base in Gibraltar
    2 program of technical growth
    3 trade monopoly in the Mediterranean
    4 firm foothold in Britain

32. The wars fought by the Romans against the people of Carthage were
    known as the
    1 Dacian Wars   3 Persian Wars
    2 Punic Wars   4 Gallic Wars

33. The African general who led his elephants across the Alps was
    1 Alexander   3 Hannibal
    2 Mithridates   4 Vercingetorix

34. The year 1979 commemorates the 1,900th anniversary of the destruction
    of Herculaneum and
    1 Pompeii   3 Brundisium
    2 Ostia   4 Capua

35. The term "Pyrrhic victory" means a conquest gained
    1 by deceit
    2 by diplomatic speeches
    3 without honor
    4 with great losses

36. The title of honor *Āfricānus* was bestowed upon *Pūblius Cornēlius
    Scīpiō* after his military success over
    1 *Mithridātēs*   3 *Ptolemaeus*
    2 *Lars Porsena*   4 *Hannibal*

37. The first triumvirate consisted of Caesar, Pompey, and
    1 Octavian   3 Lepidus
    2 Antony   4 Crassus

38. If Carthage had conquered Rome, the European civilization would
    have been
    1 Phoenician   3 German
    2 French   4 Turkish

39. Rome's first Emperor who received the title Augustus was
    1 Cassius   3 Marius
    2 Octavian   4 Regulus

40. The "*Pāx Rōmāna*" began in the reign of the emperor
    1 Augustus   3 Vespasian
    2 Tiberius   4 Marcus Aurelius

41. In the Second Punic War, who was the Roman general nicknamed
    Cunctātor?
    1 Pyrrhus   3 Lars Porsena
    2 Fabius Maximus   4 Hasdrubal

42. The second triumvirate consisted of Lepidus, Octavian, and
    1 Antony   3 Crassus
    2 Pompey   4 Cicero

43. During the Emperor Nero's reign, the city of Rome suffered widespread destruction from
    1 flood   3 fire
    2 vandalism   4 volcanic eruption

44. The gladiator who led an uprising against the Roman state was
    1 *Scaevola*   3 *Pyrrhus*
    2 *Coriolānus*   4 *Spartacus*

45. Before the founding of the Republic, the Romans were ruled by harsh kings from
    1 Spain   3 Aquitania
    2 Etruria   4 Germany

46. Which Romans could be considered the civil rights leaders of their time?
    1 *Drūsī*   3 *Scīpiōnēs*
    2 *Gracchī*   4 *Horātū*

V.   THE OCCASIONAL QUESTION

47. Dante was the first major writer to abandon Latin as the language of literature and write in the colloquial Latin of the people. The language in which he wrote was
    1 Spanish   3 Rumanian
    2 Portuguese   4 Italian

48. The educated Roman of Caesar's day was greatly influenced by the literature, philosophy, and the rhetorical style of the
    1 Greeks
    2 Etruscans
    3 Egyptians
    4 Hebrews

VI. ROMAN ENGINEERING

49. Appius Claudius began the network of roads when he constructed the
    1 *Via Valeria*
    2 *Via Sacra*
    3 *Via Hadriana*
    4 *Via Appia*

50. During the Roman occupation, Britons came to accept conveniences such as central heating and
    1 stoves
    2 gas heating
    3 indirect lighting
    4 public baths

51. An important Roman contribution to modern architecture is the
    1 flying buttress
    2 pyramid
    3 fluted column
    4 rounded arch

52. The "Main Street" of Rome was the
    1 *Via Sacra*
    2 *Via Hadriana*
    3 *Via Labicana*
    4 *Via Valeria*

53. The road leading from Rome to Brundisium is
    1 *Via Flāminia*
    2 *Via Appia*
    3 *Sacra Via*
    4 *Via Aurēlia*

VII. ROME, THE ETERNAL CITY

54. A large area in Rome which was used for athletic exercises and military training was the
    1 *Circus Maximus*
    2 *Campus Mārtius*
    3 *Colosseum*
    4 *Forum*

55. Where was the *Circus Maximus* located?
    1 in the *Campus Mārtius*
    2 outside of Rome on the Appian Way
    3 in the area of St. Peter's Basilica
    4 between the Palatine and Aventine Hills

56. Gladiatorial combats took place in the
    1 *Basilica Iulia*   3 *Forum Rōmānum*
    2 *Campus Mārtius*   4 *Colosseum*

57. What is another name for the Flavian Amphitheater?
    1 *Colosseum*   3 *Pantheon*
    2 *Circus Maximus*   4 *Campus Martius*

58. The commercial and political center of ancient Rome was the
    1 *Thermae*   3 *Forum*
    2 *Theātrum Pompeī*   4 *Templum Apollinis*

59. An eternal flame was kept burning in the temple of
    1 Mars   3 Saturn
    2 Ceres   4 Vesta

60. Modern health spas remind us of Roman
    1 *carceres*   3 *thermae*
    2 *basilicae*   4 *lūdī*

61. Which is correctly associated with its description?
    1 *cūria*—the senate house
    2 *basilica*—the slave barracks
    3 *rōstra*—the prison
    4 *peristylum*—a heated bath

62. The harbor of Rome was named
    1 *Ōstia*   3 *Herculaneum*
    2 *Capua*   4 *Antium*

63. A famous hill in Rome is the
    1 Florentine   3 Capitoline
    2 Verrine   4 Appennine

64. In Rome, public records were stored in the
    1 *Comitium*   3 *Tabulārium*
    2 *Cūria*   4 *Tulliānum*

65. Which hill in Rome was the site of the residences of famous citizens?
    1 Capitoline   3 Janiculum
    2 Esquiline   4 Palatine

66. Rome is situated on seven
    1 hills
    2 volcanos
    3 walls
    4 fortresses

67. In Rome, tenement houses were known as
    1 *casae*
    2 *vīllae*
    3 *īnsulae*
    4 *tabernae*

VIII. ROMAN HOMES

68. The *tablīnum* was a characteristic feature of a Roman
    1 ship
    2 garment
    3 house
    4 road

69. In homes of the wealthy and in most public baths, a *hypocaustum* furnished
    1 air-conditioning
    2 light
    3 music
    4 heat

70. The kitchen of a Roman house was called the
    1 *tablīnum*
    2 *culīna*
    3 *ātrium*
    4 *peristȳlum*

71. In a Roman house, the office of the master was called
    1 *impluvium*
    2 *trīclinīum*
    3 *tablīnum*
    4 *ātrium*

72. At a Roman dinner party, the standard number of people dining at a table was
    (1) 6
    (2) 9
    (3) 15
    (4) 23

IX. ROMAN DRESS

73. The garment worn by a Roman to indicate that he was a nominee for public office was known as a *toga*
    1 *pīcta*
    2 *candida*
    3 *praetexta*
    4 *virīlis*

74. What was the name for the knee-length indoor garment worn by Roman men?
    1 *stola*
    2 *palla*
    3 *toga*
    4 *tunica*

75. A Roman matron's outdoor garment was called the
    1 *toga praetexta*   3 *tunica*
    2 *palla*   4 *toga candida*

76. The costume of a Roman woman was called the
    1 *solea*   3 *toga*
    2 *stola*   4 *subligāculum*

X. ROMAN TIME AND NUMBERS

77. The Roman day started about
    (1) 1 a.m.   (3) noon
    (2) 6 a.m.   (4) midnight

78. The Roman date *pr. Kal. Apr.* refers to
    1 March 27   3 April 4
    2 March 31   4 April 12

79. *Idibus Iuniīs* refers to June
    1 first   3 third
    2 tenth   4 thirteenth

80. The Roman date *non Apr.* refers to April
    (1) 1   (3) 15
    (2) 5   (4) 25

81. What year is equivalent to the Roman numeral MCMLXVII?
    (1) 1652   (3) 1872
    (2) 1747   (4) 1967

82. In the Roman calendar, the *Kalends* always fell on the
    1 first   3 seventh
    2 fifth   4 fifteenth

83. The Roman date *ante diem VII Īdūs Decembres* refers to
    1 December 7   3 December 15
    2 December 13   4 December 20

XI. ROMAN GEOGRAPHY

84. Which sea was called "Mare Nostrum" by the Romans?
    1 Caspian   3 Mediterranean
    2 North   4 Adriatic

85. The sea which separates Greece from Asia Minor is called the
    1 Red   3 Tyrrhenian
    2 Black   4 Aegean

86. In its earliest period, the Roman world was limited to a section of
    1 *Magna Graecia*   3 *Latium*
    2 *Hispania*   4 *Sardinia*

XII. THE ROMAN MILITARY

87. What was the name given to the Roman infantry unit?
    1 *equitēs*   3 *peditēs*
    2 *aciēs*   4 *fabrī*

88. The largest unit in the Roman army was called the
    1 *legiō*   3 *centuria*
    2 *cohors*   4 *decuria*

89. The *fossa* and *agger* were parts of the Roman
    1 *peditēs*   3 *auxilia*
    2 *castra*   4 *equitēs*

90. In Caesar's army, the scouts were known as
    1 *auxilia*   3 *sagittārū*
    2 *explōrātōrēs*   4 *funditōrēs*

XIII. ROMAN LITERATURE

91. Much of our knowledge of mythology comes from Ovid's work entitled
    1 *Metamorphōsēs*   3 *Noctēs Atticae*
    2 *Ab Urbe Conditā*   4 *Epitomae*

92. Who was a noted Roman historian?
    1 Horace   3 Lucretius
    2 Livy   4 Plautus

93. Both Plautus and Terrence were famous Roman
    1 senators   3 consuls
    2 lieutenant-generals   4 authors of comedy

94. Romans assimilated, adapted, and transmitted Greek culture to posterity through the prose of Cicero and the poetry of
   1 Livy
   2 Gellius
   3 Vergil
   4 Homer

95. The author of the love poems to Lesbia was
   1 Archias
   2 Catullus
   3 Petronius
   4 Terence

96. The events surrounding the Catilinarian conspiracy were written about by both Cicero and
   1 Livy
   2 Tacitus
   3 Suetonius
   4 Sallust

XIV. THE ROMAN POLITICAL STRUCTURE

97. The Latin expression *cursus honōrum* referred to Roman
   1 political offices
   2 courts
   3 gladiatorial awards
   4 roads

98. According to the *Cursus Honōrum*, the highest office a Roman could be elected to was the
   1 consulship
   2 quaestorship
   3 tribuneship
   4 praetorship

99. After their term of office, Roman consuls were expected to
   1 retire to private life
   2 advise the senate for a year
   3 govern a province for a year
   4 serve in the army

100. A present-day treasurer is comparable to an ancient Roman
   1 *aedīlis*
   2 *praetor*
   3 *lēgātus*
   4 *quaestor*

101. As *aedīlis*, Caesar was in charge of the
   1 state religion
   2 public games
   3 jury system
   4 state treasury

102. The *praetor* was a Roman
   1 mayor
   2 judge
   3 ambassador
   4 paymaster

103. In times of extreme public danger, the consuls appointed a "dictator" with supreme power for a period of
   1 three months
   2 six months
   3 three years
   4 four years

104. A Roman *quaestor* would lose prestige if his province had a shortage of
    1 milk   3 grain
    2 wine   4 water

105. As a safeguard against tyranny, the Roman Republic was established
    with a system of
    1 secret police and informers
    2 military supervision of elections
    3 two elected consuls
    4 restricted voting privileges

106. A present-day commissioner of public works might closely compare
    his post with a Roman
    1 *aedīlis*   3 *quaestor*
    2 *praetor*   4 *pontifex maximus*

107. What was the length of the term of office of an elected Roman consul?
    (1) 1 year   (3) 10 years
    (2) 6 years   (4) 4 years

XV. ROMAN EXPRESSIONS AND ABBREVIATIONS

108. Which words were often spoken by the Roman gladiators before
    combat?
    1 *Nōs moritūrī tē salūtāmus.*
    2 *In hōc signō vincēs.*
    3 *Dīvide et imperā.*
    4 *Pāx vōbīscum.*

109. Which Latin expression best illustrates the concern with physical
    fitness?
    1 *Mēns sāna in corpore sānō.*
    2 *Manus manum lavat.*
    3 *Vestis virum reddit.*
    4 *Semper fidēlis.*

110. The term applied to membership on a committee gained automatically
    because of an office already held is
    1 ex officio   3 ex post facto
    2 de jure   4 prima facie

111. What is the meaning of the abbreviation S.P.Q.R.?
    1 Senators for a Citizens' Republic
    2 Senate and the Roman People
    3 Senate's Popular Quirinal Republic
    4 By Decree of the Senate

112. A monument dedicated to a dead person would be likely to bear the abbreviation
    1 *in mem.*   3 *cf.*
    2 *D.D.*   4 *p.m.*

113. Which expression describes the athlete whose name appears on the honor roll?
    1 *novus ōrdō seclōrum*
    2 *mēns sāna in corpore sānō*
    3 *errāre est hūmānum*
    4 *ars longa, vīta brevis*

114. An inference that does not follow from the original statement is a
    1 *nōn compos mentis*
    2 *persōna nōn grāta*
    3 *nōn sequitur*
    4 *nē plūs ultrā*

115. After the swift campaign against Pharnacēs, Caesar exclaimed
    1 *"Vēni, vīdī, vīcī"*
    2 *"Et tū Brūte"*
    3 *"Alea iacta est"*
    4 *"In hōc signō vincēs"*

XVI. CICERO, HIS LIFE, WORKS, STYLE

116. In which of his writings does Cicero extol the glory of the liberal arts?
    1 *Dē Officiīs*   3 *Prō Archiā*
    2 *In Catilinam*   4 *In C. Verrem*

117. In the Civil War of 49 B.C., Cicero joined the side of
    1 Marius   3 Pompey
    2 Sulla   4 Scipio

118. The *Philippics* of Cicero were a direct attack upon
    1 Julius Caesar   3 Mark Antony
    2 Crassus   4 Lepidus

119. A speech delivered *Ad Iūdicēs* was being addressed to
    1 the slaves   3 a jury
    2 a public assembly   4 the senators

120. As a result of Verres' corrupt practices as governor of Sicily, he suffered
    1 corporal punishment   3 execution
    2 imprisonment   4 exile

121. Cicero and Demosthenes are most closely associated with
    1 military conquest   3 poetry
    2 oratory   4 social reform

122. Which stylistic device is illustrated in the quotation "Nōn feram, nōn patiar, nōn sinam"?
    1 chiasmus   3 hendiadys
    2 anaphora   4 antithesis

123. In Cicero's speeches, which rhetorical figure was signaled by the use of the verbs, *omittō*, *praetereō* and *praetermittō*?
    1 chiasmus   3 litotes
    2 preterition   4 synecdoche

124. The conclusion of a Roman oration was the
    1 *argumentātiō*   3 *nārrātiō*
    2 *exordium*   4 *perōrātiō*

125. The close friend to whom Cicero wrote many letters was
    1 Catiline   3 Hortensius
    2 Atticus   4 Verres

126. The great orator and patriot silenced by Mark Antony was
    1 Marcus Tullius Cicero 3 Cato the Elder
    2 Augustus Caesar   4 Demosthenes

127. The literary work *Dē Senectūte* is one of Cicero's best known
    1 biographies   3 poems
    2 essays   4 letters

XVII. JULIUS CAESAR

128. According to legend, Caesar's last words just prior to his death were
    1 *Ālea iacta est*   3 *Vēnī, vīdī, vīcī*
    2 *Nōlō contendere*   4 *Et tū, Brūte*

129. When crossing the Rubicon, Caesar said:
   1 *"Ālea iacta est."*   3 *"Vēnī, vīdī, vīcī."*
   2 *"Et tū, Brūte."*   4 *"Ō tempora, ō mōrēs."*

130. Whom did Caesar defeat in the final battle of the Gallic wars?
   1 Pyrrhus   3 Alexander
   2 Tarquinius   4 Vercingetorix

131. Antony and Cleopatra were defeated by Octavian at the battle of
   1 Pharsalus   3 Munda
   2 Zama   4 Actium

132. Calpurnia was the wife of
   1 Marius   3 Caesar
   2 Octavius   4 Cicero

133. "Crossing the Rubicon" means
   1 making an irrevocable decision
   2 taking an unexpected trip
   3 outwitting an enemy
   4 admitting defeat

134. In the Gallic War, Labienus was the leader of
   1 a barbaric German tribe
   2 the foreign auxiliaries
   3 one of Caesar's legions
   4 the civilian traders

135. The Druids in the Gallic states served as
   1 priests and judges   3 doctors
   2 farmers   4 merchants and traders

Procedure

These seventeen catagories of questions are not the only ones that can be tested but, based on experience, they are the major categories. Remember my suggestion: phrase questions for yourself regarding as many choices as you can. For example, in question 131 above, the correct answer was the battle at Actium. You should ask yourself: What happened at Pharasalus? at Zama? at Munda? Any one of these three places could be the answer for another question.

Answer Key

1. 1	26. 3	51. 4	76. 2	101. 2	126. 1
2. 2	27. 3	52. 1	77. 2	102. 2	127. 2
3. 4	28. 3	53. 2	78. 2	103. 2	128. 4
4. 3	29. 1	54. 2	79. 4	104. 3	129. 1
5. 1	30. 4	55. 4	80. 2	105. 3	130. 4
6. 4	31. 3	56. 4	81. 4	106. 1	131. 4
7. 3	32. 2	57. 1	82. 1	107. 1	132. 3
8. 1	33. 3	58. 3	83. 1	108. 1	133. 1
9. 2	34. 1	59. 4	84. 3	109. 1	134. 3
10. 2	35. 4	60. 3	85. 4	110. 1	135. 1
11. 4	36. 4	61. 1	86. 3	111. 2	
12. 2	37. 4	62. 1	87. 3	112. 1	
13. 3	38. 1	63. 3	88. 1	113. 2	
14. 4	39. 2	64. 3	89. 2	114. 3	
15. 3	40. 1	65. 4	90. 2	115. 1	
16. 4	41. 2	66. 1	91. 1	116. 3	
17. 4	42. 1	67. 3	92. 2	117. 3	
18. 1	43. 3	68. 3	93. 4	118. 3	
19. 3	44. 4	69. 4	94. 3	119. 3	
20. 4	45. 2	70. 2	95. 2	120. 4	
21. 1	46. 2	71. 3	96. 4	121. 2	
22. 1	47. 4	72. 2	97. 1	122. 2	
23. 4	48. 1	73. 2	98. 1	123. 2	
24. 3	49. 4	74. 4	99. 3	124. 4	
25. 2	50. 4	75. 2	100. 4	125. 2	

POST SCRIPTUM

I sincerely hope my suggestions will prove helpful as you practice using the eight complete Regents Examinations in the second section of the book, and especially helpful as you take the examination itself. And finally, in the words of the poet Catullus, addressed to his beloved brother,

AVE ATQUE VALE.

Examination   June 1990

Comprehensive Latin

PART I

DIRECTIONS (1–15): *Do not write a translation of the following passage; read it through carefully several times to ascertain its meaning. Then in the spaces provided, write the* number *of the alternative that best translates each underlined expression as it is used in the passage.* [15]

<u>Nesciō quō nōmine appellem</u> <u>bellum Spartacō duce gestum.</u> <u>Servī id</u>
       (1)   (2)
<u>pugnāvērunt et gladiātōrēs id imperāvērunt.</u> <u>Hoc bellum erat magna</u>
                        (3)   (4)
<u>calamitās Rōmāna.</u>

Spartacus et <u>trīgintā sociī eiusdem fortūnae</u> ā Capuā effūgērunt. <u>Decem</u>
                               (5)
<u>mīlia servōrum undique vocātōrum</u> mox convēnērunt. Prīmō montem
                  (6)
Vesuvium occupāvērunt. <u>Cum ibi obsidērentur,</u> intrā montem ipsum
                                       (7)
dēscendērunt et, <u>exitū cēlātō ēgressī,</u> castra ducis Rōmānī subitō
                        (8)
oppugnāvērunt. Tum <u>gladiīs tēlīsque sibi factīs</u> multās vīllās, vīcōs, oppida
                               (9)
per tōtam Campāniam vastāvērunt. <u>Ut meliōrem exercitum habērent,</u>
                                                      (10)
equitātus equōrum ferōrum parātus est. Servī et gladiātōrēs multa
proelia gerēbant. Post proelia mīlitēs Spartacī fascēs et <u>īnsignia dē</u>
<u>praetōribus capta</u> ad Spartacum dētulērunt.
(11)
Ille, exercitū Lentulī victō <u>castrīsque Publī Cassī dēlētīs,</u> urbem Rōmam
                                          (12)
oppugnāre cōnstituit. <u>Pulsus autem ā Liciniō Crassō,</u> in extrēma Ītāliae
                             (13)
cum sociīs properāvit. Cum in Siciliam effugere parārent, nāvēs obtinēre
nōn potuērunt.

1

Cōnstitērunt, igitur, et impetum in exercitum Rōmānōrum fēcērunt. Ad
(14)
mortem pugnāvērunt. Spartacus ipse in prīmō agmine fortissimē pugnāns
(15)
occīsus est.

— L. Annaeus Flōrus, *Bellum Spartacum*, II, viii
(adapted)

1 Nesciō quō nōmine appellem
   1 I don't know by what name I should call
   2 I called a name I do not know
   3 I don't know what his name is
   4 I am calling a name he doesn't know   1____

2 bellum Spartacō duce gestum
   1 Spartacus led the established war
   2 the war waged with Spartacus as leader
   3 the war avoided by Spartacus the leader
   4 the leader aroused Spartacus to war   2____

3 Servī id pugnāvērunt et gladiātōrēs id
imperāvērunt.
   1 They fought with the slaves and commanded
     the gladiators.
   2 The slaves also gave orders to the gladiators
     who were fighting.
   3 The slaves fought with the gladiators and
     also commanded them.
   4 Slaves fought it and gladiators commanded it.   3____

4 Hoc bellum erat magna calamitās Rōmāna.
   1 That was a war of great importance to Rome.
   2 This war was great for Rome's confidence.
   3 This war was a great Roman disaster.
   4 That misfortune caused a great war for the
     Romans.   4____

5 trīgintā sociī eiusdem fortūnae
   1 thirty allies with that money
   2 the same thirty fortunate comrades
   3 the fortunes of the same thirty comrades
   4 thirty allies of the same fortune   5____

6 Decem mīlia servōrum undique vocātōrum
   1 Ten thousand slaves called from all
     directions
   2 Ten thousand called the slaves from all
     directions
   3 The slaves were summoned ten miles from
     all sides
   4 Slaves from all sides summoned ten thousand   6____

7 Cum ibi obsidērentur
   1 Although they were attacking there
   2 Since they were besieged there
   3 Because they were hidden in that place
   4 After they were observed in that place   7____

8 exitū cēlātō ēgressī
   1 having left by a secret exit
   2 hiding themselves near the exit
   3 having stopped by the exit in order to hide
   4 an exit not visible to those who were leaving   8____

9 gladiīs tēlīsque sibi factīs
   1 swords and weapons were found there
   2 in addition to swords they made weapons
   3 with swords and weapons made for
     themselves
   4 swords were made as their weapons   9____

10 Ut meliōrem exercitum habērent
   1 In order to enlist a larger army
   2 In order that he might not leave anything for
     the larger army
   3 In order that they might have a better army
   4 In order that the army might have something
     better   10____

11 īnsignia dē praetōribus capta
   1 because of the praetors the emblems were
     captured
   2 and the praetors captured the emblems
   3 the praetors were captured with their
     emblems
   4 emblems captured from the praetors   11____

12 castrīsque Publī Cassī dēlētīs
   1 they destroyed the camp and Publius Cassius
   2 and after the camp of Publius Cassius had
     been destroyed
   3 and after Publius Cassius destroyed the camp
   4 toward the destroyed camp of Publius
     Cassius   12____

13 Pulsus autem ā Liciniō Crassō
   1 Meanwhile, Licinius Crassus was beaten
   2 Meanwhile, he fled from Licinius Crassus
   3 However, having been driven back by
     Licinius Crassus
   4 He was joined, however, by Licinius Crassus   13____

14 Cōnstitērunt, igitur, et impetum in exercitum
   Rōmānōrum fēcērunt.
   1 Therefore, the Romans stopped making an
     attack on the army.

   2 They stopped, therefore, and made an attack
     against the army of the Romans.
   3 The army of the Romans, therefore, decided
     to make an attack.
   4 And, therefore, they planned to make the
     army of the Romans attack.   14____

15 in prīmō agmine fortissimē pugnāns
   1 fighting very bravely in the first column
   2 fighting the first man in the column very
     bravely
   3 in the beginning the column fighting bravely
   4 first in the column was a very brave fighter   15____

PART II

DIRECTIONS (16–25): *Do not write a translation of the following passages;
read them through carefully several times to ascertain their meaning. Base
your answers on the content of each passage only. Your answers do not have
to be complete sentences; a word or phrase may suffice. Write in English
your answer to each question.* [10]

C. Plīnius Canīniō Rūfō Suō S.

   Nuper nuntiātus est Sīlius Ītalicus in suā vīllā Neāpolītānā vītam fīnisse.
Valētūdō eius erat tam mala ut diūtius vīvere nollet; itaque edere
recūsāvit.

   Vīta Sīlī ante aegritūdinem et senectūtem fuerat beāta et fēlix. Ex līberīs
duōbus fīlius minor mortuus est, sed maior fīlius *flōrēns* atque etiam
consulāris erat. Sīlius Ītalicus, ipse cōnsulāris, Asiam aequē administrāvit,
et Rōmam cum glōriā revēnit. Ā prīncipibus cīvitātis multum salutābātur
et amābātur. Coāctus ob valētūdinem in lectō iacēre, diēs ultimōs
consumēbat in doctissimīs sermōnibus cum amīcīs atque in librīs
scribendīs. Tandem ob senectūtem ab urbe discessit et in Campāniā
habitābat.

   Complūrēs vīllās habēbat in quibus erant et multī librī et statuae et
imāginēs. Poētam Vergilium maximē amābat et ad sepulchrum eius
Neāpolī saepe adībat.

   Sīlius ā Nerōne factus est cōnsul ultimus; ultimus ex omnibus, quōs
Nerō cōnsulēs fēcerat, ē vītā dēcessit. Valē.

Plīnius, Epistulae, III, 7
(adapted)

flōrēns — prosperous

16 What recent announcement does Pliny report?

17 What had Silius decided to do because of his
   poor health?

18 What sort of life had Silius lived earlier?

19 What happened to Silius' younger son?

20 What relative of Silius became consul during
   Silius' lifetime?

21 What had Silius Italicus done after his
   consulship that allowed him to return to Rome
   in glory?

22 Name *one* of two activities that helped Silius
   pass the time during his illness.

23 Where did Silius keep large collections of
   books and statuary?

24 What place did Silius usually visit when he was
   in Naples?

25 What made Silius' consulship unique?

PART III

DIRECTIONS (26–35): *Read the following passage carefully but do* not *write a translation. Below the passage there are several questions or incomplete statements. For each, select the alternative that best answers the question or completes the statement* on the basis of the information given in the passage, *and write its* number *in the space provided.* [15]

Marcelle, tibi dīcāmus quī sit ōrātor optimus ut tuum fīlium, Getam, *ērudīre* possīs. Nullus ōrātor.esse optimus potest nisi vir bonus est quī nōn modo potestātem dīcendī habeat sed etiam sapientiam et omnēs animī virtūtēs. Eius vīta rēcta honestaque esse dēbet. Optimus ōrātor est ille vir quī possit publicās prīvātāsque rēs administrāre, quī urbēs regere cōnsiliīs, quī cīvitātēs lēgibus mūnīre, quī tandem urbēs iūdiciīs *ēmendāre.*
Igitur pater optimam spem dē suō fīliō semper habēre dēbet. Sit pater magister dīligentissimus. Nōlī putāre paucissimōs hominēs vim intellegendī tenēre. Nam *contrā* tu cognōvistī multōs hominēs ad docendum et ad discendum esse parātōs. Doctī et intellegentēs esse dēbent parentēs, nōn modo pater sed māter etiam. Cornēlia enim, Gracchōrum māter, dīcitur duōbus fīliīs multam ēloquentiam dedisse. Etiam dīcunt Laeliam in loquendō paternam ēlegantiam dēmōnstrāvisse, et tandem Hortensiam, Q. Hortensiī fīliam, apud Triumvirōs ōrātiōnem habuisse quae hodiē ā multīs legitur.

—Quīntiliānus, *Īnstitūtiō Ōrātōria*, I, Prologue 1. 5-8.
(adapted)

ērudīre — to educate
ēmendāre — to reform, improve
contrā — on the contrary

26 Quis est Marcellus?

    1 clārus poēta   3 dux mīlitum
    2 pater Getae   4 fīlius Getae   26____

27 Cūr scrīpsit Quīntiliānus ad Marcellum
Victōrium?

    1 ut Marcellus fīlium bene ēducāret
    2 quod Quīntiliānus pecūniam voluit
    3 ut Marcellus Rōmam venīret
    4 quod Quīntiliānus auxilium dēsīderāvit   27____

28 Ōrātor perfectus esse dēbet vir
   1 laetus et contentus
   2 senex et pauper
   3 fortis et fēlīx
   4 bonus et doctus   28 _____

29 Optimus ōrātor rēs bene gerit et in forō et
   1 domī   3 in templīs
   2 in bellō   4 in marī   29 _____

30 Quō modō ōrātor urbēs cōnfirmābit?
   1 mūrīs et exercitū
   2 lēgibus et sententiīs
   3 armīs et tēlīs
   4 sacrificiīs et auguriīs   30 _____

31 Quis esse dēbet optimus magister?
   1 filius   3 iūdex
   2 pater   4 ōrātor   31 _____

32 Quid habēre dēbent et māter et pater?
   1 imperium   3 scientiam
   2 pecūniam   4 amōrem   32 _____

33 Quid Cornēlia filiīs suīs dedit?
   1 potestātem loquendī
   2 dōnum aurī
   3 multam pecūniam
   4 vītam pācis   33 _____

34 Quem Laelia imitāta est?
   1 Gracchōs   3 Cornēliam
   2 filiōs suōs   4 patrem suum   34 _____

35 Ōrātiō ab Hortensiā habita posteā erat
   1 statim dēlēta
   2 causa mortis Triumvirōrum
   3 saepe lecta
   4 dēclārātiō bellī   35_____

PART IV

DIRECTIONS (36–45): *In the space provided, write the* number *of the word
or expression that, when inserted in the blank, makes* each *sentence grammatically correct.*   [10]

36 Tōtum negōtium _____ cōnfectum est.
   1 servus   3 servōs
   2 ā servō   4 servum   36_____

37 Octāviānus appellābātur _____.
   1 Augustō   3 Augustus
   2 Augustum   4 Augustī   37_____

38 Spē salūtis _____, Gallī dē suīs finibus
   discessērunt.
   1 relictā   3 relinquerētur
   2 relinquebātur   4 relictam esse   38_____

39 Rōmānī pugnam sine _____ spectāvērunt.
   1 timor   3 timōrem
   2 timōre   4 timōris   39_____

40 Hic pōns est longior quam _____.
   1 ille   3 illī
   2 illum   4 illō   40_____

41 Iūlia est puella _____ Balbus pecūniam
   dedit.
   1 cui   3 quam
   2 quī   4 quōs   41____

42 Cīvēs ad forum veniunt ut Cicerōnem
   _____.
   1 audīre   3 audīvissent
   2 audientēs   4 audiant   42____

43 Mercātōrēs vidērunt _____.
   1 nāvēs suae incendēbantur
   2 ut nāvēs suae incēnsae essent
   3 nāvēs suās incēnsās esse
   4 ad nāvēs suās incendendās   43____

44 Tanta tempestās orta est ut nautae nāvigāre
   nōn _____.
   1 possunt   3 potuisse
   2 poterant   4 possent   44____

45 Sī uxōrem inveniat, Orpheus eam domum
   _____.
   1 redūcere   3 redūxerat
   2 redūcat   4 redūcēns   45____

PART V

DIRECTIONS (46–57): *Read the passage below carefully, but do not write a
translation. Below the passage there are several questions or incomplete
statements. Choose 10 of these questions or statements, and in the space
provided, write the number of the word or expression that best answers the
question or completes the statement.* [10]

Quam ob rem, iūdicēs, cīvitās vērō gaudēret sī T. Annius tenēns
sanguineum gladium super caput suum clāmāret: "Venīte, quaesō, atque
audīte, cīvēs! P. Clōdium interfēcī; hōc gladiō et hāc dextrā manū ā
cervīcibus vestrīs ita reppulī eius furōrem, quem nūllīs lēgibus, nūllīs
5 iūdiciīs sustinēre poterāmus ut per mē sōlum honor et lībertās manērent."
Nunc enim quis est quī nōn probet, quī nōn laudet, quī nōn dīcat et
sentiat T. Annium ūnum post hominum memoriam dēfendisse rem
pūblicam et servāvisse populum Rōmānum, tōtam Ītaliam, nātiōnēs
omnēs? Mandāte hoc memoriae, iūdicēs. Sī P. Clōdius vīveret, nūlla pāx,
10 nūlla laetitia esset in hāc cīvitāte.

—Cicerō, *Prō Milōne*, 28
(adapted)

46 Cicero delivered this speech to

1 senators   3 the Roman people
2 jurors   4 all nations   46____

47 *T.* (line 1) stands for the name

1 *Titus*   3 *Tibullus*
2 *Tīrō*   4 *Tiberius*   47____

48 The Latin phrase *tenēns sanguineum gladium*
(lines 1 and 2) is best translated as

1 reaching for a sharp sword
2 holding one hundred swords
3 reaching for the shield and sword
4 holding a bloody sword   48____

49 The singular imperative form of the Latin verb
Venīte (line 2) is

1 *venīre*   3 *venī*
2 *vēnit*   4 *venīs*   49____

50 What did Cicero dramatize?
1 the swearing of an oath
2 a retreat from battle
3 the murder of Publius Clodius
4 the rage of the soldiers   50____

51 Which Latin word is similar in meaning to
   interfēcī (line 3)?
   1 *necāvī*   3 *discessī*
   2 *recēpī*   4 *laudāvī*   51____

52 The Latin phrase *hōc gladiō.* (line 3) is an
   example of an ablative of
   1 personal agent   3 comparison
   2 means   4 manner   52____

53 Which rhetorical figure is illustrated in the
   Latin expression *nullīs lēgibus, nullīs iūdicīs*
   (lines 4 and 5)?
   1 simile   3 metaphor
   2 chiasmus   4 anaphora   53____

54 What tense and mood are the Latin words
   probet, laudet, and *dīcat* (line 6)?
   1 present indicative
   2 present subjunctive
   3 future indicative
   4 perfect subjunctive   54____

55 What is the third principal part of the Latin
   word *vīveret* (line 9)?
   1 *vītāvī*   3 *vīxī*
   2 *vīcī*   4 *vīdī*   55____

56 Which Latin word is similar in meaning to
   laetitia (line 10)?
   1 *sapientia*   3 *fortitūdō*
   2 *tristitia*   4 *gaudium*   56____

57 Clodius can best be described as
   1 dangerous to the state
   2 beneficial to the citizens
   3 respected by Cicero
   4 a hero to Annius   57____

PART VI

DIRECTIONS (58–67): *For each sentence below, write, in the longer space provided, a Latin word with which the italicized word is associated by derivation. Any form of the appropriate Latin word, except prefixes and suffixes, will be acceptable. Then write, in the shorter space provided, the number preceding the word or expression that best expresses the meaning of the italicized word.* [10]

58 I always remember my grandfather as being rather *taciturn*.

    1 silent   3 harsh
    2 sad   4 active

58 _____   _____

59 Customers noticed the *acrid* odor coming from the store.

    1 fragrant   3 enticing
    2 unusual   4 sharp

59 _____   _____

60 I was not present at the *colloquy* yesterday afternoon.

    1 incident   3 performance
    2 conversation   4 party

60 _____   _____

61 *Desperation* was evident in the look on the actor's face.

    1 determination   3 hopelessness
    2 pride   4 fatigue

61 _____   _____

62 The attorney *retracted* her words.

    1 took back   3 repeated
    2 shouted   4 emphasized

62 _____   _____

63 Human knowledge is *finite*.

    1 uncertain   3 essential
    2 limited   4 valuable

63 _____   _____

64 Most of the spectators thought that the decision of the umpire was *untenable*.

    1 unexpected   3 appropriate
    2 predictable   4 indefensible

64 _____   _____

65 The small company was having *pecuniary* problems.

    1 staffing   3 transportation
    2 financial   4 maintenance

65 _____   _____

66 The physician had difficulty diagnosing the *incipient* illness.

    1 minor   3 beginning
    2 unusual   4 recurring

66 _____   _____

67 The engineer was an *urbanist*.

    1 city planner
    2 bridge builder
    3 electrical specialist
    4 railroad conductor

67 _____   _____

DIRECTIONS (68–72): *For each italicized English derivative, write, in the space provided, the number preceding the word or expression that best states the meaning of the prefix.* [5]

68 *Superscript* is written

    1 under   3 after
    2 above   4 beside   68____

69 To *permeate* is to pass

    1 over   3 through

    2 in front of   4 around   69 ____

70 *Effusion* is a pouring

    1 back   3 out

    2 into   4 around   70 ____

71 To *attract* is to draw

    1 apart   3 down

    2 back   4 towards   71 ____

72 To *contradict* is to speak

    1 against   3 for

    2 radically   4 repeatedly   72 ____

DIRECTIONS (73–77): *For each italicized abbreviation in questions 73 through 77, select the word or expression, chosen from the list below, that most accurately expresses the meaning of the abbreviation, and write its number in the space provided.* [5]

English Meanings

    1 which was to be shown

    2 that is

    3 for the time being

    4 and the others

    5 note well

    6 written after

    7 after noon

Abbreviations

73 et al.   73 ____   76 P.S.   76 ____

74 Q.E.D.   74 ____   77 pro tem   77 ____

75 p.m.   75 ____

PART VII

DIRECTIONS (78–107): *Select 20 of the following statements or questions. In the space provided, write the number of the word or expression that best answers the question or completes the statement.* [20]

78 Which office was in the *cursus honōrum*?
  1 *dictātor*   3 *cēnsor*
  2 *praetor*   4 *tribūnus*   78_____

79 Who was the severe censor of morals who hated Carthage and frequently declared, *"Carthāgō dēlenda est!"*?
  1 Camillus   3 Fabricius
  2 Cato   4 Brutus   79_____

80 What is the term for the bundle of rods with an ax, the symbol of the chief magistrates' absolute power?
  1 *imperium*   3 *stilus*
  2 *sella curūlis*   4 *fascēs*   80_____

81 The members of the First Triumvirate were Caesar, Pompey, and
  1 Octavian   3 Crassus
  2 Brutus   4 Cassius   81_____

82 Who was the young Roman general famed for his defeat of Hannibal in Africa?
  1 Scipio   3 Pompey
  2 Minucius   4 Caesar   82_____

83 Who was the famous Roman dictator who left his farm to defend Rome against the *Aequī*?
  1 Cincinnatus   3 Horatius
  2 Regulus   4 Scaevola   83_____

84 Caesar's famous words, "*Ālea iacta est!*" were
said at which event in his life?
1 invasion of Britain
2 crossing the Rubicon River
3 battle of Zela
4 fall of Alesia   84____

85 What is the legendary date of the founding of
Rome?
(1) 776 B.C.   (3) 509 B.C.
(2) 753 B.C.   (4) 27 B.C.   85____

86 The Sibylline books contained
1 drama handed down through many
generations
2 the names of all Romans who had served as
consuls
3 the laws of the Twelve Tables
4 sayings of the oracle that concerned the fate
of Rome   86____

87 *Augurēs, vestālēs,* and *haruspicēs* were all
associated with ancient Roman
1 amusements   3 religion
2 education   4 agriculture   87____

88 A *strigilis* would most likely be found in the
1 *ātrium*   3 *hortus*
2 *bibliothēca*   4 *thermae*   88____

89 Which phrase was associated with the menu of
a Roman dinner from beginning to end?
1 *pānem et circēnsēs*
2 *ab ōvō usque ad māla*
3 *festīnā lentē*
4 *carpe diem*   89____

90 The study or office of the master of the Roman
house was called the

1 *culīna*   3 *ātrium*
2 *impluvium*   4 *tablīnum*   90____

91 The men who patrolled Rome as police and
firefighters were known as

1 *aedīlēs*   3 *lībertīnī*
2 *vigilēs*   4 *prōcōnsulēs*   91____

92 An appointment made by a Roman for
a.d. III Īd. Apr. would be kept on

1 April 11   3 April 2
2 April 16   4 March 30   92____

93 *Gaius*, *Marcus*, and *Publius* were all examples
of Roman

1 *cognōmina*   3 *praenōmina*
2 *nōmina*   4 *agnōmina*   93____

94 The Golden Apples sought by Hercules were
guarded by maidens called

1 Hesperides   3 Sirens
2 Caryatids   4 Harpies   94____

95 The owl, helmet, and spear are related to
which Roman deity?

1 Minerva   3 Juno
2 Venus   4 Ceres   95____

96 According to myth, who was the first person to
fly?

1 Minos   3 Daedalus
2 Midas   4 Camillus   96____

97 The craftsman-god, called *Hephaestus* by the
Greeks, was known to the Romans as
1 *Neptūnus*   3 *Sāturnus*
2 *Mars*   4 *Vulcānus*   97____

98 The son of Apollo, considered to be the father
of medicine, was
1 Cephalus   3 Faunus
2 Aeneas   4 Aesculapius   98____

99 Jason was able to acquire the golden fleece
with the help of
1 Medusa   3 Medea
2 Aeëtes   4 Pelias   99____

100 The epic poem the *Aeneid* was written by
1 Horace   3 Demosthenes
2 Homer   4 Vergil   100____

101 Cicero studied acting techniques with a famous
actor in order to refine his oratorical skills.
Who was that actor?
1 Roscius   3 Verres
2 Sulla   4 Tiro   101____

102 Many classical myths were preserved in the
Metamōrphōsēs written by the Roman poet
1 Sallust   3 Livy
2 Ovid   4 Vergil   102____

103 Plautus and Terence were writers of
1 comedy   3 history
2 tragedy   4 biography   103____

104 The *spīna* and *mētae* would be found in the
    1 *Via Appia*   3 *Circus Maximus*
    2 *Colossēum*   4 *Tabulārium*   104____

105 Which phrase is the famous inscription on the
floor mosaic of a Pompeian *vestibulum*?
    1 *quid prō quō*   3 *cavē canem*
    2 *mementō morī*   4 *festīnā lentē*   105____

106 The round temple in the Roman Forum was
dedicated to
    1 Vesta
    2 Castor and Pollux
    3 Janus
    4 Jupiter Stator   106____

107 The Pantheon, commissioned by Marcus
Agrippa, is most famous for its great
    1 arch   3 columns
    2 dome   4 sculpture   107____

Answers   June 1990

Comprehensive Examination in Latin

PART I

(Allow a total of 15 credits, one credit for each of the following.)

(1) 1	(4) 3	(7) 2	(10) 3	(13) 3
(2) 2	(5) 4	(8) 1	(11) 4	(14) 2
(3) 4	(6) 1	(9) 3	(12) 2	(15) 1

PART II

(Allow a total of 10 credits, one credit for each of the following.)

(16) Silius Italicus had ended his life.
(17) refuse to eat (since he wished to live no longer)
(18) fortunate, happy
(19) He had died.
(20) his older son
(21) He administered Asia justly.
(22) (learned) conversations with his friends, writing books
(23) in several villas (in Campania)
(24) the tomb of the poet Vergil
(25) He was the last consul appointed by Nero. He was the last of Nero's consuls to die.

PART III

(Allow a total of 15 credits, one and one-half credits for each of the following.)

(26) 2	(28) 4	(30) 2	(32) 3	(34) 4
(27) 1	(29) 1	(31) 2	(33) 1	(35) 3

PART IV

(Allow a total of 10 credits, one credit for each of the following.)

(36) 2	(38) 1	(40) 1	(42) 4	(44) 4
(37) 3	(39) 2	(41) 1	(43) 3	(45) 2

PART V

(Allow a total of 10 credits, one credit for each of 10 of the following.)

(46) 2	(48) 4	(50) 3	(52) 2	(54) 2	(56) 4
(47) 1	(49) 3	(51) 1	(53) 4	(55) 3	(57) 1

PART VI

(Allow a total of 20 credits. For questions 58–67, allow one-half credit for each correct answer in each column.)

(58) taceō, tacitus	1	(63) fīniō, fīnis	2
(59) acer	4	(64) teneō	4
(60) colloquium, loquor	2	(65) pecūnia	2
(61) dēspērō, spērō, spēs	3	(66) incipiō, capiō	3
(62) retrahō, tractō	1	(67) urbs, urbānus	1

(For questions 68–77, allow one credit for each of the following.)

(68) 2	(70) 3	(72) 1	(73) 4	(75) 7	(77) 3
(69) 3	(71) 4		(74) 1	(76) 6	

PART VII

(Allow a total of 20 credits, one credit for each of 20 of the following.)

(78) 2	(83) 1	(88) 4	(93) 3	(98) 4	(103) 1
(79) 2	(84) 2	(89) 2	(94) 1	(99) 3	(104) 3
(80) 4	(85) 2	(90) 4	(95) 1	(100) 4	(105) 3
(81) 3	(86) 4	(91) 2	(96) 3	(101) 1	(106) 1
(82) 1	(87) 3	(92) 1	(97) 4	(102) 2	(107) 2

Examination   June 1991

Comprehensive Latin

PART I

Part I is administered at the school's convenience at some time before the written test is given. You are asked to read aloud a passage of Latin for the teacher to judge on the basis of your proficiency in the spoken language. [5 credits]

PART II

DIRECTIONS: *Your teacher will read aloud a short passage in Latin. Listen carefully to this first reading. Then your teacher will read the passage in short phrases with a pause after each phrase. After each pause, write, in Latin, the phrase read by your teacher. Do not write a translation of the   passage.*

There will be no penalty for improper use of macrons or capitalization. After you have completed writing the passage in Latin, your teacher will read the entire passage one more time so that you may check your work. [5 credits]

*The passage that the teacher reads will be found in **Answers, Part II** at the end of this examination.*

PART III

Answer the questions in Part III according to the directions for Parts IIIA, IIIB, IIIC, AND IIID. [40 credits]

PART IIIA

DIRECTIONS (**1–10**): *Do not write a translation of the following passage; read it through carefully several times to ascertain its meaning. Then, in the spaces provided, write the number of the alternative that best translates each underlined expression as it is used in the passage.* [10]

Interior pars Britanniae ab eīs inhabitātur quī nātī sunt in īnsulā. Maritima pars habitātur ab eīs quī bellī īnferendī causā ex Belgiō trānsīverant. Quī omnēs nōminibus cīvitātum appellantur ex quibus pervēnērunt. Bellō gestō, ibi mānsērunt, et agrōs colere coepērunt. Est multitūdō hominum, plurimaque aedificia simillima Gallicīs et animālium magnus numerus. Ūtuntur aut aere aut aurō aut ferrō prō pecūniā.

Ex omnibus Britannīs hūmānissimī sunt quī Cantium inhabitant. Haec regiō est martitima et similis Galliae moribus est. Incolae in parte interiōrī frūmenta nōn colunt, sed lacte et carne vīvunt; *pellēs* animālium gerunt. Omnēs vērō Britannī corpora colōrant et in pugnā sunt horribilēs propter colōrem caeruleum. Capillī sunt longī et omnis pars corporis *rāsa est* praeter caput et *labrum superius*.

> — Caesar, *Dē Bellō Gallicō*, V, 12-14.
> (adapted)

pellēs — from *pellis*, skin, pelt
rāsa est — from *rādō*, shave
labrum superius — upper lip

1 ab eīs inhabitātur quī nātī sunt in īnsulā

   1 is inhabited by those who were born on the island
   2 is owned by those who conquered the island
   3 kept those who were native people in solitude
   4 is considered isolated by many who live there

1_____

2 quī bellī īnferendī causā ex Belgiō trānsīverant

   1 who had transferred the war from Belgium
   2 whose cause was taken up by Belgium
   3 who had come over from Belgium for the sake of waging war
   4 when a fierce war was brought for that reason to Belgium

2_____

3 omnēs nōminibus cīvitātum appellantur ex
  quibus pervēnērunt
  1 every citizen is called by name to come to
    that place
  2 every state was called on to contribute from
    what each had
  3 all the citizens were called by name and they
    came
  4 all are called by the names of the states from
    which they came   3_____

4 Bellō gestō
  1 Before the war began
  2 After the war had been waged
  3 Since the war was interrupted
  4 Although the war was announced   4_____

5 aedificia simillima Gallicīs
  1 buildings smaller than the Gauls'
  2 fewer temples than in Gaul
  3 buildings very much like the Gauls'
  4 more rustic buildings than those in Gaul   5_____

6 Ūtuntur aut aere aut aurō aut ferrō prō pecūniā.
  1 Either bronze or gold is carried by their
    sheep.
  2 They use bronze or gold or iron for money.
  3 Bronze or iron is worn in their ears.
  4 They use bronze or gold to pay for their
    sheep.   6_____

7 hūmānissimī sunt quī Cantium inhabitant
  1 the wealthiest men live there in Kent
  2 Kent has the most people
  3 human affairs are most cherished in Kent
  4 the most civilized are those who live in Kent   7_____

8 frūmenta nōn colunt
  1 do not live in the fields
  2 do not enjoy pleasures
  3 do not cultivate grain
  4 do not teach agriculture   8____

9 lacte et carne vīvunt
  1 live on milk and meat
  2 search for bread and milk
  3 avoid milk and bread
  4 milk and meat are scarce   9____

10 in pugnā sunt horribilēs propter colōrem
   caeruleum
  1 on account of the heat, they are frightened
  2 they are frightening in battle because of their
    blue color
  3 because of the dark color, they are horrified
  4 a fearful battle was fought in the heat of the
    day   10____

PART IIIB

DIRECTIONS (**11–20**): *Do not write a translation of the following passage;
read it through carefully several times to ascertain its meaning. Base your
answers on the content of the passage only. Your answers do not have to be
complete sentences; a word or phrase may suffice. In the spaces provided,
write in English your answer to each question.* [10]

C. Plīnius Cornēliō Tacitō Suō

Rīdēbis dē hōc. Mihi nōn crēdēs. Ego scrīptor etiam sum *vēnātor*.
Etiam tria animālia pulcherrima cēpī. "Plīnius, vēnātor?" dīcis. Ita, ego ipse;
nōn tamen *omnīnō* ab ōtiō et quiēte discēdēbam. Ad *rētia* sedēbam; nōn

erant sagittae aut pīlum aut lancea prope mē, sed stilus et papȳrus. Exspec-
tābam in silvā et scrībēbam, ut, sī rētia vacua remanērent, reportārem tamen
tabellās plēnās.

Hoc genus studī est bonum grātumque; animus agitātiōne et mōtū corporis excitātur. In silvā etiam est sōlitūdō et illud silentium, quod *vēnātiōnī*
datur; haec omnia sunt bonae cōndiciōnēs studī et scrībendī. Ergō tū, cum ad
vēnātiōnem ībis, fer tēcum et panem et vīnum et tabellās. Inveniēs nōn
sōlum Diānam, deam vēnātiōnis, sed etiam Minervam, deam sapientiae, in
montibus et silvīs habitāre. Valē.

— Plinius, *Epistulae I*, vi
(adapted)

vēnātor — hunter
omnīnō — completely
rētia — from *rēte*, hunting net
vēnātiōnī — from *vēnātiō*, hunt

11 How does the writer expect the recipient of the
letter to react?   11_____

12 What evidence shows that Pliny was a successful
hunter?   12_____

13 Name *one* hunting weapon that Pliny says was
not near him on the hunt.   13_____

14 In addition to hunting gear, name *one* other item
that Pliny took with him.   14_____

15 What did Pliny do while he was sitting and
waiting for the nets to be filled?   15_____

16 What did Pliny hope to bring back if his hunting
were unsuccessful?   16_____

17 What is a benefit that the forest offers to Pliny's
study?   17_____

18 Name *one* thing that Pliny suggests should be brought to the hunt to eat or drink.   18_____

19 In contrast to Diana, how is Minerva described?   19_____

20 According to the writer, where can Diana and Minerva be found?   20_____

PART IIIC

DIRECTIONS (**21–30**): *Read the following passage carefully, but do* not *write a translation. Below the passage, there are several questions or incomplete statements. For each, select the alternative that best answers the question or completes the statement on the basis of the* information *given in the passage, and write its* number *in the space provided.* [10]

Agamemnōn cum Menelāō frātre et ducibus Graecīs ad Trōiam nāvigāre cōnstituit ut Helenam, uxōrem Menelāī, referret quam Paris rapuerat. Tempestās eōs in portū Graecō retinēbat. Diāna tempestātem mīserat quod Agamemnōn sacram *cervam* Diānae vulnerāverat et contrā Diānam male locūtus erat. Agamemnōn *haruspicēs* convocāvit et consuluit. Tum *Calchās* haruspex respondit Īphigenīam, fīliam Agamemnonis, sacrificandam esse. Rē audītā, Agamemnōn fīliam suam interficere *rēcūsāvit*. Tunc Ulixēs hoc cōnsilium cēpit: Ulixēs ipse cum Diomēde missus est ut Īphigenīam ad portum Graecum dūceret. Ulixēs, cum ad Clytaemnēstram, mātrem Īphigenīae, vēnisset, falsē nūntiāvit Achillem in mātrimōnium Īphigenīam ductūrum esse. Cum Ulixēs Īphigenīam in portum Graecum dūxisset et Agamemnōn eam sacrificāre nōn iam rēcūsāret, Diāna puellam servāvit et Īphigenīam per nūbēs in terram longīnquam dētulit. Ibique Īphigenīam templī suī *sacerdōtem* fēcit.

— Hyginus, *Fabulae*, XCVIII
(adapted)

cervam — from *cerva*, doe, female deer
haruspicēs — from *haruspex*, soothsayer, prophet, fortune teller
Calchās — a famous Greek prophet
rēcūsāvit — from *rēcūsō*, refuse
sacerdōtem — from *sacerdōs*, priestess

21 Agamemnōn ad Trōiam īre voluit ut
  1 domum redīret
  2 Menelāum interficeret
  3 Helenam rēciperet
  4 Paridem servāret   21____

22 Ā quō Helena capta erat?
  1 ā Menelāō   3 ab Ulixe
  2 ā Paride   4 ab Achille
                                     22____

23 Graecī in portū manēbant
  1 cum navigāre nōn possent
  2 quod Paris eōs manēre iussit
  3 cum nāvēs incēnsae essent   23____
  4 dum ducēs sē armant

24 Diāna erat īrāta et tempestātem effēcit
  1 quod Trōiānī in suō portū erant
  2 cum haruspicēs convocātī essent
  3 quod Calchās Iphigenīam accūsāverat
  4 cum Agamemnōn animal sacrum necāre
    temptāvisset
                                     24____

25 Quid petīvit Agamemnōn in hāc rē difficilī?
  1 dōnum ā Menelāō
  2 navem et mīlitēs
  3 consilium ab haruspicibus
  4 pācem cum hostibus   25____

26 Calchās Agamemnonī dīxit
  1 Diānam semper īrātam futūram esse
  2 Clytaemnestram ad aram ventūram esse
  3 haruspicēs nihil scīre
  4 fīliam Agamemnonis interficiendam esse   26____

27 Cum prīmum verba Calchantis audīvīsset,
   Agamemnōn
   1 Īphigenīam sacrificāre nōluit
   2 clāmāre violenter incēpit
   3 contrā hostēs statim pugnāvit
   4 nāvēs subitō solvit   27____

28 Ulixēs in animō habuit
   1 pācem cum hostibus facere
   2 Paridem ē castrīs ēicere
   3 ad portum Īphigenīam ferre
   4 Clytaemnēstram interficere   28____

29 Ulixēs Clytaemnēstrae dīxit
   1 Achillem Īphigenīam esse uxōrem cupere
   2 Diomēdem Īphigenīam amāre
   3 Agamemnōnem ad Trōiam nāvigāvisse
   4 Paridem Helenam retulisse   29____

30 Quis tandem Īphigenīam servāvit?
   1 pater   3 Achilles
   2 Diāna   4 Clytaemnēstra   30____

PART IIID

DIRECTIONS (**31–42**): *Read the passage below carefully, but do not write a translation. Below the passage, there are several questions or incomplete statements. Choose 10 of these questions or statements, and in the space provided, write the* number *of the word or expression that best answers the question or completes the statement.* [10]

Tyrannus Pīsistratus dīcitur prīmus posuisse publicē librōs ad legendum Athēnīs. Deinde Athēniēnsēs ipsī dīligenter numerum librōrum auxērunt. Sed posteā, Xerxēs Athēnās occupāvit et, tōtā urbe praeter *arcem* incēnsā,

5

illam omnem librōrum cōpiam abstulit et librōs portāvit in Persās. Multōs
post annōs Seleucus rēx cūrāvit ut eī librī omnēs Athēnās referrentur.

Posteā ingēns numerus librōrum in Aegyptō ab Ptolemaeīs rēgibus
collēctus est — prope mīlia septingenta librōrum. Sed eī omnēs, dum urbs
Alexandrīa bellō vastātur, forte ā mīlitibus auxiliāriīs Rōmānīs incēnsī sunt.

— Gellius, *Noctēs Atticae*, Book VII, XVII
(adapted)

arcem — from *arx*, citadel

31 What does the author say about the tyrant
Pisistratus?
1 He was the first to establish a public library.
2 He publicly punished those who read books.
3 He read books to the children of Athens.
4 He destroyed all the books in Athens.   31_____

32 What rhetorical device appears in line 1?
1 anaphora   3 alliteration
2 litotes   4 chiasmus   32_____

33 The Latin word *posuisse* (line 1) is
1 a subjunctive   3 an imperative
2 an infinitive   4 a participle   33_____

34 Which is the best translation for the Latin phrase
ad legendum (line 1)?
1 for reading   3 by reading
2 must be read   4 about to read   34_____

35 The first principal part of the Latin verb *auxērunt*
(line 2) is
1 *agō*   3 *augeō*
2 *audeō*   4 *audiō*   35_____

36 What did Xerxes do after Athens had been destroyed by fire?
1 He burned all the remaining books.
2 He demanded a larger supply of books.
3 He transported the books from Athens to Persia.
4 He asked Seleucus to care for the books.   36_____

37 The Latin word *abstulit* (line 4) is a compound of the preposition *ab* and the verb
1 *teneō*   3 *laetor*
2 *sum*   4 *ferō*   37_____

38 Which Latin expression means the opposite of *multōs post annōs* (lines 4 and 5)?
1 *semper*   3 *saepe*
2 *brevī tempore*   4 *iterum et iterum*   38_____

39 Which word is associated by derivation with a Latin word in the sentence *Multōs . . . referrentur* (lines 4 and 5)?
1 announce   3 reference
2 military   4 liberate   39_____

40 The action of King Seleucus is best described as
1 honorable   3 cowardly
2 cruel   4 hasty   40_____

41 Which Latin word is omitted but is understood with *eī omnēs* (line 7)?
1 *rēgēs*   3 *urbēs*
2 *librī*   4 *Aegyptī*   41_____

42 What does Gellius say about the Ptolemies'
collection of books?

1 It was not very large.
2 It was removed from Rome.
3 It pertained only to war.
4 It was burned by soldiers.   42____

PART IV

Answer the questions in Part IV according to the directions for Parts IVA,
IVB, IVC, and IVD. [30 credits]

PART IVA

DIRECTIONS (**43–52**): *In the space provided, write the number of the
word or expression that, when inserted in the blank, makes each sentence
grammatically correct.* [10]

43 Māter omnium _____ artium sapientia est.

1 bonā   3 bonārum
2 bonī   4 bonam   43____

44 Cūrā, _____, tē ipsum.

1 medicus   3 medicum
2 medice   4 medicō   44____

45 Magnae rēs nōn fiunt sine _____.

1 perīculum   3 perīculōrum
2 perīcula   4 perīculō
                                                    45____

46 Malum est cōnsilium _____ mūtārī nōn
potest.
1 quod   3 quae
2 quī   4 quem   46_____

47 Puella _____ magnō cum studiō persuāsit.
1 matre   3 matris
2 matrem   4 matrī   47_____

48 Hīs rēbus _____, Caesar ad portum
pervēnit.
1 cōnstituat   3 cōnstituere
2 cōnstitūtīs   4 cōnstituendum   48_____

49 Sōcratēs putābat sē _____ cīvem tōtīus
mundī.
1 erat   3 esset
2 esse   4 fuisset   49_____

50 Nōlī _____ ad forum!
1 īte   3 īre
2 ībant   4 īret   50_____

51 Mīlitēs tam dēfessī erant ut nōn iam iter
facere _____.
1 cuperent   3 cupiēbant
2 cupīvērunt   4 cupiant   51_____

52 Sī cīvēs ad Cūriam hodiē vēnissent, duōs novōs
cōnsulēs _____.
1 vidēbant   3 vident
2 vidēbunt   4 vīdissent   52_____

PART IVB

DIRECTIONS (**53–62**): *This part contains two passages in English in which words associated by derivation with Latin words are italicized. Below each passage, there are several questions or incomplete statements. For each, select the alternative that best answers the question or completes the statement, and write its number in the space provided.* [10]

The restorer's *credo* is like the physician's: First, do no harm. The treatment is to lift layers of Rome's dust, sooty grease from burning candle tallow, and other substances — even the *residue* of Greek wine used as a cleaning *solvent* some 275 years ago. All have *obscured* Michelangelo's Promethean work.

— *National Geographic*

53 The English word *credo* is associated by derivation with *crēdō*, the Latin word that means
1 burn
2 condone
3 believe
4 declare

53____

54 The root of the English word *residue* is associated by derivation with which Latin word paired with its English meaning?
1 *saliō* — leap
2 *sedeō* — sit
3 *scindō* — cut
4 *siccō* — dry up

54____

55 The English word *solvent* is associated by derivation with which Latin word paired with its English meaning?
1 *sōl* — sun
2 *salveō* — be well
3 *ventus* — wind
4 *solvō* — loosen

55____

56 The English word *obscured* is associated by derivation with *obscūrus*, the Latin word that means
1 careless
2 insecure
3 dark
4 observed

56____

To the 19th-Century mind, with its *penchant* for the *scientific* and the mechanical, the camera was the supreme mechanism, a trap for facts. Capable of capturing high detail, *operated* with a *minimum* of human *intervention*, it seemed from the first to have a special purchase on the truth. William Henry Fox Talbot, the Englishman who was one of photography's inventors, was merely summing up what would become the judgment of the day when he called his new *process* the "pencil of nature."

— *Time*

57 In the English words *penchant* and *scientific*, the -*nt*- is associated with the -*nt*- of the Latin present active participle. What is the English equivalent of this -*nt*-?

1 -ing   3 we
2 -ed   4 you   57____

58 The English word *scientific* is associated by derivation with which Latin word paired with its English meaning?

1 *sentiō* — feel   3 *sciō* — know
2 *servō* — save   4 *scrībō* — write   58____

59 The English word *operated* is associated by derivation with which Latin word whose meaning is *work*?

1 *ratiō*   3 *peragō*
2 *erat*   4 *opus*   59____

60 The word *minimum* is an English word and also the superlative form of the Latin word

1 *malus*   3 *bonus*
2 *parvus*   4 *multus*   60____

61 The English word *intervention* is associated by derivation with the Latin words

1 *inter* and *veniō*   3 *inter* and *vendō*
2 *in* and *terra*   4 *in* and *terminus*   61____

62 The English word *process* is associated by derivation with which Latin word paired with its
English meaning?

1 *capiō* — take   3 *caedō* — kill
2 *cadō* — fall   4 *cēdō* — move   62____

PART IVC

DIRECTIONS (**63–67**): *For each sentence below, write, in the longer space
provided, a Latin word with which the italicized word is associated by derivation. Any form of the appropriate Latin word, except prefixes and suffixes,
will be acceptable. Then, in the shorter space provided, write the number preceding the word or expression that best expresses the meaning of the italicized
word.* [5]

63 The senator made a *vehement* speech.

1 boring   3 long
2 powerful   4 gloomy   63____

64 Who is the most *loquacious* student in the class?

1 intelligent 3 talkative
2 popular   4 shy   64____

65 After the accident, the skier suffered from
vertigo.

1 memory loss   3 dizziness
2 back pain   4 headache   65____

66 Because of the *ire* of both neighbors, there was
no easy solution to the argument.

1 anger   3 mistrust
2 stubbornness 4 pride   66____

67 The speaker's *tenacity* helped him to win the debate.

   1 humor   3 cautiousness

   2 experience   4 persistence   67_____

PART IVD

DIRECTIONS (**68–72**): *Each italicized word below has an important basic Latin root as its source. For each word, choose the meaning of its basic Latin root and write its number in the space provided.* [5]

68 *dictionary*

   1 lead   3 say

   2 know   4 write   68_____

69 *umbrella*

   1 wave   3 entrance

   2 rain   4 shadow   69_____

70 *demonstrable*

   1 show   3 warn

   2 collect   4 hold   70_____

71 *recipe*

   1 seek   3 throw

   2 send   4 take   71_____

72 *protract*

   1 wait   3 think

   2 drag   4 fear   72_____

PART V

DIRECTIONS (**73–102**): *Select 20 of the following statements or questions. In the space provided, write the* number *of the word or expression that best answers the question or completes the statement.*   [20 credits]

History and Public Life

73 In the painting shown below, who is sitting alone as Cicero denounces him for conspiring to over‑ throw the Republic?

    1 Verres   3 Manilius

    2 Archias   4 Catiline   73_____

74 The last of the seven kings of Rome was

    1 Greek   3 Carthaginian

    2 Helvetian   4 Etruscan   74_____

75 What disaster occurred in Rome in 64 A.D. dur‑ ing the reign of Nero?

    1 a fire   3 a flood

    2 an earthquake   4 a volcanic eruption   75_____

76 In order to become a lawyer or a politician, a Roman spent the greatest part of his education studying
   1 geography   3 oratory
   2 mathematics   4 music   76____

77 A general who had won a major victory was honored with the title
   1 *centuriō*   3 *cōnsul*
   2 *imperātor*   4 *lēgātus*   77____

78 Caesar's opponent in the Civil War, whom he defeated in the battle of Pharsalus, was
   1 Pompey   3 Marius
   2 Sulla   4 Brutus   78____

79 In the power struggle after the death of Caesar, who was victorious over Mark Antony in the battle of Actium?
   1 Cassius   3 Cato
   2 Lepidus   4 Octavian   79____

80 According to legend, Hannibal, Hasdrubal, and Hanno were from the nation founded by
   1 Hadrian   3 Priam
   2 Dido   4 Orgetorix   80____

81 A victory gained with extensive losses is called
   1 Pyrrhic   3 Philippic
   2 Ciceronian   4 Pompeian   81____

82 What is reported to have been said by Caesar after his swift defeat of Pharnaces, king of Pontus?

1 *"Et tū, Brūte."*
2 *"Vēnī, vīdī, vīcī."*
3 *"Ālea iacta est."*
4 *"In hōc signō vincēs."*   82____

Daily Life

83 What did the Romans call the type of shop shown in the illustration below?

1 *taberna*   3 *templum*
2 *tablīnum*   4 *thermae*   83____

84 A middle-class Roman merchant was of the socioeconomic order known as

1 *optimātēs*   3 *plēbēs*
2 *equitēs*   4 *senātōrēs*   84____

85 The purple-bordered toga, worn by young boys
and certain government officials, was called the
1 *toga virīlis*   3 *toga praetexta*
2 *toga candida*   4 *toga sordida*   85____

86 On which day would the Roman date *a.d. III Īd.
Oct.* fall?
1 September 3   3 October 5
2 September 29   4 October 13   86____

87 At a large Roman dinner party, how many people
generally reclined on each *lectus*?
1 twelve   3 three
2 six   4 four   87____

Myths and Legends

88 Which mythological creatures are shown in the
illustration below?

1 furies   3 satyrs
2 centaurs   4 harpies   88____

89 According to Roman mythology, Orpheus went to the underworld to bring back his wife. What was his wife's name?

1 Eurydice   3 Penelope
2 Psyche   4 Lavinia   89____

90 The six Vestal Virgins were priestesses of the goddess of the

1 hunt   3 harvest
2 hearth   4 moon   90____

91 Who was the two-faced god of doorways?

1 Lar   3 Chiron
2 Ares   4 Janus   91____

92 One of the accomplishments of Theseus was killing the

1 Nemean Lion   3 Minotaur
2 Medusa   4 Lernean Hydra   92____

93 What was the name of the king's daughter who helped Jason win the Golden Fleece?

1 Medea   3 Cassandra
2 Ariadne   4 Andromeda   93____

94 What was the name of the river in the underworld that dead souls had to cross?

1 *Rhēnus*   3 *Styx*
2 *Xanthus*   4 *Tiberis*   94____

Literature

95 In the mosaic illustrated below, the seated figure represents the poet who wrote of the love story of Dido and Aeneas.

What is the poet's name?
1 Vergil   3 Catullus
2 Homer   4 Hesiod   95____

96 The Roman historian who wrote extensively about the Punic Wars was
1 Livy   3 Sallust
2 Tacitus   4 Caesar   96____

97 The Roman who wrote an eyewitness account of
the eruption of Mount Vesuvius in 79 A.D. was
   1 Seneca   3 Lucretius
   2 Cicero   4 Pliny   97____

98 Who were two popular writers of ancient Roman
comedies?
   1 Vergil and Homer
   2 Plautus and Terence
   3 Horace and Catullus
   4 Plato and Aristotle   98____

Architecture and Art

99 On which hill was the Temple of Jupiter
Optimus Maximus?
   1 Palatine   3 Aventine
   2 Esquiline   4 Capitoline   99____

100 Law courts often met in the
   1 *palaestra*   3 *basilica*
   2 *Campus Martius*   4 *Āra Pācis*   100____

101 The dungeon of the *Carcer* in Rome was called
the
   1 *Tulliānum*   3 *Rostra*
   2 *Cloāca Maxima*   4 *Domus Aurea*   101____

102 In the model of the Circus Maximus shown in the illustration below, what is the name of the structure in the middle, around which the chariots raced?

1 *carcerēs*   3 *quadrīgae*

2 *spīna*   4 *tabulārium*   102____

Answers   June 1991

Comprehensive Examination in Latin

PART I
(Allow a total of 5 credits for this part.)

PART II
(Allow a total of 5 credits, one-half credit for each of the following 10 italicized words.)

Terentia tibi/ et *saepe*/ et maximās/ agit *grātiās*./ Id est *mihi* grātissimum./ Ego *vīvō* miserrimus/ et maximō *dolōre* cōnficior./ Ad tē/ *quid* scrīban / *nesciō*./ Sī enim es Rōmae/ *iam* mē adsequī/ nōn potes/ sīn es in viā/ cum *eris*/ mē adsecūtus/ cōram agēmus/ quae erunt *agenda*./ Cūrā ut valeās.

PART IIIA
(Allow a total of 10 credits, one credit for each of the following.)

(1) 1	(3) 4	(5) 3	(7) 4	(9) 1
(2) 3	(4) 2	(6) 2	(8) 3	(10) 2

PART IIIB
(Allow a total of 10 credits, one credit for each of the following.)

(11) by laughing; by not believing
(12) He captured three very beautiful animals.
(13) arrows, spear, lance
(14) stylus (pen), papyrus (paper)
(15) He wrote.
(16) full tablets
(17) the mind is stimulated by exercise and movement of the body; solitude and silence are there
(18) bread, wine
(19) Minerva is the goddess of wisdom.
(20) living in the mountains and the woods

PART IIIC
(Allow a total of 10 credits, one credit for each of the following.)

(21) 3	(23) 1	(25) 3	(27) 1	(29) 1
(22) 2	(24) 4	(26) 4	(28) 3	(30) 2

PART IIID
(Allow a total of 10 credits, one credit for each of 10 of the following.)

(31) 1	(34) 1	(37) 4	(39) 3	(41) 2
(32) 3	(35) 3	(38) 2	(40) 1	(42) 4
(33) 2	(36) 3			

PART IVA
(Allow a total of 10 credits, one credit for each of the following.)

(43) 3	(45) 4	(47) 4	(49) 2	(51) 1
(44) 2	(46) 1	(48) 2	(50) 3	(52) 4

PART IVB
(Allow a total of 10 credits, one credit for each of the following.)

(53) 3	(55) 4	(57) 1	(59) 4	(61) 1
(54) 2	(56) 3	(58) 3	(60) 2	(62) 4

PART IVC
(Allow a total of 5 credits, one-half credit for each correct answer in each space.)

(63) vehemēns, vehō, mēns   2
(64) loquor, loquax   3
(65) vertō, vertīgō   3
(66) ira   1
(67) teneō, tenax   4

PART IVD
(Allow a total of 5 credits, one credit for each of the following).

(68) 3	(69) 4	(70) 1	(71) 4	(72) 2

PART V
(Allow a total of 20 credits, one credit for each of 20 of the following).

(73) 4	(78) 1	(83) 1	(88) 2	(93) 1	(98) 2
(74) 4	(79) 4	(84) 2	(89) 1	(94) 3	(99) 4
(75) 1	(80) 2	(85) 3	(90) 2	(95) 1	(100) 3
(76) 3	(81) 1	(86) 4	(91) 4	(96) 1	(101) 1
(77) 2	(82) 2	(87) 3	(92) 3	(97) 4	(102) 2

Examination   June 1992

Comprehensive Latin

PART I

Part I is administered at the school's convenience at some time before the written test is given. You are asked to read aloud a passage of Latin for the teacher to judge on the basis of your proficiency in the spoken language. [5]

PART II

DIRECTIONS: *Your teacher will read aloud a short passage in Latin. Listen carefully to this first reading. Then your teacher will read the passage in short phrases with a pause after each phrase. After each pause, write, in Latin, the phrase read by your teacher. Do* not *write a translation of the passage.*

There will be no penalty for improper use of macrons or capitalization. After you have completed writing the passage in Latin, your teacher will read the entire passage one more time so that you may check your work. [5]

The passage that the teacher reads will be found in **Answers, Part II** , *at the end of this examination.*

PART III

Answer the questions in Part III according to the directions for Parts IIIA, IIIB, IIIC, and IIID. [40]

PART IIIA

DIRECTIONS (**1–10**): *Do* not *write a translation of the following passage; read it through carefully several times to ascertain its meaning. Then, in the spaces provided, write the* number *of the alternative that best translates each underlined expression as it is used in the passage.* [10]

In Cūriā L. Tarquinius multā cum audāciā ōrātiōnem habēbat. <u>Cum</u>

<u>huic ōrātiōnī intervēnisset</u>, Servius, quī ōlim fuerat servus, sed nunc erat

(1)

rēx, statim ā vestibulō Cūriae māgnā vōce rogāvit, "<u>Quid est hoc reī</u>,

(2)   (3)

Tarquinī? Rēx sum. Quā audāciā tū senātōrēs vocāre ausus es <u>aut in meā</u>

<u>sēde cōnsīdere?</u>"

(4)

Tarquinius ferōciter ad haec respondit sē <u>patris suī sēdem tenēre</u> ac

(5)   (6)

filium rēgis esse multō meliōrem rēgem quam filium servī. Clāmōrēs

oriēbantur et <u>concursus populī in Cūriam contendit</u>.

(7)

Tum necessitāte Tarquinius ūltima audēre coāctus est. Ille, <u>multō et</u>

<u>aetāte et vīribus validior</u>, Servium arripuit atque ē Cūriā tulit et per

(8)

gradūs in viam dēiēcit; inde in Cūriam rediit. Sociī rēgis fūgērunt. Servius,

cum ipse sōlus domum redīret, <u>ab eīs quī ab Tarquiniō missī erant</u>

(9)

interficitur.

Servius Tullius rēgnāvit annōs quattuor et quadrāgintā. <u>Inde L.</u>

<u>Tarquinius rēgnāre coepit</u>, cui Superbus erat cognōmen.

(10)

— Livy, *Ab Urbe Conditā*, I, XLVIII — XLVIX

(adapted)

1 Cum huic ōrātiōnī intervēnisset
  1 Although his speech had been heard
  2 Since this speech had begun
  3 When he had interrupted this speech
  4 When that speech had been repeated   1____

2 statim ā vestibulō Cūriae māgnā vōce rogāvit

   1 suddenly, near the entrance of the senate-
     house, a loud voice spoke
   2 immediately asked in a loud voice from the
     entrance of the senate-house
   3 by the entrance of the senate-house,
     suddenly a loud sound arose
   4 immediately they were shouting with loud
     voices near the entrance of the senate-house   2_____

3 Quid est hoc rēī, Tarquinī?

   1 Where is this race, Tarquinius?
   2 How is this king, Tarquinius?
   3 What is this situation, Tarquinius?
   4 Why is that important to the king,
     Tarquinius?   3_____

4 aut in meā sēde cōnsīdere

   1 or to sit in my seat
   2 or sat in my seat
   3 and seated in my seat
   4 and then sat in my seat   4_____

5 Tarquinius ferōciter ad haec respondit

   1 Tarquinius was fiercely criticized for this
   2 Tarquinius fiercely responded to this
   3 He fiercely answered this for Tarquinius
   4 The reply was fiercely made to Tarquinius
     about these matters   5_____

6 sē patris suī sēdem tenēre
  1 that she occupied her father's home
  2 to lead them to their father's seat
  3 he was held at his father's home
  4 that he was holding his father's seat   6____

7 concursus populī in Cūriam contendit
  1 a crowd of people hastened into the
    senate-house
  2 an attack of the people occurred near the
    senate-house
  3 he hastens to the senate-house with a crowd
    of people
  4 the people prepared a racecourse near the
    senate-house   7____

8 multō et aetāte et vīribus validior
  1 much stronger both in age and in strength
  2 and at a much stronger age
  3 in summer the men seemed much stronger
  4 and many stronger men were equal   8____

9 ab eīs quī ab Tarquiniō missī erant
  1 from the ones who were sent to Tarquinius
  2 from those whom Tarquinius had sent
  3 by those who had been sent by Tarquinius
  4 to those who were sent by Tarquinius   9____

10 Inde L. Tarquinius rēgnāre coepit
  1 Then Lucius Tarquinius captured the
    kingdom
  2 At last he ordered Lucius Tarquinius to rule
  3 Finally Lucius Tarquinius forced him to rule
  4 Then Lucius Tarquinius began to rule   10____

PART IIIB

DIRECTIONS (**11–20**): *Do not write a translation of the following passage; read it through carefully several times to ascertain its meaning. Base your answers on the content of the passage only. Your answers do not have to be complete sentences; a word or phrase may suffice. In the space provided, write in English your answer to each question.* [10]

Est in librīs Graecīs fābula dē epistulā sēcrētā ab virō Āsiāticō missā. Vir Āsiāticus fuit Histiaeus nōmine, nātus in terrā longinquā dē familiā nōbilī. Āsiam tunc tenēbat imperiō rēx Darīus. Is Histiaeus, cum in rēgiā apud Darīum esset, cuidam amīcō rēs occultās et sēcrētās scrībere furtim volēbat.

Igitur Histiaeus hōc modō litterās mittere constituit. Servum suum diū oculōs aegrōs et īnfirmōs habentem vocat. Servus bene vidēre nōn poterat. Histiaeus *capillum* omnem ex capite servī, *tamquam* oculōrum cūrae et valētūdinis causā, removet. Deinde Histiaeus in caput servī formās litterārum scrīpsit. Hīs litterīs scrīptīs, servum domī suae retinuit, dum capillus incrēsceret. Ubī capillī satis longī erant, Histiaeus iubet servum īre ad amīcum, et, "Cum ad eum vēneris," inquit, "eum rogā ut capillum ab capite tuō removeat, sīcut ego fēcī." Servus, ut imperātum erat, ad amīcum venit et iussum dominī efficit. Atque amīcus nōn frūstrā capillum servī remōvit. Ita litterae inventae sunt, et amīcus Histiaeī nuntiōs sēcrētōs facile lēgit.

capillum — from *capillus*, hair   — Gellius, *Noctēs Atticae* XVII, ix
tamquam — as if   (adapted)

11 What was the topic of the story in the Greek books?

_____

12 How does the author describe Histiaeus, the man from Asia?

_____

13 Who was Darius?

_____

14 What did Histiaeus want to do?

_____

15 What health problem did Histiaeus' slave have?

_____

16 Under the pretense of improving the slave's health, what did Histiaeus first do to the slave?

_____

_____

17 What was the real purpose of this action?

_____

_____

18 Why did Histiaeus keep the slave at home for a while?

_____

_____

19 What was the slave told to ask Histiaeus' friend to do?

_____

_____

20 What was the final result of the mission?

_____

_____

PART IIIC

DIRECTIONS (21–30): *Read the following passages carefully, but do* not *write a translation. Below each passage, there are several questions or incomplete statements. For each, select the alternative that best answers the question or completes the statement on the basis of the* information given in the passage, *and write its* number *in the space provided.* [10]

Ōlim serpēns iacēbat super terram frīgidam, et serpēns multum frīgēbat. Homō quīdam, amōre animālium mōtus, accēpit serpentem et posuit in *sinum* suum ad *calefaciendum*. Serpēns calefactus hominem dentibus fortiter vulnerābat. Et homō ait, "Quārē ita male mē oppugnāvistī? Quia prō bonō tuō in sinū meō tē collocāvī." Rēspondit serpēns, "Nōnne scīs semper esse inimīcitiam inter genus meum et tuum, et odium quoque?"

Eōdem modō is, quī malam nātūram habet, cum potest, semper nātūram suam exercet. Nōlī iuvāre neque amāre umquam hominem tibi adversum; nōlī mandāre eī tē ipsum.

sinum — from *sinus*, lap   — Odo Ceritonēnsis, *Aesopica*, 588
calefaciendum — from *calefaciō*, make warm   (adapted)

21 Serpēns erat in perīculō quod erat
    1 aetāte confectus   3 frīgidissimus
    2 leō in silvā   4 graviter vulnerātus   21____

22 Vir quī serpentem accēpit

   1 plēnus erat timōris
   2 bonus et benignus erat
   3 volēbat perīre
   4 serpentem interficere voluit   22_____

23 In sinū suō homō serpentem posuit ut

   1 cibum eī daret
   2 eum melius vidēret
   3 fortitūdinem dēmōnstrāret
   4 serpēns fieret calidus   23_____

24 Hōc factō, serpēns repentē

   1 dē sinū discessit
   2 hominem vulnerāre constituit
   3 in terram intrāvit
   4 mortuus est   24_____

25 Homō nōn intellexit cūr serpēns

   1 eum aggressus esset
   2 auxilium rogāvisset
   3 loquī potuisset
   4 celeriter exīvisset   25_____

26 Quid docet haec fābula?

   1 Semper adiuvā inimīcum tuum.
   2 Da salūtem hostibus.
   3 Crēde tē semper salvum esse perīculīs.
   4 Nōlī adversāriō tuō auxilium dare.   26_____

    M. Minuciō Rūfō et P. Cornēliō consulibus, bellum Pūnicum secundum contrā Romānōs gestum est ab Hannibale, Carthāginiēnsium duce quī Saguntum cōpiīs suīs expugnāverat. Rōmānī lēgātōs Carthāginem mīsērunt ut mandārētur Hannibalī nē bellum contrā sociōs populī Rōmānī gereret. Dūra respōnsa ā Carthāginiēnsibus data sunt. Saguntīnīs victīs, bellum Carthāginiēnsibus indictum est.

— Eutropius, *Breviārium*, III, 7
(adapted)

27 Quis erat M. Minucius Rūfus?
1 consul Rōmānus
2 dux Carthāginiēnsium
3 lēgātus Saguntīnōrum
4 amīcus Hannibalis   27____

28 Quid fēcit Hannibal?
1 ad Rōmānōs auxilium mīsit
2 in oppidō Saguntō habitābat
3 exercitum contrā Saguntum dūxit
4 Carthāginem oppugnāvit   28____

29 Hannibal et Carthāginiēnsēs volēbant
1 pācem cum Rōmānīs facere
2 bellum contrā sociōs Rōmānōrum gerere
3 domum redīre
4 cum consulibus loquī   29____

30 Quandō bellum contrā Carthāginiēnsēs
   indictum est?
1 postquam Rūfus mortuus est
2 priusquam respōnsa data sunt
3 postquam Carthāginiēnsēs Saguntīnōs
   vīcērunt
4 antequam Hannibal cum P. Cornēliō
   locūtus est   30____

PART IIID

DIRECTIONS (**31–42**): *Read the passage below carefully, but do not write a translation. Below the passage, there are several questions or incomplete statements. Choose 10 of these questions or statements, and in the space provided, write the number of the word or expression that best answers the question or completes the statement.* [10]

Autrōnius veniēbat ad mē et saepe veniēbat, multīs cum lacrimīs, mē
ōrāns ut sē dēfenderem. Commemorābat sē fuisse meum condiscipulum in
pueritiā, familiārem in adulescentiā, collēgam in quaestūrā. Ego multum
etiam Autrōnium iūveram; atque ille mē multum. Quibus rēbus, iūdicēs,
5 ita mōtus sum ut memōriam eius in mē iniūriae paene dēpōnerem; nam ab
eō missus erat C. Cornēlius quī mē, in meā domō, in conspectū uxōris ac
līberōrum meōrum, necāre volēbat.

Sī tamen ego dē mē sōlō cōgitāvissem, illīus Autrōnī lacrimīs ac precibus
commōtus essem. Tum autem putāre coepī dē patriā, dē vestrīs perīculīs,
10 dē urbe templīsque, dē īnfantibus, matrōnīs, virginibus; tum etiam in
animum meum veniēbat memōria incendiōrum, tēlōrum, caedis, cīvium
sanguinis. Tum dēnique eī resistēbam; tum dēnique arbitrābar mē
numquam hominem cīvibus urbīque tam īnfestum, tam scelestum, tam
maleficum dēfendere posse.

— Cicerō, Prō Sullā, 18–20.
(adapted)

31 A synonym for the Latin word *ōrāns* (line 2) is
   1 *vidēns*   3 *capiēns*
   2 *oriēns*   4 *petēns*   31_____

32 What did Cicero indicate about himself and
Autronius?
   1 They had known each other since boyhood.
   2 They had recently met.
   3 They had taught in the same school.
   4 They had come from related families.   32_____

33 A synonym for the Latin word *familiārem* (line 3)
is
   1 *patrem*   3 *mercātōrem*
   2 *magistrum*   4 *amīcum*   33_____

34 Which is the superlative form of the Latin word
multum (line 4)?
   1 *plūs*   3 *plūrimum*
   2 *optimum*   4 *māius*   34_____

35 The first principal part of the Latin word *iūveram*
   (line 4) is
   1 *iungō*   3 *iūrō*
   2 *iubeō*   4 *iuvō*   35_____

36 In this passage, Cicero is talking to
   (1) Autronius   (3) C. Cornelius
   (2) judges   (4) his wife   36_____

37 Which English word is derived from the Latin
   word *necāre* (line 7)?
   1 unique   3 internecine
   2 negative   4 nectar   37_____

38 According to the passage, Cicero said that
   Autronius sent C. Cornelius to
   1 kill Cicero while his wife and children
     watched
   2 arrest Cicero's wife in the presence of her chil-
     dren
   3 see Cicero's wife and children
   4 instruct Cicero's wife to watch his children   38_____

39 Which Latin word is an antonym for *numquam*
   (line 13)?
   1 *nunc*   3 *simul*
   2 *semper*   4 *ōlim*   39_____

40 Which figure of speech is illustrated in the Latin
   expression *tam īnfestum, tam scelestum, tam
   maleficum* (lines 13 and 14)?
   1 chiasmus   3 simile
   2 personification 4 anaphora   40_____

41 What does Cicero explain in this passage?
  1 why he is unable to defend Autronius
  2 why he never was a classmate of Autronius' in
     school
  3 why Autronius never leaves the city
  4 why Autronius moved Cornelius to tears   41____

42 Cicero concludes that Autronius is
  1 a faithful friend   3 a good citizen
  2 an evil man   4 a poor judge   42____

PART IV

Answer the questions in Part IV according to the directions for Parts IVA,
IVB, IVC, and IVD. [30]

PART IVA

DIRECTIONS (**43–52**): *In the space provided, write the* number *of the word
or expression that, when inserted in the blank, makes* each *sentence grammatically correct.* [10]

43 Quid ēgistī in urbe, _____?
  1 amīce   3 amīcō
  2 amīcōs   4 amīcum   43____

44 Omnia mala exempla ex _____ orta sunt.
  1 rēs bonae   3 rēbus bonīs
  2 rēs bonās   4 rērum bonārum   44____

45 Melior tūtiorque est certa pāx quam _____.
  1 spērāta victōria   3 spērātam victōriam
  2 spērātīs victōriīs   4 spērātās victōriās   45____

46 Cincinnātus dēligēbātur _____.
  1 dictātōrem   3 dictātor
  2 dictātōris   4 dictātōre   46____

47 Meum donum nōn est grātum _____.
   1 māter   3 ad mātrem
   2 mātrī   4 mātre   47____

48 Fortis imperator, populum Rōmānum _____!
   1 servātur   3 servāte
   2 servā   4 servātus   48____

49 Putō tē hoc _____.
   1 facis   3 factus esset
   2 fēcistī   4 fēcisse   49____

50 Sī senātōrēs ōrātōrem _____, eum
   laudāvissent.
   1 audīvisse   3 audīre
   2 audiunt   4 audīvissent   50____

51 Imperātor persuādēbit mīlitibus nē _____.
   1 fugiant   3 fugite
   2 fūgērunt   4 fugientēs   51____

52 Nōmine _____, dē tē fābula narrātur.
   1 mūtātō   3 mūtantem
   2 mūtāre   4 mūtandus   52____

PART IVB

DIRECTIONS (**53–62**): *This part contains a passage in English in which
words associated by derivation with Latin words are italicized. Below the passage, there are several questions or incomplete statements. For each, select the
alternative that best answers the question or completes the statement, and
write its number in the space provided.* [10]

It is Mars, the blood-red *specter* in the nighttime sky, that *continues* to
reign in the imagination. It has *inspired* some of the best science fiction, from
Edgar Rice Burrough's romantic tales of John Carter and his exploits on
Barscom to Ray Bradbury's eerily beautiful "Martian Chronicles." For that
5   matter, Mars is the only planet with a candy bar named after it.

In "Mars Beckons," John Noble Wilford, a science *correspondent* for "The New York Times" and twice a Pulitzer Prize winner, writes on the historic myths, *current speculations* and scientific facts of this *celebrated* planet. More *important*, he weighs the question that, not too long ago, only spaceflight
10 *aficionados* dared to ask publicly: When do we go to Mars in person and directly seek the truth behind the *legend*?

— *The New York Times Book Review*

53 Which Latin word, paired with its English meaning, is associated by derivation with the word *specter* (line 1) and *speculations* (line 8)?
1 *pectō* — comb   3 *spectō* — look at
2 *spargō* — sprinkle   4 *pecūnia* — money   53_____

54 The English word *continues* (line 1) is associated by derivation with the Latin word
1 *tondeō*   3 *contemnō*
2 *teneō*   4 *contrahō*   54_____

55 The origin of the spelling of the English word *reign* (line 2) is best explained by referring to its association with the Latin word
1 *regnō*   3 *regredior*
2 *ignis*   4 *rigidus*   55_____

56 Which Latin word, paired with its English meaning, is associated by derivation with the English word *inspired* (line 2)?
1 *spērō* — hope   3 *spondeō* — pledge
2 *spernō* — reject   4 *spīrō* — breathe   56_____

57 Which Latin word is associated by derivation with the English word *correspondent* (line 6)?
1 *corripiō*   3 *respondeō*
2 *corrigō*   4 *rēspiciō*   57_____

58 The English word *current* (line 8) is associated by
   derivation with *currō*, the Latin word that means
   1 care for   3 give back
   2 estimate   4 run   58_____

59 The English word *celebrated* (line 8) is associated
   by derivation with the Latin word
   1 *celerō*   3 *labōrō*
   2 *celebrō*   4 *līberō*   59_____

60 The English word *important* (line 9) contains the
   Latin word that means
   1 they place   3 they carry
   2 they can   4 they seek   60_____

61 Which Latin word, paired with its English
   meaning, is associated by derivation with the
   Spanish and English word *aficionados* (line 10)?
   1 *faciō* — do   3 *afferō* — bring to
   2 *fingō* — shape   4 *affundō* — pour   61_____

62 The English word *legend* (line 11) is associated
   by derivation with *legō*, the Latin word that
   means
   1 compel   3 admire
   2 read   4 bind   62_____

PART IVC

DIRECTIONS (**63–67**): *For each sentence below, write, in the longer space
provided, a Latin word with which the italicized word is associated by derivation. Any form of the appropriate Latin word, except prefixes and suffixes,
will be acceptable. Then write in the shorter space provided, the number preceding the word or expression that best expresses the meaning of the italicized
word.* [5]

63 The young consumer made a *judicious* choice in deciding what to buy.
   1 unusual   3 wise
   2 impulsive   4 inconsistent

63_____   _____

64 The commentator's remark on the radio was *ludicrous*.
   1 absurd   3 important
   2 upsetting   4 insensitive

64_____   _____

65 The patient was diagnosed as having an *auditory* problem.
   1 allergy   3 speech
   2 vision   4 hearing

65_____   _____

66 The athlete's anger upon losing the game was *transitory*.
   1 irrational   3 excessive
   2 temporary   4 obvious

66_____   _____

67 We were all amazed by the *fortitude* shown by the stranger.
   1 courage   3 charm
   2 curiosity   4 compassion

67_____   _____

PART IVD

DIRECTIONS (**68–72**): *For each Latin expression used in English, write, in the space provided at the left, the number of the English translation, chosen from the list below, that most nearly has the same meaning.* [5]

	Latin Expression	English Translation
68_____	68 *status quō*	1 by virtue of office
69_____	69 *dē iure*	2 a necessity
70_____	70 *sine quā nōn*	3 without preparation
71_____	71 *quid prō quō*	4 the existing state
72_____	72 *ex tempore*	5 something for another thing
		6 according to law
		7 prepared for all things

PART V

DIRECTIONS (**73–102**): *Select 20 of the following statements or questions. In the space provided, write the* number *of the word or expression that best answers the question or completes the statement.* [20]

History and Public Life

73 In the procession of an important Roman shown in the illustration below, what were the men carrying the fasces called?

1 lictors

2 praetors

3 augurs

4 clients

73_____

74 The year 509 B.C. marked the beginning of the Roman
    1 kingdom   3 empire
    2 republic   4 dictatorship   74____

75 Who were known for advocating social reform for the Plebeians?
    1 *Horātū*   3 *Fabū*
    2 *Drusī*   4 *Gracchī*   75____

76 Which civilization greatly influenced early Roman culture and flourished in the area just north of the emerging Roman state?
    1 Samnite   3 Ligurian
    2 Greek   4 Etruscan   76____

77 Near the end of his life, Cicero delivered a series of speeches, known as the *Philippics*, in which he attacked
    1 Antony   3 Atticus
    2 Clodius   4 Cato   77____

78 The home of Vercingetorix was
    1 Spain   3 Gaul
    2 Germany   4 Britain   78____

79 In the third century B.C., Rome's greatest military and political rival was
    1 Greece   3 Carthage
    2 Persia   4 Gaul   79____

80 The usual length of a consul's term in office was
    (1) 1 year   (3) 5 years
    (2) 2 years   (4) 10 years   80____

81 Who said that he found Rome a city of bricks and
left it a city of marble?

1 Nero   3 Titus

2 Augustus   4 Trajan   81_____

82 The first office of the *cursus honōrum*, tradition-
ally held by an aspiring politician, was

1 dictator   3 praetor

2 consul   4 quaestor   82_____

Daily Life

83 In the illustration below, two slaves are helping
the *matrōna* dress.

What were these slaves called?

1 *ancillae*   3 *vīlicī*

2 *paedagōgī*   4 *nōmenclātōrēs*   83_____

84 Who typically wore masks such as the two shown in the illustration below?

1 priests
2 gladiators
3 soldiers
4 actors

84_____

85 The Latin phrase *ab ōvō usque ad māla* refers to Roman

1 clothing
2 architecture
3 food
4 law

85_____

86 Which road led south from Rome to Brundisium?

1 Via Flaminia
2 Via Sacra
3 Via Aurelia
4 Via Appia

86_____

87 For relaxation, Romans spent much of their leisure time in the

1 *Thermae*
2 *Templa*
3 *Cloāca*
4 *Tulliānum*

87_____

88 In the homes of the wealthy, scrolls were usually located in the

1 *culīna*
2 *triclīnium*
3 *bibliothēca*
4 *ālae*

88_____

Myths and Legends

89 What is the name of the man, shown in the illustration below, who solved the riddle of the Sphinx?

1 Oedipus   3 Hermes

2 Agamemnon   4 Aeneas   89____

90 Who received the punishment of not being able to reach the food and drink that appeared just beyond his grasp?

1 Tantalus

2 Sisyphus

3 Midas

4 Croesus   90____

91 The illustration below shows the Roman goddess of the Moon and the hunt.

What was the name of this goddess?
1 Juno   3 Diana
2 Minerva   4 Ceres   91____

92 What was the name of the Gorgon whose face was deadly to look upon?
1 Hecate   3 Andromache
2 Medusa   4 Hecuba   92____

93 Which woman's name is synonymous with fidelity?
1 Helen   3 Penelope
2 Medea   4 Circe   93____

94 Who ferried the dead across a river in the underworld?
1 Orpheus   3 Aeneas
2 Eurydice   4 Charon   94_____

Literature

95 Who was the Greek orator who influenced
Cicero?
1 Aristotle   3 Quintilian
2 Demosthenes   4 Socrates   95_____

96 The term "oral tradition," as applied to antiquity,
refers to
1 fathers passing along family secrets to their
sons
2 stories being told and retold by minstrels or
bards
3 orators delivering speeches in the forum in
very loud tones
4 Romans relying on word-of-mouth transmis-
sion of current events, in the absence of
printed media   96_____

97 The story of Aeneas' flight from Troy is told by
the epic poet
1 Homer   3 Vergil
2 Terence   4 Horace   97_____

98 Who said, "*Ō tempora! Ō mōrēs!*" when he was
exasperated with the state of Roman society?
1 Cato   3 Pompey
2 Agrippa   4 Cicero   98_____

Architecture and Art

99 The illustration below shows a Roman speakers' platform.

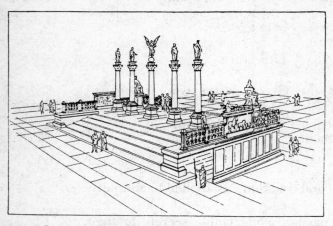

What was this platform called?

1 *rostra*   3 *carcer*

2 *balneae*   4 *rēgia*   99_____

100 The type of artwork practiced by the Romans in which individual colored tiles or stones are arranged so as to make a picture is known as

1 engraving   3 relief

2 fresco   4 mosaic   100_____

101 Which type of building, used for the law courts, lends its floor plan and name to modern churches?

1 *rostra*   3 *domus*

2 *basilica*   4 *taberna*   101_____

102 Which type of building was the original Roman Colosseum?

1 theater   3 shrine

2 amphitheater   4 temple   102_____

Answers   June 1992

Comprehensive Examination in Latin

PART I
(Allow a total of 5 credits for this part.)

PART II
(Allow a total of 5 credits, one-half credit for each of the following 10 italicized words.)

Haec est prīma aetās / populī Rōmānī / et quasi *īnfantia* / quam *habuit*/ sub *rēgibus* septem/ quādam fātōrum industriā / tam *variīs* ingeniō / ut rēī publicae rātiō / et *ūtilitās* postulābat. / Nam quid/ Rōmulō *ardentius*? / Tālī opus fuit/ ut invāderet *rēgnum*./ Quid Numā religiōsius? / Ita rēs *poposcit* / ut ferōx populus / deōrum metū *mītigārētur*./

PART III
PART IIIA
(Allow a total of 10 credits, one credit for each of the following.)

(1) 3	**(3)** 3	**(5)** 2	**(7)** 1	**(9)** 3
(2) 2	**(4)** 1	**(6)** 4	**(8)** 1	**(10)** 4

PART IIIB
(Allow a total of 10 credits, one credit for each of the following.)
(11) a secret letter (sent by an Asian man, Histiaeus)
(12) He was born in a faraway land (of a noble family).
(13) the king (of Asia)
(14) write secret, hidden things to a certain friend
(15) unhealthy (weak) eyes
(16) removed all the hair from his head
(17) to write the forms of the letters on the slave's head
(18) to let his hair grow back
(19) to remove the hair from his head again
(20) The letter was found (and the secret messages easily read).

PART IIIC
(Allow a total of 10 credits, one credit for each of the following.)

(21) 3	**(23)** 4	**(25)** 1	**(27)** 1	**(29)** 2
(22) 2	**(24)** 2	**(26)** 4	**(28)** 3	**(30)** 3

PART IIID
(Allow a total of 10 credits, one credit for each of 10 of the following.)

(31) 4	(33) 4	(35) 4	(37) 3	(39) 2	(41) 1
(32) 1	(34) 3	(36) 2	(38) 1	(40) 4	(42) 2

PART IV
PART IVA
(Allow a total of 10 credits, one credit for each of the following.)

(43) 1	(45) 1	(47) 2	(49) 4	(51) 1
(44) 3	(46) 3	(48) 2	(50) 4	(52) 1

PART IVB
(Allow a total of 10 credits, one credit for each of the following.)

(53) 3	(55) 1	(57) 3	(59) 2	(61) 1
(54) 2	(56) 4	(58) 4	(60) 3	(62) 2

PART IVC
(Allow a total of 5 credits, one-half credit for each correct answer in each space.)

(63) iūdicō, iūdex, iūs   3   (66) trānseō, eō, trānsitus   2
(64) lūdō, lūdus   1   (67) fortis, fortitūdō, fortiter   1
(65) audiō, audītor   4

PART IVD
(Allow a total of 5 credits, one credit for each of the following.)

(68) 4	(69) 6	(70) 2	(71) 5	(72) 3

PART V
(Allow a total of 20 credits, one credit for each of 20 of the following.)

(73) 1	(78) 3	(83) 1	(88) 3	(93) 3	(98) 4
(74) 2	(79) 3	(84) 4	(89) 1	(94) 4	(99) 1
(75) 4	(80) 1	(85) 3	(90) 1	(95) 2	(100) 4
(76) 4	(81) 2	(86) 4	(91) 3	(96) 2	(101) 2
(77) 1	(82) 4	(87) 1	(92) 2	(97) 3	(102) 2

Examination   June 1993

Comprehensive Latin

PART I

Part I is administered at the school's convenience at some time before the written test is given. You are asked to read aloud a passage of Latin for the teacher to judge on the basis of your proficiency in the spoken language. [5 credits]

PART II

DIRECTIONS: *Your teacher will read aloud a short passage in Latin. Listen carefully to this first reading. Then your teacher will read the passage in short phrases with a pause after each phrase. After each pause, write, in Latin, the phrase read by your teacher. Do not write a translation of the passage.*

There will be no penalty for improper use of macrons or capitalization. After you have completed writing the passage in Latin, your teacher will read the entire passage one more time so that you may check your work. [5 credits]

*The passage that the teacher reads will be found in **Answers, Part II**, at the end of this examination.*

PART III

Answer the questions in Part III according to the directions for Parts IIIA, IIIB, IIIC, and IIID. [40 credits]

PART IIIA

DIRECTIONS (**1–10**): *Do not write a translation of the following passage; read it through carefully several times to determine its meaning. Then, in the space provided, write the* number *of the choice that best translates each underlined expression as it is used in the passage.* [10]

Spectā, M. Antōnī, sī tibi placet, aliquandō rem pūblicam. Cōnsīderā quī

sint tuī maiōrēs, nōn quibuscum vīvās; temptā mēcum redīre in reī
   (1)   (2)

pūblicae grātiam, sī id facere volēs. Sed tū dē tē arbitrāberis; ego dē mē
                                              (3)   (4)

loquar.

Ego adulēscēns dēfendī rem pūblicam; ego senex eam nōn relinquam;
                                          (5)

nōn timuī gladiōs Catilīnae, nōn pertimēscam tuōs. Sed etiam vītam meam

dabō, sī lībertās cīvitātis meā morte retinērī potest. Ego enim *abhinc* annōs
               (6)

prope vīgintī, hōc ipsō in templō, dīxī mortem *cōnsulārī* nōn posse esse

immātūram; nunc, cum sim senex, id vērius dīcere possum. Mors, patrēs
                                        (7)

cōnscrīptī, mihi quaerenda est, quod perfēcī eās rēs quās cōnātus eram.

Tamen haec duo cupiō: ūnum, ut cum mors ad mē vēnerit sciam populum
          (8)   (9)

Rōmānum esse līberum; alterum, ut omnēs bonī recipiant id quod dē rē
      (10)

pūblicā mereant.

— Cicero, *In Antōnium*, II, 46
(adapted)

abhinc — ago
cōnsulārī — from *cōnsulāris*, ex-consul
immātūram — too early

1 Cōnsīderā quī sint tuī maiōrēs
  1 Think of those younger than you
  2 Your elders are the ones who were
    considered
  3 Consider who your ancestors are
  4 Your ancestors are greater than you are   1_____

2 temptā mēcum redīre in reī publicae grātiam
 1 try to give thanks to me and the republic
 2 try to go back to the republic gratefully
 3 try to lead me back into favor with the
   republic
 4 try to return with me into the favor of the
   republic   2_____

3 tū dē tē arbitrāberis
 1 you will think about yourself
 2 you must think only of yourself
 3 it may be thought about you
 4 when you think about yourself   3_____

4 ego dē mē loquar
 1 I force myself to speak about this
 2 I will speak about myself
 3 I can make a place for myself to speak
 4 I must speak concerning this place   4_____

5 ego senex eam nōn relinquam
 1 I, indeed, will not abandon the old man
 2 I, an old man, will not abandon it
 3 he, an old man, did not rely on me
 4 in my old age, I do not rely on this   5_____

6 sī lībertās cīvitātis meā morte retinērī potest
 1 if the citizens' freedom is not lost by my
   death
 2 if the freedom of my citizens may be lost
   after my death
 3 if a free republic is not gained because of my
   death
 4 if the freedom of the state can be retained
   by my death   6_____

7 id vērius dīcere possum
  1 it scares me to say it
  2 I probably should tell him the truth
  3 I am able to say it more truly
  4 it enables me to speak courageously   7____

8 Tamen haec duo cupiō
  1 At last, I have achieved these two things
  2 Nevertheless, I want these two things
  3 I need these two things so greatly
  4 Although these two things are essential   8____

9 cum mors ad mē vēnerit
  1 when death comes to me
  2 although I escaped death
  3 since death will turn from me
  4 when death had deceived me   9____

10 sciam populum Rōmānum esse līberum
  1 I know that the child is of the Roman people
  2 the Roman people know that they are free
  3 the people know that the child is a Roman
  4 I know that the Roman people are free   10____

PART IIIB

DIRECTIONS (**11–20**): *Do not write a translation of the following passage; read it through carefully several times to determine its meaning. Base your answers on the content of the passage only. Your answers do not have to be complete sentences; a word or phrase may suffice. In the spaces provided, write in English your answer to each question.* [10]

Ōlim complūrēs lēgātī Prūsiae, rēgis Bīthȳniae, et quīdam senātōrēs Rōmānī cēnābant apud Flāminīnum cōnsulem Rōmānum, et omnēs dē Hannibale loquēbantur. Ūnus ē lēgātīs dīxit Hannibalem in Prūsiae rēgnō esse. Senātōrēs, maximō timōre dē Hannibale commōtī, cōnstituērunt mittere in Bīthȳniam lēgātōs quī Prūsiam rēgem rogārent ut trāderet Rōmānīs Hannibalem. Itaque lēgātī Rōmānī in Bīthȳniam ad Prūsiam rēgem īvērunt.

Rēx ā lēgātīs Rōmānīs rogātus nōn negāvit Hannibalem adesse, et Rōmānī ductī sunt ad hoc aedificium in quō Hannibal hōc tempore inerat. Hūc cum Rōmānī vēnissent, puer ab iānuā prōspiciēns Hannibalī dīxit multōs mīlitēs Rōmānōs advenīre. Hannibal puerō imperāvit ut omnēs iānuās aedificiī circumīret, ac statim nūntiāret *num* aedificium undique *obsidērētur*. Cum puer renūntiāvisset omnēs exitūs occupātōs esse, Hannibal sēnsit sē ā Rōmānīs petī neque vītam sibi diūtius retinendam esse. Nē ab hostibus interficerētur, sūmpsit venēnum et hōc modō vītam suam termināvit.

— Nepos, *Vita Hannibalis,* xxiii, 12
(adapted)

num — whether
obsidērētur — from *obsideō*, besiege, blockade

11 What were Prusias' envoys and the Roman senators doing together?

_____

_____

12 What information about Hannibal did one of Prusias' envoys report?

_____

_____

13 How did the Roman senators feel when they learned the news?

_____

_____

14 For what purpose did the senators decide to send
   Roman envoys to Bithynia?

_____

_____

15 Where were the Roman envoys taken?

_____

_____

16 What did the boy looking out from the doorway
   observe?

_____

_____

17 Name *one* thing Hannibal ordered the boy to do.

_____

_____

18 What did the boy report as a result of this order?

_____

_____

19 Name *one* thing Hannibal realized upon hearing
   this news.

_____

_____

20 What action did Hannibal take after hearing the
   news?

_____

_____

PART IIIC

DIRECTIONS (**21–30**): *Read the following passages carefully, but do* not
write a translation. Below each passage, there are several questions or incom-
plete statements. For each, select the choice that best answers the question or
completes the statement on the basis of the information given in the passage,
and write its number in the space provided. [10]

Dēmētrius philosophus dē *panthērā* scrībit. Quīdam vir hanc panthēram iacentem in mediā viā petentemque auxilium vīdit. Hic vir timōre currere coepit; animal autem circumambulābat, sine dubiō auxilium petēns et dolōre affectum. Parvī *catulī* panthērae procul in fossam altam ceciderant. Vir dolōrem panthērae sēnsit et panthēram nōn timuit, eamque secūtus est quō dūxit. Cum causam dolōris intellēxit et spem suae salūtis, parvōs catulōs, līberōs panthērae, ex fossā līberāvit. Ut grātiās ageret, ea panthēra virum ad viam redūxit et virō nōn nocuit; benignitātem dēmōnstrāvit, quae etiam in genere hūmānō rāra est.

— Pliny, *Historiae Nātūrālēs* VIII, xxi, 59–60
(adapted)

panthērā — from *panthēra*, panther, wild cat
catulī — from *catulus*, cub, offspring

21 Cūr iacēbat panthēra in mediā viā?

   1 ad virōs oppugnandōs
   2 ut auxilium obtinēret
   3 quod nox appropinquābat
   4 dormiendī causā   21_____

22 Panthērā vīsā, quid statim fēcit vir?

   1 Incēpit fugere.
   2 Eam necāre temptāvit.
   3 Saxa iēcit.
   4 Cum eā locūtus est.   22_____

23 Quō panthēra virum dūxit?

   1 in spēluncam ubi panthēra habitābat
   2 ad locum in quō māgnum praemium erat
   3 domum virī ipsīus
   4 ad fossam in quā erant līberī suī   23_____

24 Quid fēcit vir prō panthērā in hōc locō?

   1 Magnam pecūniam invēnit.
   2 Multum cibum panthērae dedit.
   3 Līberōs panthērae servāvit.
   4 Multa animālia necāvit.   24_____

25 Quō modō panthēra virō grātiās ēgit?
   1 Panthēra virum vulnerāvit.
   2 Panthēra ā virō pecuniam quaesīvit.
   3 Panthēra līberōs virī invēnit.
   4 Panthēra virum ad iter retulit.   25____

Evanthēs, auctor Graecus, scrībit hanc fābulam: vir quīdam ad flūmen
quoddam dūcitur et, vestibus in arbore suspēnsīs, per aquam natat atque
abit in dēserta vasta. Hīc trānsformātur in lupum et cum cēterīs lupīs in
dēsertīs vastīs congregātur per annōs IX; quō in tempore sī nullōs
hūmānōs videt, revertitur ad idem flūmen, trāns flūmen natat, et formam
hominis recipit. Vir revenit; ecce homo, senior autem est novem annīs.
Evanthēs addit hoc quoque mīrābilius: virum recipere eandem vestem!

                                    — Pliny, *Historiae Nātūrālēs* VIII, xxxiv, 81
                                                   (adapted)

26 Quid facit vir quīdam ad flūmen ductus?
   1 Arborem celeriter ascendit.
   2 Vestīmenta in arbore ponit.
   3 In silvam fugit.
   4 Aquam bibit ē flūmine.   26____

27 Quid facit vir, postquam flūmen trānsit?
   1 Arborēs ē silvā removet.
   2 Novās vestēs petit.
   3 Discēdit in terram vastam.
   4 Domum currit.   27____

28 Quid virō accidit in hōc locō novō?
   1 Barbarī eum inveniunt.
   2 Animālia eum necant.
   3 Vir moritur.
   4 Vir lupus fit.   28____

29 Sī vir redīre vult, nōn dēbet
  1 hominēs vidēre   3 fābulās narrāre
  2 cibum edere   4 novās vestēs gerere   29_____

30 Quid accidit huic virō post IX annōs?
  1 Aquam eandem bibit.
  2 Fīlium prōcreat.
  3 Vir hūmānus iterum fit.
  4 In canem mūtātur.   30_____

PART IIID

DIRECTIONS (**31–42**): *Read the passage below carefully, but do not write a translation. Below the passage, there are several questions or incomplete statements. Choose 10 of these questions or statements, and, in the space provided, write the number of the word or expression that best answers the question or completes the statement.* [10]

C. Plīnius Maesiō Maximō suō salūtem dīcit.

  Tibi scrīpseram perīculum esse in *tacitīs suffrāgiīs*. Iam factum est.
Proximīs comitiīs inventa sunt multa ioca et verba obscēna scripta in
quibusdam *tabellīs*. Etiam, in locō candidātōrum nōminum, nōmina
aliōrum virōrum scripta erant. Senātus īrā commōtus clāmāvit scelestum
5 virum quī haec scrīpsisset pūniendum esse. Ille vir, tamen, sē cēlāvit.
Fortasse fuit inter cīvēs indignantēs et īrātōs.
  Quid putāmus hunc virum domī facere quī in suffrāgiīs pūblicīs sē gessit
tam fūrtim? Audetne haec hic vir quod sēcum putat: "Quis enim umquam
sciet?" Petīvit tabellās, stilum accēpit, verba sēcrēta scrīpsit; nēmō
10 umquam sciet.
  Quō tē vertere potes ut remedium inveniās? Ubīque mala sunt acerrima;
remedia nōn satis fortia! Valē.
                                              — Pliny, *Epistulae*, IV, XXV.5–XXVII.1
                                                                     (adapted)

tacitīs suffrāgiīs — from *tacitum suffrāgium*, secret ballot
tabellīs — from *tabella*, ballot

31 The heading suggests that one is about to read
  1 a biography   3 a poem
  2 an oration   4 a letter   31_____

32 What was found written on the tablets?
1 jokes and obscene words
2 proposed laws
3 titles of books
4 political slogans   32____

33 In which tense and voice is *scripta erant* (line 4)?
1 imperfect active   3 perfect passive
2 pluperfect passive   4 future active   33____

34 The Latin word *commōtus* (line 4) is a participle describing
1 *īrā*   3 *senātus*
2 *virum*   4 *nōmina*   34____

35 Which English word is associated by derivation with the Latin word *īrātōs* (line 6)?
1 irate   3 itinerant
2 reiterate   4 deteriorate   35____

36 The Latin phrase *putāmus hunc virum domī facere* (line 7) contains
1 an indirect statement
2 an indirect question
3 a purpose clause
4 a result clause   36____

37 In which case is the Latin word *domī* (line 7)?
1 nominative   3 locative
2 accusative   4 vocative   37____

38 According to Pliny, in what manner has the man behaved?
1 bravely   3 thoughtfully
2 truthfully   4 disgracefully   38____

39 A person who is motivated by the idea expressed
by the Latin phrase *nēmō umquam sciet* (lines 9
and 10) is someone who is
1 intellectual   3 heroic
2 sneaky·   4 hasty   39_____

40 Which figure of speech is illustrated in the sentence *Quō tē vertere potes ut remedium inveniās*
(line 11)?
1 anaphora   3 rhetorical question
2 alliteration   4 personification   40_____

41 The author concludes that remedies to such
problems as he has described are
1 very helpful   3 too weak
2 plentiful   4 unnecessary   41_____

42 What is the main theme of this passage?
1 the abuse of voting privileges
2 unjust accusations
3 the role of the senate
4 public versus private life   42_____

PART IV

Answer the questions in Part IV according to the directions for Parts IVA,
IVB, IVC, and IVD. [30 credits]

PART IVA

DIRECTIONS (**43–52**): *In the space provided, write the number of the word
or expression that, when inserted in the blank, makes each sentence grammatically correct.* [10]

43 Hostēs _____ pugnant.
1 gladiīs   3 gladius
2 cum gladiīs   4 gladiōrum   43_____

44 Rōmulus in casā Faustulī _____ habitāvit.

   1 multōrum annōrum   3 multīs annīs

   2 multī annī   4 multōs annōs   44____

45 Quid tibi vīs, _____?

   1 Marcus   3 Marcum

   2 Marce   4 Marcō   45____

46 Nihil est certius quam _____.

   1 mors   3 mortem

   2 morte   4 mortis   46____

47 Puella _____ dōnum dat.

   1 pater   3 patrī

   2 patre   4 ad patrem   47____

48 In Circum Maximum ībimus ut spectāculum

   _____.

   1 vidēre   3 vīdimus

   2 vīdissēmus   4 videāmus   48____

49 Tantā fortitūdine locūtus est ut omnēs eum

   _____.

   1 laudāvisse   3 laudābuntur

   2 laudārent   4 laudāte   49____

50 Cum amīcī _____, Gallī auxilium rogābant.

   1 vēnissent   3 venī

   2 venīre   4 venient   50____

51 Interim Caesarī nūntiāvit _____ Rōmā
vēnisse.

   1 lēgātī   3 lēgātōs

   2 lēgātōrum   4 lēgātīs   51____

52 Quis hoc potest _____?

   1 videntem   3 videt

   2 vidēre   4 videat   52____

PART IVB

DIRECTIONS (**53–62**): *This part contains two passages in English in which words associated by derivation with Latin words are italicized. Below each passage, there are several questions or incomplete statements. For each, select the choice that best answers the question or completes the statement, and write its number in the space provided.* [10]

During the depths of winter, sea ice in the Northern Hemisphere covers almost six million square miles, or *approximately* twice the size of the *conterminous* United States. A computer-generated image based on satellite *data* depicts the average *maximum* ice cover for February. It shows the entire Arctic Ocean frozen over, with *tentacles* of ice *extending* as far south as Hudson Bay and the Labrador Sea.

                                                       — *National Geographic*

53 The English word *approximately* is associated by derivation with *proximus*, the Latin word that means

   1 nearest   3 empty

   2 favorable   4 quickest   53____

54 Which Latin prefix and word are associated by derivation with the English word *conterminous*?

   1 *con* and *terminus*   3 *con* and *teneō*

   2 *contra* and *ministrō*   4 *contrā* and *minus*   54____

55 The English word *data* is associated by derivation with the fourth principal part of the Latin word

   1 *doceō*   3 *doleō*

   2 *dīcō*   4 *dō*   55____

56 The English word *maximum* is the superlative
form of the Latin word
1 *multus*   3 *magnus*
2 *melior*   4 *malus*   56____

57 Which Latin word meaning *stretch* is associated
by derivation with the English words *tentacles*
and *extending?*
1 *temptō*   3 *exterreō*
2 *tendō*   4 *extollō*   57____

Civilizations have always influenced and enriched one another *culturally*
through borrowing, osmosis and *acculturation*. With the development of
intercontinental communications networks and the audiovisual *media*, the
speed at which these *processes* take place is *accelerating* at a tremendous
rate. Music, a source of enjoyment which transcends linguistic barriers, is
one of the more positive *aspects* of these exchanges.
                                              – A World of Music

58 The English words *culturally* and *acculturation*
are associated by derivation with *cultus*, the
fourth principal part of the Latin word
1 *conferō*   3 *colō*
2 *collocō*   4 *colloquor*   58____

59 The English word *media* is a borrowed Latin
word whose Latin meaning is
1 middle   3 method
2 manner   4 mobile   59____

60 The English word *processes* is associated by derivation with both the prefix and the root of the
Latin word
1 *prōgredior*   3 *prōdūcō*
2 *prōcidō*   4 *prōcēdō*   60____

61 The English word *accelerating* is associated by
derivation with the Latin words
1 *ac* and *cella*   3 *ab* and *cēlō*
2 *ad* and *celer*   4 *as* and *celsus*   61____

62 The word *aspects* is associated by derivation with
   the Latin word that means
   1 breathe   3 hope for
   2 scatter   4 look at   62_____

   PART IVC

   DIRECTIONS (**63–67**): *For each sentence below, write, in the longer space
   provided, a Latin word with which the italicized word is associated by derivation. Any form of the appropriate Latin word, except prefixes and suffixes,
   will be acceptable. Then, write, in the shorter space provided, the number preceding the word or expression that best expresses the meaning of the italicized
   word.* [5]

63 Doctors had already administered the *potent*
   medicine to a number of patients.
   1 expensive   3 experimental
   2 powerful   4 dangerous

63 _____   _____

64 The speaker's remarks were quite *malicious*.
   1 thoughtful   3 surprising
   2 humorous   4 evil

64 _____   _____

65 We were all able to learn from *subsequent* experi-
   ences.
   1 unpleasant   3 later
   2 repeated   4 ordinary

65 _____   _____

66 The hikers followed a *perilous* route.
   1 dangerous   3 historic
   2 easy   4 scenic

66 _____   _____

67 Effective communication is related in part to one's *diction*.

1 manner of speaking   3 listening skills
2 accuracy of spelling   4 writing ability

67 _____   _____

PART IVD

DIRECTIONS (**68–72**): *For each italicized English derivative, write, in the space provided, the number preceding the word or expression that best states the meaning of the prefix.* [5]

68 The English word *degrade* has the Latin root that means *step* and the Latin prefix that means

1 ahead   3 across
2 into   4 down   68_____

69 The English word *revoke* has the Latin root that means *call* and the Latin prefix that means

1 forward   3 after
2 back   4 toward   69_____

70 The English word *educe* has the Latin root that means *lead* and the Latin prefix that means

1 in   3 out
2 above   4 together   70_____

71 The English word *circumvent* has the Latin root that means *come* and the Latin prefix that means

1 around   3 behind
2 in front of   4 through   71_____

72 The English word *suppose* has the Latin root that means *put* and the Latin prefix that means

1 upon   3 before
2 against   4 under   72_____

PART V

DIRECTIONS (**73–102**): *Select* 20 *of the following statements or questions. In the space provided, write the* number *of the word or expression that best answers the question or completes the statement.* [20 credits]

History and Public Life

73 The illustration below shows three Gallic priests.

What were these Gallic priests called?

1 *Haruspicēs*   3 *Praetōrēs*

2 *Augurēs*   4 *Druidī*   73_____

74 Who were responsible for the maintenance of the structure shown in the illustration below?

1 aediles   3 praetors

2 consuls   4 tribunes   74_____

75 Which officials were responsible for determining
   the size of the population and for reviewing the
   moral conduct of individuals and the Roman
   state at large?

   1 lictors   3 censors
   2 tribunes   4 consuls   75____

76 The regular sequence of political offices leading
   to the consulship was known as the

   1 *senātus cōnsultum*   3 *mōs māiōrum*
   2 *cursus honōrum*   4 *praefex fabrum*   76____

77 Who stopped the Etruscans at the bridge on the
   Tiber River?

   1 Horatius
   2 Tarquinius Superbus
   3 Marcus Cato
   4 Pyrrhus   77____

78 A catastrophic fire in A.D. 64 devastated Rome
   during the reign of

   1 Augustus   3 Marcus Aurelius
   2 Caligula   4 Nero   78____

79 Augustus' stepson, who succeeded him as emperor, was

   1 Tiberius   3 Nero
   2 Caligula   4 Nerva   79____

80 Vercingetorix was defeated by Caesar at the
   battle of

   1 Pharsalus   3 Alesia
   2 Zama   4 Actium   80____

81 The Roman hero who thrust his right hand into fire to prove his courage was

1 Cincinnatus   3 Manlius Torquatus

2 Regulus   4 Mucius Scaevola   81____

82 Because no one in his family had held public office before, Cicero was known as a

1 *novus homō*   3 *plēbs*

2 *pater patriae*   4 *lībertus*   82____

Daily Life

83 What did the Romans call the good luck charm around the neck of the girl shown in the illustration below?

1 *galea*   3 *palla*

2 *bulla*   4 *stola*   83____

84 What is the name of the instruments, shown in the illustration below, that a Roman schoolboy would have used to write upon his *tabella*?

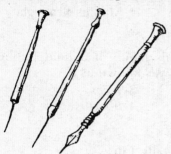

1 *stilus*   3 *cēra*
2 *volūmen*   4 *plūma*   84_____

85 The *dēnārius*, common during much of the Roman Republic, was a

1 type of garment
2 silver coin
3 style of haircut
4 merchant ship   85_____

86 The Roman girls and women who dedicated at least 30 years of their lives to keep the sacred fire burning were priestesses of

1 Vesta
2 Saturn
3 Castor and Pollux
4 Ceres   86_____

87 The illustration below shows a consul who is about to throw a *mappa* (handkerchief) to signal the start of a chariot race.

Where is the most likely place for the chariot race to have taken place?

1 Forum
2 Circus Maximus
3 Colosseum
4 Pantheon

87_____

88 The illustration below shows an inscription.

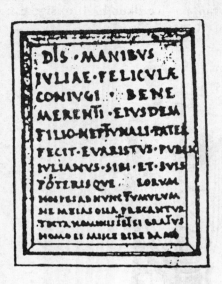

The inscription begins with the words that would
typically be carved on
1 an aqueduct
2 a public bath
3 a shop front
4 a tomb   88____

89 The Nones of March were on the
   (1) 5th
   (2) 7th
   (3) 13th
   (4) 15th   89____

Myths and Legends

90 Who was the hero, shown on the vase painting below, who was tied to the mast of the ship so that he could enjoy without danger the deadly song of the Sirens?

1 Aeneas	3 Ulysses
2 Hercules	4 Bellerophon

90____

91 The Roman god with the unusual head, shown in the illustration below, was the god of beginnings and endings.

Who was this god?

1 Mercury	3 Mars
2 Jupiter	4 Janus

91____

92 The ferryman in the underworld who conveyed
dead souls across the Styx was
1 Rhadamanthus
2 Cerberus
3 Charon
4 Pluto   92_____

93 The Trojan prophetess doomed always to tell the
truth and never to be believed was
1 Cassandra
2 Ariadne
3 Hecuba
4 Andromache   93_____

94 When Daphne was pursued by Apollo and could
not escape, she was turned into a
1 cow
2 weeping rock
3 laurel tree
4 harpy   94_____

Literature

95 Who were the two most famous authors of
Roman comedies?
1 Vergil and Lucan
2 Catullus and Propertius
3 Lucretius and Seneca
4 Plautus and Terence   95_____

96 The illustration below shows Ovid, who wrote the *Ars Amātōria*.

What other work of literature did Ovid write?
1 *Aeneid*   3 *Bucolics*
2 *Metamorphoses*   4 *Annals*   96_____

97 Who wrote about the history of Rome from earliest times?
1 Juvenal   3 Petronius
2 Livy   4 Martial   97_____

98 The *Dē Senectūte, Dē Amīcitiā,* and *Dē Nātūrā Deōrum* were written by

    1 Cicero   3 Horace

    2 Sallust   4 Vergil   98_____

Architecture and Art

99 The illustration below shows the Roman Forum.

Which road went through the Forum?

    1 *Via Appia*

    2 *Via Aurēlia*

    3 *Via Flāminia*

    4 *Via Sacra*   99_____

100 The illustration below shows the top of one type
of column commonly used in Roman architecture.

Which architectural order is used on the capital
of this column?

1 Doric   3 Corinthian
2 Ionic   4 Egyptian   100_____

101 The opening in the roof of the atrium, through
which rainwater fell into a pool below, was called
the

1 *peristȳlium*   3 *culīna*
2 *compluvium*   4 *ālae*   101_____

102 The Flavian Amphitheater was popularly known
as the

1 *Cūria*   3 *Pantheon*
2 *Cloāca*   4 *Colossēum*   102_____

Answers June 1993

Comprehensive Examination in Latin

PART I
(*Allow a total of 5 credits for this part.*)

PART II
(*Allow a total of 5 credits, one-half credit for each of the following 10 italicized words.*)

Est enim *amīcitia* / nihil aliud / nisi omnium *dīvīnārum* / hūmānārumque *rērum* / cum benevolentiā / et cāritāte cōnsēnsiō; / *quā* quidem / haud sciō an / *exceptā* sapientiā / nihil melius / *hominī* sit / ā dīs *immortālibus* datum. / Dīvitiās / aliī *praepōnunt*, / bonam aliī valētūdinem, / *aliī* potentiam, / aliī *honōrēs*, / multī etiam voluptātēs./

PART III
PART IIIA
(*Allow a total of 10 credits, one credit for each of the following.*)

(1) 3	(3) 1	(5) 2	(7) 3	(9) 1
(2) 4	(4) 2	(6) 4	(8) 2	(10) 4

PART IIIB
Note: Not all of the acceptable answers have been included.

(*Allow a total of 10 credits, one credit for each of the following.*)
(11) dining (and talking about Hannibal)
(12) that Hannibal was in Prusias' kingdom
(13) They were moved by a very great fear of Hannibal.
(14) to ask King Prusias to hand over Hannibal to the Romans
(15) to the building where Hannibal was
(16) that many Roman soldiers were coming
(17) to go around to all the doors of the building (and to announce whether the building was being blockaded from all sides)
(18) that all the exits were occupied
(19) that he was being sought by the Romans (and that he should no longer hold on to life)
(20) He took poison (and in this way ended his life).

PART IIIC
(Allow a total of 10 credits, one credit for each of the following.)

(21) 2	(23) 4	(25) 4	(27) 3	(29) 1
(22) 1	(24) 3	(26) 2	(28) 4	(30) 3

PART IIID
(Allow a total of 10 credits, one credit for each of 10 of the following.)

(31) 4	(33) 2	(35) 1	(37) 3	(39) 2	(41) 3
(32) 1	(34) 3	(36) 1	(38) 4	(40) 3	(42) 1

PART IV

PART IVA
(Allow a total of 10 credits, one credit for each of the following.)

(43) 1	(45) 2	(47) 3	(49) 2	(51) 3
(44) 4	(46) 1	(48) 4	(50) 1	(52) 2

PART IVB
(Allow a total of 10 credits, one credit for each of the following.)

(53) 1	(55) 4	(57) 2	(59) 1	(61) 2
(54) 1	(56) 3	(58) 3	(60) 4	(62) 4

PART IVC
Note: Not all of the acceptable answers have been included.

(Allow a total of 5 credits, one-half credit for each correct answer in each space.)

(63) potēns, possum   2   (66) perīculum   1
(64) malus   4   (67) dīcō   1
(65) subsequor, sequor   3

PART IVD
(Allow a total of 5 credits, one credit for each of the following.)

(68) 4	(69) 2	(70) 3	(71) 1	(72) 4

PART V

(Allow a total of 20 credits, one credit for each of 20 of the following.)

(73) 4	(78) 4	(83) 2	(88) 4	(93) 1	(98) 1
(74) 1	(79) 1	(84) 1	(89) 2	(94) 3	(99) 4
(75) 3	(80) 3	(85) 2	(90) 3	(95) 4	(100) 2
(76) 2	(81) 4	(86) 1	(91) 4	(96) 2	(101) 2
(77) 1	(82) 1	(87) 2	(92) 3	(97) 2	(102) 4

Examination   June 1994

Comprehensive Latin

PART I

Part I is administered at the school's convenience at some time before the written test is given. You are asked to read aloud a passage of Latin for the teacher to judge on the basis of your proficiency in the spoken language. [5 credits]

PART II

DIRECTIONS: *Your teacher will read aloud a short passage in Latin. Listen carefully to this first reading. Then your teacher will read the passage in short phrases with a pause after each phrase. After each pause, write, in Latin, the phrase read by your teacher. Do not write a translation of the passage.*

There will be no penalty for improper use of macrons or capitalization. After you have completed writing the passage in Latin, your teacher will read the entire passage one more time so that you may check your work. [5 credits]

The passage that the teacher reads will be found in **Answers, Part II,** *at the end of this examination.*

PART III

Answer the questions in Part III according to the directions for Parts IIIA, IIIB, IIIC, AND IIID.   [40 credits]

PART IIIA

DIRECTIONS (**1–10**): *Do not write a translation of the following passage; read it through carefully several times to determine its meaning. Then, in the space provided, write the* number *of the choice that best translates each* underlined expression *as it is used in the passage.* [10]

Fuit in terrā Graeciā āctor excellentissimus quī fāmam obtinuerat.
Praestābat omnibus cēterīs clārā suā vōce. Dīcunt nōmen esse Polum. Ad
$\overline{(1)}$
omnēs urbēs Graeciae nōtās iter fēcit. Is āctor Polus maximē amātum
$\overline{(2)}$
fīlium morte āmīsit, et magnō dolōre afficiēbātur. Dolōre dēpositō, post
$\overline{(3)}$ $\overline{(5)}$
breve tempus ad scaenam rediit. Agēbat in scaenā tālī modō ut nēmō
$\overline{(6)}$
scīret illum miseriam ferre.

Eō tempore Athēnīs in fābulā nōmine "Ēlectrā" āctūrus erat. In fābulā
$\overline{(7)}$
Polus trāns scaenam urnam cum *ossibus* Orestis portāre dēbēbat. Igitur,
$\overline{(8)}$
Polus ē *sepulchrō* fīlī ossa atque urnam tulit, atque, ut fābula postulāvit,
$\overline{(9)}$
dēmōnstrābat magnum dolōrem, sed vērum dolōrem, nōn imitātum.
$\overline{(10)}$

— Aulus Gellius, *Noctēs Atticae*, VI, 5
(adapted)

ossibus — from *os*, bone
sepulchrō — from *sepulchrum*, tomb

1 Fuit in terrā Graeciā āctor excellentissimus
  1 The land in Greece was superb for an actor
  2 There was an actor in the land that spoke
    excellent Greek
  3 In the land of Greece, there was a very
    distinguished actor
  4 A superb actor came into the land of Greece   1____

2 Praestābat omnibus cēterīs clārā suā vōce.
  1 His voice appeared clear to all others.
  2 All others surpassed him in speaking ability.
  3 All others praised his voice for its
    distinctness.
  4 He surpassed all others in the clarity of his
    voice.   2____

3 Ad omnēs urbēs Graeciae nōtās iter fēcit.
1 He built important highways to all the cities
of Greece.
2 He journeyed to all the famous cities of
Greece.
3 He made forced marches to all the cities he
knew in Greece.
4 Well-known roads led to all the cities of
Greece.   3_____

4 maximē amātum fīlium morte āmīsit
1 he lost his most beloved son in death
2 he sent his son away on an important mission
3 his oldest son died of a broken heart
4 his favorite son suffered greatly before death   4_____

5 Dolōre dēpositō
1 Outwitted by trickery
2 When the plot was revealed
3 After his grief had been set aside
4 Dramatizing his sorrow   5_____

6 ad scaenam rediit
1 he left the stage
2 he remained on stage
3 he returned to the stage
4 he ran from the stage   6_____

7 Eō tempore Athēnīs in fābulā nōmine "Ēlectrā"
āctūrus erat.
1 At that time he was about to act in the play
named "Electra" at Athens.
2 At that time an Athenian actress named
"Electra" wrote the play.
3 In time the play "Electra" came to Athens.
4 The name of the play, given at that time in
Athens, was "Electra."   7_____

8 Polus trāns scaenam urnam cum ossibus
  Orestis portāre dēbēbat

  1 Orestes had to carry Polus' bones across the
    stage in a large urn
  2 Polus had to carry an urn with the bones of
    Orestes across the stage
  3 the urn with bones, which was on the stage,
    was carried across to Polus
  4 Orestes had to carry the urn full of bones
    across to Polus   8____

9 Polus ē sepulchrō fīlī ossa atque urnam tulit

  1 Polus buried his son's bones in an urn in a
    tomb
  2 Polus left the bones and the urn of his son in
    the tomb
  3 Polus left an urn at the tomb for his son's
    bones
  4 Polus brought the bones and the urn from
    his son's tomb   9____

10 dēmōnstrābat magnum dolōrem, sed vērum
   dolōrem, nōn imitātum

  1 he showed great sorrow, but real sorrow, not
    imitated
  2 he felt that his grief was not real but artificial
  3 he felt that real sorrow could not be acted
  4 he displayed great grief, but it was fictitious,
    not real   10____

PART IIIB

DIRECTIONS (**11–20**): *Do not write a translation of the following passage; read it through carefully several times to determine its meaning. Base your answers on the content of the passage only. Your answers do not have to be complete sentences; a word or phrase may suffice. In the spaces provided, write in English your answer to each question.* [10]

Rōmānī bellum contrā Latīnōs gerēbant. Latīnī erant Rōmānīs similēs linguā, mōribus, rēbus mīlitāribus. Mīlitēs Rōmānī et mīlitēs Latīnī in bellō permixtī saepe distinguī nōn poterant. Ergō nē mīlitēs errōre caperentur, cōnsulēs imperāvērunt nē quis extrā *ōrdinem*, nē contrā mandātum cōnsulum, in hostem pugnāret.

T. Manlius autem, fīlius cōnsulis, in castra hostium vēnit. Manlius in memoriā imperium nōn tenēbat et statim mīlitem inimīcum interfēcit. Cum in castra Rōmāna rediisset, ad patrem vēnit et dīxit: "Hoc fēcī, et haec arma ex hoste capta portō, pater, ut omnēs dīcant mē tuō honōre dignum esse." Quod cum cōnsul audīvisset, mīlitēs advocārī statim iussit. "Tū," inquit, "T. Manlī, neque imperium cōnsulis neque potestātem patris timuistī. Extrā ōrdinem in hostem pugnāvistī et disciplīnam mīlitārem neglexistī, quā stetit ad hunc diem rēs pūblica Rōmāna. Ī, lictor; dūc fīlium meum ad mortem. Trīste exemplum sed bonum erimus mīlitibus Rōmānīs." Tanta poena tam celeriter effēcit ut mīlitēs essent ducibus oboedientiōrēs.

— Livy, *Ab Urbe Conditā VIII*, 6.7
(adapted)

ōrdinem — from *ōrdō*, military rank, formation

11 Name *one* way in which the Latins and Romans were culturally alike.

_____

_____

12 What problem did this similarity cause?

_____

_____

13 What order did the consuls give to the Romans?

_____

_____

14 What relationship did Titus Manlius have to one of the consuls?

_____

_____

15 What action did Manlius take after entering the
     enemy camp?

     _____

     _____

16 What reason did Manlius give to the consul for
     his actions?

     _____

     _____

17–18 List *two* things the consul accused Manlius of
        having done.

     _____

     _____

19 What was the consul's punishment for Manlius?

     _____

     _____

20 What effect did this punishment have on the
     Roman soldiers?

     _____

     _____

PART IIIC

DIRECTIONS (**21–30**): *Read the following passages carefully, but do* not
*write a translation. Below each passage, there are several questions or incom-
plete statements. For each, select the choice that best answers the question or
completes the statement* on the basis of the information given in the passage,
and write its number *in the space provided.*   [10]

Cum *olīva* in urbe Graecā sē subitō ostendisset et in aliā parte urbis
aqua ē terrā ērūpisset, haec spectācula rēgem commōvērunt. Rēx igitur
mīsit nūntium ad Apollinem Delphicum, quī quaereret quid
intellegendum esset et quid faciendum esset. Ille respondit olīvam ā
Minervā datam esse, aquam ā Neptūnō, et urbem nōminandam esse ex
nōmine aut deae aut deī.
    Ōrāculō acceptō, rēx cīvēs omnēs ad *ferendum suffrāgium* convocāvit et
omnēs virī prō Neptūnō, omnēs fēminae prō Minervā suffrāgia tulērunt.
Minerva, cuius nōmen in Graeciā erat "Athēnē," vīcit.

olīva – olive tree   – Augustīnus, *Dē Cīvitāte Deī*, XVIII, 9
ferendum suffrāgium — from *suffrāgium ferre*, to cast a vote   (adapted)

21 Quid spectāculum in Graeciā vidēbātur?
  1 Aqua ē terrā ērūpit.
  2 Rēx factus est deus.
  3 Apollō appāruit.
  4 Rēx montem mōvit.   21_____

22 Quid fēcit rēx cum haec spectācula vīdisset?
  1 Mīlitēs convocāvit.
  2 Cīvēs sē movēre iussit.
  3 Nūntium ad ōrāculum Apollinis mīsit.
  4 Ipse templum Minervae vīsitāvit.   22_____

23 Rēx mox audīvit aquam esse
  1 rēgnum Minervae   3 salūtī rēgī
  2 dōnum Neptūnī   4 malam fortūnam   23_____

24 Cūr rēx cīvēs convocāvit?
  1 ut deum deamque vidērent
  2 ut deōs laudārent
  3 ut hostēs vincerent
  4 ut suffrāgium ferrent   24_____

25 Suffrāgia prō Neptūnō ferēbantur ab
  1 fēminīs   3 virīs
  2 ōrāculō   4 Minervā   25_____

26 Quae dōna dedit Minerva urbī Athēnīs?
  1 aquam et terram
  2 sapientiam et virtūtem
  3 suffrāgium et imperium
  4 olīvam et nōmen   26_____

Cicerō Atticō Salūtem Dīcit.

Trīgintā diēs iam exspectō per quōs nūllās litterās ā tē accēpī. Mihi autem erat in animō, ut tē scrīpsī, īre in Ēpīrum et ibi meum fātum exspectāre. Tē ōrō ut scrībās ad mē absentem omnia quae accidant et ut dēs litterās ā mē scrīptās ad omnēs amīcōs nostrōs. Ante diem V Kal. Novembrīs.

— Cicerō, *Epistulae Ad Atticum*, III, 21
(adapted)

27 Quid exspectābat Cicerō?
1 epistulam ab amicō
2 nūntium dē filiō
3 dōnum ē Graeciā missum
4 tempus ad scrībendum   27____

28 Cicerō cōnsilium capiēbat
1 nē ab hostibus interficerētur
2 nē nāvis delērētur
3 ut iter faceret
4 ut amīcōs vidēret   28____

29 Cicerō Atticum rogat
1 ut sēcum veniat
2 ut omnia ad sē scrībat
3 nē quid amīcīs dīcat
4 nē urbem relinquat   29____

30 Cicerō hanc epistulam scrīpsit
1 mēnse Decembrī
2 post adventum in Ēpīrō
3 post mortem Atticī
4 mēnse Octōbrī   30____

PART IIID

DIRECTIONS (31–42): *Read the passage below carefully, but do not write a translation. Below the passage, there are several questions or incomplete statements. Choose 10 of these questions or statements, and, in the space provided, write the number of the word or expression that best answers the question or completes the statement.* [10]

Prīncipiō nātūra omnibus animālibus dat et attribuit ut sē, vītam corpusque, servent. Omnia animālia et nōs hominēs vītāmus ea quae noxia et perīculōsa sunt, sed omnia quae sunt ad vīvendum necessāria petimus et parāmus — cibum, domum et aliās rēs eiusdem generis. Rēs commūnis
5 omnium animālium est cupiditās prōcreandī et deinde cūra prōcreātōrum.
  Sed inter hominem et bestiam est haec maxima dīversitās. Bestia sēnsū movētur et sē accomodat ad condiciōnēs praesentēs. Homō autem, quod potestātem rātiōnis habet, per quam cōnsequentiās cernit, facile tōtīus vītae cursum futūrum videt et rēs necessāriās praeparat.

                                                          — Cicerō, *Dē Officiīs*, I, iii–iv
                                                                    (adapted)

31 What aspect of animal nature does the author first describe?
    1 hostility   3 cooperation
    2 cleanliness   4 self-preservation   31____

32 What is the mood of the verb *servent* (line 2)?
    1 indicative   3 subjunctive
    2 infinitive   4 imperative   32____

33 The Latin word *vītāmus* (line 2) comes from the verb *vītō*, which means to avoid. Which English word is associated by derivation with the Latin word *vītāmus*?
    1 inevitable   3 enviable
    2 vitriolic   4 vital   33____

34 According to the author, what is an element
common to both humans and beasts?

1 a desire to care for their offspring
2 a desire for power over other animals
3 a need to understand their world
4 a need to communicate with their equals   34_____

35 The Latin word *maxima* (line 6) is the superlative
form of the adjective

1 *bona*   3 *magna*
2 *parva*   4 *multa*   35_____

36 Which Latin word means the opposite of
dīversitās (line 6)?

1 *amīcitia*   3 *grātia*
2 *similitūdō*   4 *gravitās*   36_____

37 The Latin word *sē* (line 7) refers to

1 *homō*   3 *sēnsū*
2 *bestia*   4 *condiciōnēs*   37_____

38 In what case is the Latin word *homō* (line 7)?

1 nominative   3 accusative
2 genitive   4 ablative   38_____

39 According to the passage, what quality allows humans to see the consequences of their actions?
1 the power of reason
2 reverence for the gods
3 the ability to interpret omens
4 communication skills   39____

40 Which Latin word, paired with its English meaning, has the same root as the Latin word *cōnsequentiās* (line 8)?
1 *cōnscendō* — climb   3 *secō* — cut
2 *sequor* — follow   4 *cōnsentiō* — agree   40____

41 In the phrase *vītae cursum* (line 9), the word *cursum* (from *currō*) implies that life is
1 a puzzle   3 a race
2 a joke   4 an act   41____

42 According to the author, what is a basic difference between humans and beasts?
1 Beasts care nothing for shelter; shelter is important to humans.
2 Beasts seek food; humans make food.
3 Beasts have no feelings; humans are motivated by feelings.
4 Beasts live in the present; humans live for the future.   42____

PART IV

Answer the questions in Part IV according to the directions for Parts IVA, IVB, IVC, and IVD. [30 credits]

PART IVA

DIRECTIONS (**43–52**): *In the space provided, write the* number *of the word or expression that, when inserted in the blank, makes* each *sentence grammatically correct.* [10]

43 Catōnem in bibliothēcā _____ vīdī.

  1 sedentēs   3 sedentis

  2 sedentium   4 sedentem   43_____

44 Rōmulus septem et trīgintā _____ rēgnāvit.

  1 annus   3 annōs

  2 annīs   4 annōrum   44_____

45 Dēbēs, _____, pārēre grammaticō.

  1 Pūblī   3 Pūbliō

  2 Pūblius   4 Pūblium   45_____

46 Puerī _____ permōtī sunt.

  1 incendiō   3 incendia

  2 incendiōrum   4 incendium   46_____

47 Scīpiō, Rōmānus ērudītissimus, _____ habitāvit.

  1 Rōma   3 Rōmam

  2 Rōmae   4 Rōmā   47_____

48 Cum fortiter _____, tamen victus est.
  1 pugnātūrus esse   3 pugnāvisset
  2 pugnāte   4 pugnārī   48____

49 Cōnsulēs, rēgibus _____, creātī sunt.
  1 expulistī   3 expellunt
  2 expulsīs   4 expulimus   49____

50 Tanta tempestās coorta est, ut nūlla nāvis
  cursum tenēre _____.
  1 potest   3 posse
  2 potuerant   4 posset   50____

51 Auxilium miserīs _____ dēbēmus.
  1 dare   3 dedimus
  2 dantem   4 datō   51____

52 Puer putat mīlitem audācem _____.
  1 erat   3 fuerit
  2 esse   4 esset   52____

PART IVB

DIRECTIONS (**53–62**): *This part contains a passage in English in which words associated by derivation with Latin words are italicized. Below the passage, there are several questions or incomplete statements. For each, select the choice that best answers the question or completes the statement, and write its number in the space provided.* [10]

DISTINCTIVE RECEPTIONS

TERRACE

Exchange vows from a celestial setting overlooking the spectacular Manhattan skyline.

5 The Terrace Restaurant, nestled atop the highest point of Manhattan, offers a breathtaking panorama of the city's major bridges and landmarks.

And the ambiance is equally impressive. An abundance of flowers
10 and fresh greenery, fine china and crystal, sparkling mirrors and glass, combine to create a fairy-tale aura.

Fete your guests on innovative French cuisine, exquisitely prepared and
15 presented with lavish attention to detail. Indoor valet parking is available.

For more information, or to visit, please call David Anderson.

212-555-9490
400 W. 119th Street, New York City

- *celestial*
- *spectacular*

- *Terrace*

- *major*

- *impressive*
- *abundance*
- *mirrors*

- *innovative*
- *prepared*
- *presented*

- *information*

53 Which Latin word, paired with its English meaning, is associated by derivation with the English word *celestial* (line 1)?

1 *cēlō* — hide   3 *caelum* — sky
2 *celerō* — hasten   4 *cella* — room

53____

54 The English word *spectacular* (line 2) is associated by derivation with *spectō*, the Latin word that means

1 hope for   3 breathe
2 look at   4 wonder   54____

55 The English word *Terrace* (line 4) is associated by derivation with the Latin word

1 *terra*   3 *terrēre*
2 *errāre*   4 *tertius*   55____

56 The English word *major* (line 7) is associated by derivation with the Latin word *maior*. Which Latin word has the opposite meaning of *maior*?

1 *melior*   3 *peior*
2 *minor*   4 *plūs*   56____

57 The English word *equally* (line 8) is associated by derivation with the Latin word

1 *aequus*   3 *quidem*
2 *aqua*   4 *quaero*   57____

58 The English word *impressive* (line 9) is associated by derivation with the fourth principal part of the Latin word

1 *impellō*   3 *praesum*
2 *prendō*   4 *premō*   58____

59 The English word *mirrors* (line 11) is associated by derivation with the Latin word

1 *morior*   3 *moror*
2 *mōlior*   4 *mīror*   59____

60 The English word *innovative* (line 13) is associated by derivation with *novus*, the Latin word that means

1 ninth   3 known
2 new   4 old   60____

61 Which Latin element, paired with its English meaning, is associated by derivation with the prefix in the English words *prepared* (line 14) and *presented* (line 15)?

1 *prae* — before
2 *procul* — far
3 *per* — through
4 *propter* — because of   61____

62 The English word *information* (line 17) contains the Latin word that means

1 strong   3 shape
2 perhaps   4 marketplace   62____

PART IVC

DIRECTIONS (**63–67**): *For each sentence below, write, in the longer space provided, a Latin word with which the italicized word is associated by derivation. Any form of the appropriate Latin word, except prefixes and suffixes, will be acceptable. Then, write, in the shorter space provided, the number preceding the word or expression that best expresses the meaning of the italicized word.* [5]

63 The witness gave an *abbreviated* account of the incident.

1 humorous   3 shortened
2 rambling   4 descriptive

63 _____   _____

64 The construction of the new highway was postponed to *pacify* the residents who were affected.

1 relocate   3 alert
2 calm   4 compensate

64 _____   _____

65 My friend was just telling me about his *incredible* experience.

1 unbelievable   3 terrible
2 rewarding   4 recent

65 _____   _____

66 The treaty negotiations were *protracted*.

1 bitter   3 cut off
2 friendly   4 drawn out

66 _____   _____

67 There was an *ostentatious* display of awards in the office.

1 small   3 attractive
2 informative   4 showy

67 _____   _____

PART IVD

DIRECTIONS (**68–72**): *For each italicized Latin expression used in English, write, in the space provided, the number of the English translation, chosen from the list below, that most nearly has the same meaning.* [5]

Latin Expression

68 *ad lib.* 68_____

69 *pro tem.* 69_____

70 *et al.* 70_____

71 *cf.* 71_____

72 *e.g.* 72_____

English Translation

1 and others

2 compare

3 in the work cited

4 at pleasure

5 for example

6 around

7 for the time being

PART V

DIRECTIONS (**73–102**): *Select* 20 *of the following statements or questions. In the space provided, write the* number *of the word or expression that best answers the question or completes the statement.* [20 credits]

History and Public Life

73 The illustration below shows a quotation attributed to Julius Caesar, as written by William Shakespeare.

Shakespeare puts these words into the mouth of Julius Caesar on the occasion of

1 Caesar's assumption of the dictatorship
2 Caesar's assassination
3 Brutus' rejection of Caesar as father-in-law
4 Caesar's recognition of Brutus as one of his lost children

73____

74 *Magna Graecia* was the name given to which
geographical area?
1 northern Spain 3 central Greece
2 southern Gaul 4 southern Italy 74_____

75 In the first century B.C., civil war raged in Rome
between Marius and
1 Caesar 3 Octavian
2 Pompey 4 Sulla 75_____

76 The seaport of ancient Rome was located at the
mouth of the Tiber River and was called
1 Brundisium 3 Ostia
2 Lavinium 4 Baiae 76_____

77 Historians generally believe that Rome was
invaded by barbarians and that it fell in the year
(1) A.D. 476 (3) 44 B.C.
(2) A.D. 14 (4) 509 B.C. 77_____

78 Who admitted the Sabines into the citadel of
Rome and was crushed beneath their shields as
her reward?
1 Tarpeia 3 Cloelia
2 Sempronia 4 Camilla 78_____

79 The Roman legions occasionally marched about
25 miles in a single day. What was this forced
march called?
1 *ambulātum longum* 3 *maior adventus*
2 *magnum iter* 4 *via longissima* 79_____

80 After completing their one-year term as the chief executives of Rome, the ex-consuls were expected to

    1 retire gracefully from public service
    2 start the *cursus honōrum* again
    3 undertake wars of conquest and revenge
    4 govern Roman provinces   80____

81 The hometown of both Marius and Cicero was

    1 Tarentum   3 Arpinum
    2 Capua   4 Mediolānum   81____

82 A Roman praetor served as a

    1 priest   3 tax collector
    2 teacher   4 judge   82____

Daily Life

83 In the cartoon below, the salutation to the chicken is an adaptation of an ancient Roman greeting.

BLONDIE

This greeting is reminiscent of the one given by

    1 soldiers to their general
    2 Vestal Virgins to the Senate
    3 gladiators to the emperor
    4 slaves to the head of the household   83____

84 The words *"Ubi tū Gaius, ego Gaia"* were pro-
nounced at a Roman ceremony for a

   1 marriage   3 birth

   2 coming of age   4 death   84_____

85 Where would a Roman family worship their
Larēs and *Penātēs?*

   1 in a temple

   2 along the banks of the Tiber

   3 at the Field of Mars

   4 at home   85_____

86 An influential senator would be escorted early in
the morning to the Forum by his

   1 *familia*   3 *paedagōgus*

   2 *grammaticus*   4 *clientēs*   86_____

87 The phrase *ab ōvō usque ad māla* refers to Roman

   1 habits of dressing

   2 fondness for meals of many courses

   3 systems of agriculture

   4 shipbuilding techniques   87_____

88 The *strigilis, apodytērium,* and *tepidārium* are all
associated with Roman

   1 baths   3 schools

   2 chariot races   4 magistrates   88_____

Myths and Legends

89 Which mythological creature is shown in the cartoon below?

1 hydra   3 cyclops
2 centaur   4 harpy   89_____

90 Who was forced to roll an enormous rock uphill for eternity as a punishment for his crimes?
1 Ixion   3 Sisyphus
2 Minos   4 Tityus   90_____

91 What is the name of the Titan who is shown in
the illustration below?

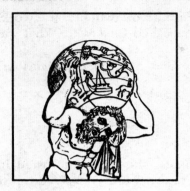

1 Prometheus	3 Tantalus
2 Epimetheus	4 Atlas

91____

92 The Greek god Hermes was known to the
Romans as

1 Mars	3 Apollo
2 Mercury	4 Bacchus

92____

93 Which name refers to something or someone so
hideously ugly that one cannot bear to gaze on it?

1 Medusa	3 Perseus
2 Bellerophon	4 Galataea

93____

94 Whom did the maiden Ariadne, daughter of King
Minos, help to escape from the Labyrinth?

1 Paris	3 Ulysses
2 Jason	4 Theseus

94____

Literature

95 Caesar was the author of two literary works about war. One was called *Civil War*. What was the other called?

   1 *Gallic Wars*   3 *Peloponnesian Wars*
   2 *Punic Wars*   4 *Pyrrhic Wars*   95_____

96 Most ancient Romans who were interested in contemporary literature were exposed to new works via

   1 the large supply of inexpensive, mass-produced editions
   2 public recitations by authors
   3 the extensive advertising program of the public libraries
   4 a program of mandatory reading instituted by Augustus   96_____

97 In a formal Roman speech, the introductory remarks were included in the

   1 *refutātiō*   3 *perōrātiō*
   2 *narrātiō*   4 *exordium*   97_____

98 When Cicero delivered speeches *ad Patrēs Cōnscrīptōs*, he was addressing the

   1 Senate   3 jury
   2 Roman people   4 prisoners   98_____

Architecture and Art

99 The illustration below shows an ancient Roman
structure that was often found in large cities. This
structure, located in Verona, was similar to one
built in Rome by a Flavian emperor.

UNIVERSITY PRINTS, BOSTON

What is this structure?
1 theater   3 amphitheater
2 basilica   4 temple   99_____

100 The hypocaust was used to
   1 sacrifice animals
   2 heat the floors and pools of the *thermae*
   3 administer medicine
   4 brand the foreheads of runaway slaves   100_____

101 The front rooms of a *domus*, facing the street,
were often
   1 used as extra dining rooms
   2 leased to shopkeepers
   3 opened up to enlarge the atrium
   4 shut off in winter to avoid heating costs   101_____

102 The famous Roman wall separating Britain from
    Scotland is named for the Emperor
1 Hadrian	3 Titus
2 Nero	4 Tiberius

                                                        102____

Answers June 1994

Comprehensive Examination in Latin

PART I
(Allow a total of 5 credits for this part.)

PART II
(Allow a total of 5 credits, one-half credit for each of the following 10 italicized words.)

Nerō meus / *mīrificās* / apud mē / tibi grātiās *ēgit*, / prorsus incrēdibilēs, / ut nūllum honōrem / sibi *habērī* / potuisse *dīceret*, / quī ā tē / praetermissus esset. / *Magnum* frūctum / ex ipsō *capiēs*; / nihil est enim / illō adulēscente / grātius. / Sed mehercule / *mihi* quoque / *grātissimum* fēcistī; / plūris enim / ex omnī nōbilitāte / nēminem faciō, / *Itaque,* / sī ea fēceris, / *quae* ille per mē / tēcum agī *voluit*, / grātissimum / mihi fēceris./

PART III
PART IIIA
(Allow a total of 10 credits, one credit for each of the following.)

(1) 3	**(3)** 2	**(5)** 3	**(7)** 1	**(9)** 4
(2) 4	**(4)** 1	**(6)** 3	**(8)** 2	**(10)** 1

PART IIIB
The answers to the questions in this part do not have to be complete sentences. A phrase or word may be sufficient for a completely correct one-credit response. Disregard errors in English. Allow no partial credit. Not all of the acceptable answers have been included.

(Allow a total of 10 credits, one credit for each of the following.)

(11) in language (customs and military affairs)

(12) The Roman soldiers and the Latin soldiers could hardly be distinguished when mixed in battle. (Soldiers might be captured by mistake.)

(13) that no one fight out of rank or against the consuls' command

(14) Titus Manlius was the consul's son.

(15) He killed an enemy soldier.

(16) that all would say that he was worthy of his father's honor

(17–18) He did not fear the consul's order; he did not fear his father's power; he fought out of rank; he neglected military discipline.

(19) death

(20) It made them be more obedient to their leaders.

PART IIIC
(Allow a total of 10 credits, one credit for each of the following.)

(21) 1	**(23)** 2	**(25)** 3	**(27)** 1	**(29)** 2
(22) 3	**(24)** 4	**(26)** 4	**(28)** 3	**(30)** 4

PART IIID
(Allow a total of 10 credits, one credit for each of 10 of the following.)

(31) 4	**(33)** 1	**(35)** 3	**(37)** 2	**(39)** 1	**(41)** 3
(32) 3	**(34)** 1	**(36)** 2	**(38)** 1	**(40)** 2	**(42)** 4

PART IV
PART IVA
(Allow a total of 10 credits, one credit for each of the following.)

(43) 4	**(45)** 1	**(47)** 2	**(49)** 2	**(51)** 1
(44) 3	**(46)** 1	**(48)** 3	**(50)** 4	**(52)** 2

PART IVB
(Allow a total of 10 credits, one credit for each of the following.)

(53) 3	**(55)** 1	**(57)** 1	**(59)** 4	**(61)** 1
(54) 2	**(56)** 2	**(58)** 4	**(60)** 2	**(62)** 3

PART IVC
(Allow credit for any correctly spelled form of the Latin word. Allow no credit for prefixes or suffixes. Not all of the acceptable answers have been included.)

(Allow a total of 5 credits, one-half credit for each correct answer in each column.)

Column I	Column II
(63) brevis	**(63)** 3
(64) pax, pacō	**(64)** 2
(65) crēdō, crēdibilis	**(65)** 1
(66) trahō (tractus)	**(66)** 4
(67) ostendō, ostentō	**(67)** 4

PART IVD
(Allow a total of 5 credits, one credit for each of the following.)

(68) 4	**(69)** 7	**(70)** 1	**(71)** 2	**(72)** 5

PART V
(Allow a total of 20 credits, one credit for each of 20 of the following.)

(73) 2	**(78)** 1	**(83)** 3	**(88)** 1	**(93)** 1	**(98)** 1
(74) 4	**(79)** 2	**(84)** 1	**(89)** 2	**(94)** 4	**(99)** 3
(75) 4	**(80)** 4	**(85)** 4	**(90)** 3	**(95)** 1	**(100)** 2
(76) 3	**(81)** 3	**(86)** 4	**(91)** 4	**(96)** 2	**(101)** 2
(77) 1	**(82)** 4	**(87)** 2	**(92)** 2	**(97)** 4	**(102)** 1

Examination   June 1995

Comprehensive Latin

PART I

Part I is administered at the school's convenience at some time before the written test is given. You are asked to read aloud a passage of Latin for the teacher to judge on the basis of your proficiency in the spoken language. [5 credits]

PART II

DIRECTIONS: *Your teacher will read aloud a short passage in Latin. Listen carefully to this first reading. Then your teacher will read the passage in short phrases with a pause after each phrase. After each pause, write, in Latin, the phrase read by your teacher. Do* not *write a translation of the passage.*

There will be no penalty for improper use of macrons or capitalization. After you have completed writing the passage in Latin, your teacher will read the entire passage one more time so that you may check your work. [5 credits]

The passage that the teacher reads will be found in **Answers, Part II,** *at the end of this examination.*

PART III

Answer the questions in Part III according to the directions for Parts IIIA, IIIB, IIIC, and IIID.   [40 credits]

PART IIIA

DIRECTIONS (**1–10**): *Do not write a translation of the following passage; read it through carefully several times to determine its meaning. Then, in the space provided, write the* number *of the choice that best translates each* underlined expression *as it is used in the passage.* [10]

Tiberiō prīncipe, quīdam *corvus*, in Castoris Pollūcisque templō nātus, (1) in vīcīnam tabernam dēvolāvit et ibi mānsit. Brevī tempore is corvus (2) (3) hūmānam locūtiōnem didicit et māne ē tabernā ēvolans in rostra in Forum (4) prīncipem Tiberium, deinde Germānicum et Drūsum Caesarēs nōminātim (5) salūtābat, posteā ad tabernam redībat. Plūrimōs annōs hoc officium (6) omnibus diēbus perficiēbat et nōtus fiēbat. Mercātor alterīus tabernae hunc corvum necāvit, sīve invidiā vīcīnae tabernae sīve īrācundiā subitā. (7) Plēbs tam īrāta erat ut prīmō mercātor expellerētur ex eā regiōne, et mox (8) interficerētur. Fūnus corvī splendidum habitum est cum pompā māgnificā (9) (10) ad Viam Appiam et ibi corvus cremātus est.

— Plinius, *Nātūrālis Historia* X, lx, 121–123
(adapted)

corvus — raven, crow

1 Tiberiō prīncipe
   1 At the mouth of the Tiber
   2 When Tiberius was emperor
   3 When the Tiber was overflowing
   4 Although Tiberius was present   1____

2 in Castoris Pollūcisque templō nātus
1 before the time of the son of Castor and Pollux
2 as Castor and Pollux were swimming near the temple
3 since Pollux was born at a time before Castor
4 born on the temple of Castor and Pollux   2____

3 in vīcīnam tabernam dēvolāvit
1 he flew down into a nearby shop
2 he did not want the tavern in the neighborhood
3 he flew down onto the defeated shopkeeper
4 he did not want to be defeated in the tavern   3____

4 is corvus hūmānam locūtiōnem didicit
1 a human taught this raven to speak
2 this raven offered wealth to a human
3 this raven learned human speech
4 this raven assumed a human position   4____

5 māne ē tabernā ēvolāns in rostra
1 wishing to remain and poke his beak out of the shop
2 poking his beak out of the shop in the morning
3 continued flying from the speakers' platform and to the shop
4 in the morning flying out of the shop onto the speakers' platform   5____

6 prīncipem Tiberium, deinde Germānicum et
Drūsum Caesarēs nōminātim salūtābat

 1 Caesar first saluted Tiberius, then he
 mentioned Germanicus and Drusus
 2 he greeted emperor Tiberius, then the
 Caesars, Germanicus and Drusus, by name
 3 immediately Tiberius and then Germanicus
 and Drusus greeted Caesar by name
 4 first Tiberius, then the Caesars, Germanicus
 and Drusus, were named in order to be
 saluted   6_____

7 Mercātor alterīus tabernae hunc corvum
necāvit

 1 The merchant killed the ravens near this
 other shop
 2 Another shop offered a reward for killing
 these ravens
 3 This raven killed a merchant in another shop
 4 A merchant of another shop killed this raven   7_____

8 Plēbs tam īrāta erat ut prīmō mercātor
expellerētur

 1 The people were so angry that at first the
 merchant was driven out
 2 However, the people who were angry drove
 out the first merchant
 3 Then the people were angry as they expelled
 the very first merchant
 4 The people became very angry and the first
 merchant was expelled   8_____

9 et mox interficerētur
  1 and soon he was killed
  2 soon he also killed them
  3 and soon they interfered
  4 soon he was even brought back   9____

10 Fūnus corvī splendidum habitum est cum
pompā māgnificā
  1 The splendor of the raven's funeral was due
    to the magnificent procession
  2 The magnificent raven lived on since its
    funeral procession was splendid
  3 The raven's splendid funeral was held with a
    magnificent procession
  4 The splendid raven had a wonderful
    ceremony for his funeral   10____

PART IIIB

DIRECTIONS (11–20): *Do not write a translation of the following passages; read them through carefully several times to ascertain their meaning. Base your answers on the content of each passage* only. *Your answers do not have to be complete sentences; a word or phrase may suffice. In the spaces provided, write in English your answer to each question.* [10]

Cum *fundum* emere cōgitābis, sīc in animō hābē: prīmum spectā quō mōdō et quā dīligentiā proximī agricolae agrōs suōs colant et labōrent. In bonā regiōne labōrāre bonum erit. Sī poteris, quaere fundum quī est sub monte, in quō sōl saepe lūcet, quī habet bonam aquam, quī est prope oppidum et viam bonam celebremque, qui in merīdiem spectat. Deinde *vīlicum* rogāre necesse erit quae opera et labōrēs iam facta sint, et quae facienda sint. Sī vīlicus dīcet servōs nōn bonōs esse aut aufūgisse et tempestātēs malās fuisse, causās et explānātiōnem postulā.

                    — Catō, *Dē Agricultūrā*, 1–2
                           (adapted)

fundum — from *fundus*, farm
vīlicum — from *vīlicus*, overseer

11 When a person buys a farm, what should be considered first?

_____

_____

12–14 The author mentions six conditions in choosing a good region to farm. Name *three* of the conditions.

_____

_____

15 What is *one* question that will be necessary to ask the overseer?

_____

_____

16 Identify *one* situation in which a prospective buyer should demand an explanation.

_____

_____

   Postrēmus omnium rēgum Rōmānōrum fuit Tarquinius, quī obtinuit cognōmen Superbum propter facta et mōrēs. Tarquinius māluit capere magis quam exspectāre rēgnum quod ā Serviō tenēbātur. Itaque Tarquinius mīsit homicīdās ut fīnīrent vītam Serviī rēgis. Potestātem scelere et crīmine captam Tarquinius nōn melius administrāvit quam acquīsīverat. Et Tullia, fīlia Serviī et uxor Tarquiniī, erat similis mōribus suō marītō. Cum haec fēmina Tarquinium, marītum et novum rēgem, salūtāret, equōs in currū dūxit trāns sanguineum corpus patris.

— Flōrus, *Epitoma*, I, 7
(adapted)

17 What did Tarquin's reputation cause him to obtain?

_____

_____

18 What specific action did the impatient Tarquin take after he decided to seize power?

_____

_____

19 Who was Tullia?

_____

_____

20 What did Tullia do when she greeted the new king?

_____

_____

PART IIIC

DIRECTIONS (**21–30**): *Read the following passage carefully, but do* not *write a translation. Below the passage, there are several questions or incomplete statements. For each, select the alternative that best answers the question or completes the statement* on the basis of the information given in the passage, *and write its* number *in the space provided.* [10]

Camillus, imperātor clārus Rōmānus, bellō in Faliscōs praeerat. Faliscī erant hostēs ferōcēs sed hominēs intellegentēs quī dīligenter docuērunt līberōs suōs.

Apud ducēs Faliscōrum erat mōs: omnēs līberōs ab eōdem magistrō doctissimō docērī. In pāce hic magister puerōs Faliscōs extrā moenia ad lūdendum et exercendum semper ēdūcēbat, et per tempus bellī eandem rem fēcit, etsi hoc perīculōsum erat. Sed ūnō diē longius prōgressus, magister eōs līberōs Faliscōs ad castra Rōmāna et ad Camillum, imperātōrem Rōmānum, perdūxit. Tum magister, "Ego," inquit, "Faliscōs līberōs in manūs Rōmānōrum trādō; nam hī puerī sunt filiī dē potentissimīs virīs Faliscīs."

Quae cum Camillus audīret, "Nec populus Rōmānus nec imperātor," inquit, "ad quōs vēnistī sunt similēs tibi, improbissime vir! Nōn contrā līberōs arma habēmus, sed contrā virōs armātōs. Virtūte et armīs et opere vincam, nōn scelere."

Deinde Camillus manūs magistrī post tergum *ligārī* iussit. Tum bacula rāmōsque puerīs dedit ut eum vulnerārent ad oppidum redeuntēs. Faliscī cum spectāculum vidērent, fīdēm Rōmānōrum et iustitiam imperātōris Rōmānī laudāvērunt et fīnem bellī facere petīvērunt.

— Līvius, *Ab Urbe Conditā* V, xxvi–xxvii
(adapted)

ligārī — from *ligō*, tie, bind

21 Quis Camillus erat?
   1 prīnceps Faliscōrum
   2 dux Rōmānōrum
   3 fīlius prīncipis Faliscōrum
   4 magister equitum   21____

22 Cum Faliscī acrēs mīlitēs essent, tamen
   1 puerōs bene ēducāvērunt
   2 numquam hostēs vīcērunt
   3 familiās in bellum dūxērunt
   4 semper pācem petīvērunt   22____

23 Quod officium habuit ūnus magister?
   1 Omnēs puerōs perīculō servāvit.
   2 Librōs Graecē scrīpsit.
   3 Erat dux Faliscōrum.
   4 Omnēs fīliōs prīncipum docuit.   23____

24 Puerī extrā moenia semper dūcēbantur
   1 ut bellum parārent
   2 ut pācem peterent
   3 ut corpora exercērent
   4 ut pugnārent   24____

25 Cur erat periculum extrā murōs?
1 Erat tempus bellī.
2 Tempestās erat mala.
3 Iter erat difficile.
4 Puerī magistrō nōn parent.   25____

26 Magister līberōs Faliscōs tulit
  1 domum   3 ad salūtem
  2 ad Rōmānōs   4 ad patrēs eōrum   26____

27 Camillus ōrātiōnem vehementem habuit
  1 contrā magistrum
  2 prō pāce perpetuā
  3 ad patrēs conscrīptōs
  4 in patriae amantēs   27____

28 Camillus erat īrātus quod
  1 magister erat fīdus Faliscus
  2 puerī in castrīs nōn exercēbant
  3 parvōs puerōs Faliscōs capere nōluit
  4 puerī erant ferōcissimī in bellō   28____

29 Cum magister ad oppidum revenīret
  1 ā puerīs vulnerātus est
  2 ā populīs laudātus est
  3 puerī eum līberāvērunt
  4 Faliscī eum interfēcērunt   29____

30 Nunc Faliscī voluērunt
  1 magistrum laudāre   3 pācem facere
  2 Rōmānōs vincere   4 puerōs vulnerāre   30____

PART IIID

DIRECTIONS (**31–42**): *Read the passage below carefully, but do* not *write a translation. Below the passage, there are several questions or incomplete statements. Choose 10 of these questions or statements, and, in the space provided, write the* number *of the word or expression that best answers the question or completes the statement.* [10]

Tullius Terentiae Suae et Tulliae S.P.D.

Vōbīs consīderandum est, cārissimae meae, dīligenter putō, quid faciātis
— utrum Rōmae remaneātis an propter multa in urbe perīcula ad mē
veniātis. Id nōn sōlum meum consilium est, sed etiam vestrum. Haec in
mentem mihi veniunt: Rōmae vōs esse salvās posse per nostrum
5   propinquum Dolābellam, quī auxilium vōbīs ferat sī violentia et
perturbātiō in urbe subitō ērumpant.
Sed rursus perterritus sum, quod videō omnēs bonōs hominēs et multōs
nostrōs amīcōs Rōmā abesse, et eōs mulierēs suās sēcum habēre. Haec
autem regiō, in quā ego sum, complūra oppida et villās sine perīculō
10   habet. Sī cōnstituātis exīre, incolumēs et laetae hīc mēcum esse possītis.
Ego nōn adhūc certus sum, quod consilium sit melius. Vōs vidēte, quid
aliae fēminae in istō locō faciant. Consīderāte hanc rem dīligentissimē
vōbīscum et cum amīcīs. Cupiō vōs facere id quod optimum esse sentiātis.
Quoque necesse est vōbīs dīcere lībertō meō Philotimō quī vōbīscum
15   manet ut domum custōdiat atque praesidium offerat.
Tandem māximē labōrāte ut valeātis, sī mē valēre vultis.

ix Kal. Febr. Formiīs.

— Cicerō. *Ad Familiārēs* XIV. xviii
(adapted)

31 To whom is this letter addressed?
 1 Terentia and Tullia
 2 Philotimus and his friends
 3 Tullius
 4 Dolabella   31_____

32 The Latin word *cārissimae* (line 1) is the superlative of the Latin adjective
 1 *calida*   3 *certa*
 2 *cāra*   4 *cūra*   32_____

33 The author of the letter feels that a decision must
   be made
      1 secretly   3 courageously
      2 quickly   4 carefully   33_____

34 In which tense and mood is the Latin word
   remaneātis (line 2)?
      1 present indicative
      2 future indicative
      3 present subjunctive
      4 perfect subjunctive   34_____

35 Which English word is associated by derivation
   with the Latin word *perīcula* (line 2)?
      1 peristyle   3 periscope
      2 perilous   4 peripheral   35_____

36 The best meaning for the phrase *Rōmae vōs esse
   salvās posse* (line 4) is
      1 that I want you safely in Rome
      2 that you are safe anyplace away from Rome
      3 that I can safely come to Rome
      4 that at Rome you can be safe   36_____

37 In which case is the Latin word *vōbīs* (line 5)?
      1 dative   3 nominative
      2 genitive   4 accusative   37_____

38 Why is the author frightened by the situation in Rome?

  1 Fires have carelessly been set throughout the city.
  2 Slaves have been causing trouble.
  3 Good men and friends are leaving Rome with their wives.
  4 Too many soldiers are staying in Rome.   38_____

39 The Latin word *quā* (line 9) refers to

  1 the author's spouse
  2 the present danger
  3 the author's location
  4 Dolabella's home   39_____

40 The Latin words *Sī cōnstituātis* (line 10) begin

  1 a result clause
  2 a purpose clause
  3 an indirect statement
  4 a conditional clause   40_____

41 What does the author wish his family to do?

  1 avoid the other women in Rome
  2 beware of friends who live in the city
  3 do what they feel is the best
  4 make a place at home for the freedmen   41_____

42 What service will Philotimus provide?

  1 He will protect Cicero's loved ones.
  2 He will sell Cicero's house.
  3 He will set the slaves free.
  4 He will offer gifts to the gods.   42_____

PART IV

Answer the questions in Part IV according to the directions for Parts IVA, IVB, IVC, and IVD. [30 credits]

PART IVA

DIRECTIONS (**43–52**): *In the space provided, write the* number *of the word or expression that, when inserted in the blank, makes* each *sentence grammatically correct.* [10]

43 Cēnābat Nerva cum _____.
   1 paucās   3 paucōrum
   2 paucōs   4 paucīs   43_____

44 Sulla appellātus est _____.
   1 dictātōrem   3 dictātōris
   2 dictātor   4 dictātōre   44_____

45 Sunt multae stēllae, _____ numquam vīdimus.
   1 quās   3 cui
   2 quī   4 cuius   45_____

46 Cleopatra nōn persuāsit _____.
   1 imperātōris   3 imperātōrī
   2 imperātōrum   4 imperātōre   46_____

47 Rēs pūblica mihi cārior est _____.
   1 fīliōs   3 fīliī
   2 fīlium   4 fīliō   47____

48 Multīs virīs _____, legēbātur ōrātiō.
   1 audientem   3 audientī
   2 audientibus   4 audientēs   48____

49 _____, Marce, civēs statim ex urbe.
   1 Dūcite   3 Ducī
   2 Ducitis   4 Dūc   49____

50 Cum Caesar Ancōnam _____, urbem relīquimus.
   1 occupāre   3 occupāvisset
   2 occupantem   4 occupāvimus   50____

51 Scīs mē _____.
   1 lūdere   3 lūdō
   2 lūdentibus   4 lūdat   51____

52 Discipulus multa rogābat ut multa _____.
   1 disceret   3 discit
   2 discet   4 disce   52____

PART IVB

DIRECTIONS **(53–62)**: *This part contains a passage in English in which words associated by derivation with Latin words are italicized. Below the passage, there are several questions or incomplete statements. For each, select the alternative that best answers the question or completes the statement, and write its number in the space provided.* [10]

Northern India saw a *florescence* of temple architecture in the seventh century *A.D.* as newly established princes underwrote the *construction* of shrines dedicated to a pantheon of Hindu and Jain *deities*. Through such *commissions*, royal patrons hoped to legitimize their claim to power and to

5 charm those gods thought to hold the key to prosperity and everlasting life. Though few of these monuments have *survived*, a wealth of temple *statuary* has come down to us, providing insight into both the religious and political life of the *region* between the eighth and thirteenth centuries A.D. This sculptural *legacy* is celebrated in "Gods, Guardians, and Lovers," now on

0 view at the Asia *Society* in New York City.

                                                    — *Archaeology*, "Visions of Paradise,"
                                                    July/August 1993

53 The English word *florescence* (line 1) is associated by derivation with the Latin word *flōs* (flower) and the Latin suffix *escere*, which means
  1 to save   3 to become
  2 to diminish   4 to harm   53_____

54 The abbreviation *A.D.* (line 2) refers to the Latin words
  1 *Ante Diēs*   3 *Agnus Deī*
  2 *Ad Datum*   4 *Annō Dominī*   54_____

55 The English word *construction* (line 2) is associated by derivation with the fourth principal part of the Latin word
  1 *struō*   3 *tribuō*
  2 *stringō*   4 *trādō*   55_____

56 The English word *deities* (line 3) is associated by
derivation with the Latin word
1 *diēs*   3 *dēiectus*
2 *deus*   4 *dētentus*   56____

57 The English word *commissions* (line 4) is associated by derivation with the fourth principal part
of the Latin word
1 *maneō*   3 *misceō*
2 *mittō*   4 *moneō*   57____

58 The English word *survived* (line 6) is associated
by derivation with the Latin word
1 *vīs*   3 *via*
2 *vincō*   4 *vīvō*   58____

59 The English word *statuary* (line 6) is associated
by derivation with the Latin word that means
1 star   3 stand
2 stone   4 sit   59____

60 Which Latin word, paired with its English meaning, is associated by derivation with the English
word *region* (line 8)?
1 *regō* — rule   3 *agō* — do
2 *regredior* — return   4 *gignō* — bring forth   60____

61 Which Latin word, paired with its English meaning, is associated by derivation with the English
word *legacy* (line 9)?
1 *lectus* — couch   3 *lūceō* — shine
2 *lēx* — law   4 *largus* — abundant   61____

62 The English word *Society* (line 10) is associated
by derivation with the Latin word
1 *socius*   3 *sacer*
2 *sacculus*   4 *sēcūrus*   62____

PART IVC

DIRECTIONS (**63–67**): *For each sentence below, write, in the longer space provided, a Latin word with which the italicized word is associated by derivation. Any form of the appropriate Latin word, except prefixes and suffixes, will be acceptable. Then, write, in the shorter space provided, the number preceding the word or expression that best expresses the meaning of the italicized word.* [5]

63 The weather conditions intensified the *tristful* atmosphere of the gathering.

   1 playful   3 stormy
   2 bright   4 sad

63 _____   _____

64 The revolt is in its *incipient* stage.

   1 beginning   3 violent
   2 final   4 dormant

64 _____   _____

65 The report was a *dominant* factor in the board's decision.

   1 disruptive   3 main
   2 minor   4 surprise

65 _____   _____

66 No one listened to the *admonitions* of the speaker.

   1 promises   3 stories
   2 warnings   4 excuses

66 _____   _____

67 The judge remained *obdurate* when the defendant asked for mercy.

   1 shocked   3 sympathetic
   2 hardhearted   4 cautious

67 _____   _____

PART IVD

DIRECTIONS (**68–72**): *For each italicized Latin expression used in English, write, in the space provided, the* number *of the English translation, chosen from the list below, that most nearly has the same meaning.* [5]

68 To extract is to draw

    1 into   3 out
    2 under   4 before   68_____

69 To circumnavigate is to sail

    1 around   3 in front of
    2 by   4 away   69_____

70 To collaborate is to work

    1 above   3 on
    2 across   4 with   70_____

71 To intervene is to come

    1 down   3 after
    2 between   4 together   71_____

72 A recession is a going

    1 back   3 near
    2 toward   4 up   72_____

PART V

DIRECTIONS (**73–102**): *Select* 20 *of the following statements or questions. In the space provided, write the* number *of the word or expression that best answers the question or completes the statement.* [20 credits]

History and Public Life

73 The illustration below shows a wall painting from a tomb near Rome. This painting is evidence that the early Italian neighbors of the Romans had achieved a high level of sophistication.

Who were these early Italian neighbors of the Romans?

1 Gauls   3 Trojans
2 Phoenicians   4 Etruscans   73 _____

74 The coins shown below depict a Gaul and the date, the Ides of March.

These coins honor the memory of
1 Gaius Julius Caesar
2 Marcus Tullius Cicero
3 Graeus Pompeius Magnus
4 Publius Terentius Afer   74_____

75 The illustration below shows a typical scene in ancient Rome.

What activity is shown in this illustration?
1 a wealthy freedman being carried by his slaves to a dinner party
2 a foreign dignitary being welcomed to the Senate in the traditional fashion
3 a Roman elected official traveling with his official retinue
4 a traditional Roman funeral procession   75_____

76 According to legend, which event occurred in 509 B.C.?
1 the assassination of Caesar
2 the beginning of the Republic
3 the establishment of the Empire
4 the founding of Rome   76_____

77 Who was the Roman general who was victorious against Hannibal, the Carthaginian?
1 Cornelius Sulla   3 Scipio Africanus
2 Emperor Nero   4 Gaius Marius   77_____

78 Cicero's greatest political service to the Republic was his crushing of the rebellion planned by
1 Pompey   3 Catiline
2 Vercingetorix   4 Spartacus   78_____

79 The Roman magistrate whose primary responsibility was the management of the treasury was the
1 aedile   3 consul
2 praetor   4 quaestor   79_____

80 Which island was a rich source of grain and became Rome's first province?
1 Crete   3 Cyprus
2 Sicily   4 Delos   80_____

81 The *legiōnēs, cohortēs,* and *manipulī* were divisions of the Roman

1 patricians   3 plebs
2 government   4 army   81____

82 What were the "Twelve Tables"?

1 the earliest written code of Roman law
2 the traditional dining arrangement in a Roman home
3 the booths where citizens voted in elections for tribunes
4 the bronze lists of consuls posted in the Forum   82____

Daily Life

83 Which room is shown in the illustration below?

1 *tablīnum*   3 *culīna*
2 *triclīnium*   4 *cubiculum*   83____

84 Wealthy Romans often had lavish country houses
called
1 *casae*   3 *tabernae*
2 *vīllae*   4 *īnsulae*   84_____

85 What would a Roman man wear while he was
running for public office?
1 *toga virīlis*   3 *toga picta*
2 *toga praetexta*   4 *toga candida*   85_____

86 The illustration below shows the supplies that a
Roman boy would take to school.

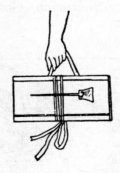

The supplies shown in the illustration are a wax
tablet and a
1 *corona*   3 *stilus*
2 *tēlum*   4 *pīlum*   86_____

87 The Roman numeral MCMLXXIV is equivalent
   to
   (1) 1858   (3) 1974
   (2) 1934   (4) 2124   87_____

88 The Ides of January falls on January
   1 first   3 ninth
   2 seventh   4 thirteenth   88_____

89 The slave who guarded the entrance to a house
   was the
   1 *lictor*   3 *paedagōgus*
   2 *iānitor*   4 *ancilla*   89_____

Myths and Legends

90 The symbols shown in the illustration below were
   inspired by Greek deities.

   Who are the Roman deities associated with Ares
   and Aphrodite?
   1 Mars and Venus   3 Apollo and Diana
   2 Jupiter and Juno   4 Neptune and Ceres   90_____

91 The illustration below shows Hercules killing a nine-headed monster. This monster is associated with the water of a swamp.

What was this monster called?
1 Minotaur   3 Cerberus
2 Centaur   4 Hydra   91____

92 The leader of the Argonauts, who captured the Golden Fleece, was
1 Hercules   3 Jason
2 Ulysses   4 Theseus   92____

93 Navigation in the narrow passage between Italy and Sicily has always been treacherous. The ancient Romans and Greeks believed that the dangers in these waters were caused by two monsters. These monsters were
1 Deucalion and Pyrrha
2 Castor and Pollux
3 Pyramus and Thisbe
4 Scylla and Charybdis   93____

94 What gift is referred to in the expression "I fear
the Greeks especially bearing gifts"?
1 Trojan horse
2 golden apples
3 belt of Hippolyta
4 weapons of the Cyclopes   94_____

95 The illustration below shows the hero of Homer's
Iliad. This hero was a famous Greek warrior who
was vulnerable only in his heel.

Who was this Greek warrior?
1 Achilles   3 Patroclus
2 Hector   4 Aeneas   95_____

Literature

96 The illustration below shows a woman sitting on a tripod and predicting the future. Many ancient authors referred to this scene in their works.

The occasion shown in the scene is a

1 ritual sacrifice of animals by a priestess
2 consultation of the oracle at Delphi
3 meeting between a bride-to-be and her aged groom
4 ritual bath of a goddess

96_____

97 Which author wrote a vast and famous collection of myths in which there are many transformations?

1 Caesar 3 Lucretius
2 Vergil 4 Ovid 97____

98 What is the name given to a work, such as the *Aeneid*, that is a long narrative poem recounting the deeds of a legendary or historical hero?

1 tragedy 3 satire
2 epic 4 lyric 98____

Architecture and Art

99 The inscription on the building shown below states that it was built by Marcus Agrippa. This building is remarkable for its domed roof.

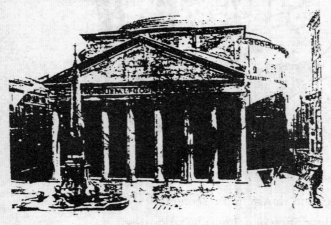

What is this building called?

1 Pantheon 3 Temple of the Divine Julius
2 Colosseum 4 Temple of Vespasian 99____

100 The illustration below shows a floor plan.

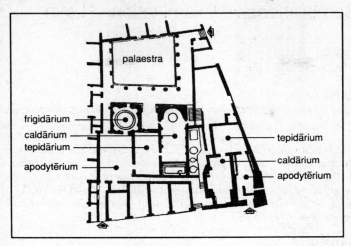

This illustration is a floor plan of a
1 temple   3 bath
2 house   4 theater   100____

101 After the age of 15, young Romans would con-
secrate the *bulla*, which they had worn from in-
fancy, to their household gods. These household
gods were known as the
1 *Amōrēs*   3 *Pontificēs*
2 *Olympicī*   4 *Larēs*   101____

102 The Roman athletic and military training area
was located at the
1 Colosseum   3 Forum
2 Campus Martius   4 Circus Maximus   102____

Answers June 1995

Comprehensive Examination in Latin

PART I
(Allow a total of 5 credits for this part.)

PART II
(Allow a total of 5 credits, one-half credit for each of the following 10 italicized words.)

Quod nōs in Ītaliam / salvōs *vēnisse* gaudēs, / perpetuō *gaudeās* velim; / sed perturbātī / dolōre *animī* / magnīsque *inūuriīs* / metuō nē / id cōnsilī cēperimus, / quod nōn facile / *explicāre* possīmus. / Quārē, / quantum *potes*, / adiuvā; / quid autem possis, / mihi in *mentem* / nōn vēnit. / In viam / quod tē dēs / hōc tempore, / *nihil* est. / Et longum est *iter* / et nōn tūtum, / et nōn videō, /*quid* prōdesse possīs, / sī vēneris. / Valē.

PART III
PART IIIA
(Allow a total of 10 credits, one credit for each of the following.)

(1) 2	**(3)** 1	**(5)** 4	**(7)** 4	**(9)** 1
(2) 4	**(4)** 3	**(6)** 2	**(8)** 1	**(10)** 3

PART IIIB
The answers to the questions in this part do not have to be complete sentences. A phrase or word may be sufficient for a completely correct one-credit response. Disregard errors in English. Allow no partial credit. Not all of the acceptable answers have been included.

(Allow a total of 10 credits, one credit for each of the following.)
- **(11)** how and with what diligence the neighboring farmers work and cultivate their fields
- **(12–14)** located at the foot of a mountain; where the Sun often shines; has good water; is near a town; near a good, well-traveled road; faces south
- **(15)** what work has already been done; what must be done
- **(16)** if the slaves are not good or have fled; if the weather has been bad
- **(17)** the last name "Superbus," "the Proud"
- **(18)** He sent murderers to end King Servius' life.
- **(19)** the daughter of Servius (and the wife of Tarquin)
- **(20)** She led horses in a chariot over the bloody body of her father.

PART IIIC
(Allow a total of 10 credits, one credit for each of the following.)

(**21**) 2	(**23**) 4	(**25**) 1	(**27**) 1	(**29**) 1
(**22**) 1	(**24**) 3	(**26**) 2	(**28**) 3	(**30**) 3

PART IIID
(Allow a total of 10 credits, one credit for each of 10 of the following.)

(**31**) 1	(**33**) 4	(**35**) 2	(**37**) 1	(**39**) 3	(**41**) 3
(**32**) 2	(**34**) 3	(**36**) 4	(**38**) 3	(**40**) 4	(**42**) 1

PART IV

PART IVA
(Allow a total of 10 credits, one credit for each of the following.)

(**43**) 4	(**45**) 1	(**47**) 4	(**49**) 4	(**51**) 1
(**44**) 2	(**46**) 3	(**48**) 2	(**50**) 3	(**52**) 1

PART IVB
(Allow a total of 10 credits, one credit for each of the following.)

(**53**) 3	(**55**) 1	(**57**) 2	(**59**) 3	(**61**) 2
(**54**) 4	(**56**) 2	(**58**) 4	(**60**) 1	(**62**) 1

PART IVC
(Allow credit for any correctly spelled form of the Latin word. Allow no credit for prefixes or suffixes. Not all of the acceptable answers have been included.)

(Allow a total of 5 credits, one-half credit for each correct answer in each column.)

Column I	Column II
(**63**) tristis	(**63**) 4
(**64**) incipiō, capiō	(**64**) 1
(**65**) dominus, domus	(**65**) 3
(**66**) admoneō, moneō	(**66**) 2
(**67**) durus	(**67**) 2

PART IVD
(Allow a total of 5 credits, one credit for each of the following.)

(**68**) 3	(**69**) 1	(**70**) 4	(**71**) 2	(**72**) 1

PART V

(Allow a total of 20 credits, one credit for each of 20 of the following.)

(**73**) 4	(**78**) 3	(**83**) 2	(**88**) 4	(**93**) 4	(**98**) 2
(**74**) 1	(**79**) 4	(**84**) 2	(**89**) 2	(**94**) 1	(**99**) 1
(**75**) 3	(**80**) 2	(**85**) 4	(**90**) 1	(**95**) 1	(**100**) 3
(**76**) 2	(**81**) 4	(**86**) 3	(**91**) 4	(**96**) 2	(**101**) 4
(**77**) 3	(**82**) 1	(**87**) 3	(**92**) 3	(**97**) 4	(**102**) 2

Examination   June 1996

Comprehensive Latin

PART I

Part I is administered at the school's convenience at some time before the written test is given. You are asked to read aloud a passage of Latin for the teacher to judge on the basis of your proficiency in the spoken language. [5 credits]

PART II

DIRECTIONS: *Your teacher will read aloud a short passage in Latin. Listen carefully to this first reading. Then your teacher will read the passage in short phrases with a pause after each phrase. After each pause, write, in Latin, the phrase read by your teacher. Do* not *write a translation of the passage.*

There will be no penalty for improper use of macrons or capitalization. After you have completed writing the passage in Latin, your teacher will read the entire passage one more time so that you may check your work. [5 credits]

The passage that the teacher reads will be found in **Answers, Part II,** *at the end of this examination.*

PART III

Answer the questions in Part III according to the directions for Parts IIIA, IIIB, IIIC, and IIID.   [40 credits]

1

PART IIIA

DIRECTIONS (1–10): *Do not write a translation of the following passage; read it through carefully several times to determine its meaning. Then, in the space provided, write the* number *of the choice that best translates* each *underlined expression* as it is used in the passage. [10]

Nam ut *Archiās* prīmum excessit ex pueritiā atque ab eīs artibus et lūdīs
<u>(1)</u>
quibus aetās puerīlis *solet* formārī, contulit sē ad studium scrībendī. Prīmum
<u>(2)</u>
vīxit *Antiochīae*, nam nātus est ibi nōbilī familiā. (Haec urbs erat quondam
<u>(3)</u>
nōta et cōpiōsa cum ērudītissimīs hominibus et līberālissimīs studiīs.)

Archiās celeriter incēpit superāre omnēs glōriā ingeniī.
<u>(4)</u>

Posteā, in cēterīs partibus Āsiae Graeciaeque adventūs Archiae

celebrantur sīc ut admīrātiō hominis superāret fāmam. Ītalia erat tum plēna

Graecārum artium ac disciplīnārum. Haec studia in Latiō illō tempore
<u>(5)</u>
vehementius colēbantur quam nunc in eīsdem oppidīs. Itaque Tarentīnī huic

cīvitātem cēteraque praemia dōnāvērunt. Omnēs quī poterant iūdicāre aliquid
<u>(6)</u>
dē ingeniīs putāvērunt Archiam esse dignum amīcitiā atque laudātiōne.
<u>(7)</u>
Cum esset iam nōtus, Archiās vēnit Rōmam, Mariō et Catulō cōnsulibus.
<u>(8)</u>
Prīmum, intellēxit eōs cōnsulēs maximās rēs ad scrībendum prōvidēre posse.
<u>(9)</u>
Statim *Lūcullī* recēpērunt eum in suam domum. Propter suum ingenium et

nātūram et virtūtem, Archiās afficiēbātur summō honōre. Nōn solum eī quī
<u>(10)</u>
studēbant discere atque audīre aliquid, sed etiam eī quī discere simulābant,

Archiam laudāvērunt.

— Cicerō, *Prō Archiā Poētā*, III
(adapted)

Archiās, Archiae, m. — a Greek poet
solet — from *soleō, solēre*, to be accustomed
Antiochīae — from *Antiochīa,ae*, f., the city of Antioch
Lūcullī, Lūcullōrum, m. — the Lucullan family

1 ut Archiās prīmum excessit ex pueritiā

    1 as soon as Archias grew out of boyhood
    2 so that Archias as a youth might be chosen first
    3 as Archias for the first time excelled as a youth
    4 so that Archias' boyhood was considered first   1 _____

2 contulit sē ad studium scrībendī

    1 his desire to write left him
    2 as eagerness for writing overtook him in this way
    3 since he considered writing most important
    4 he proceeded to the study of writing   2 _____

3 nam nātus est ibi nōbilī familiā

    1 indeed he sailed there with a high-ranking family
    2 for he was born there of a noble family
    3 also he reported here with important families
    4 when he found noble families here   3 _____

4 superāre omnēs glōriā ingeniī

    1 the genius of all was glorified
    2 to surpass all in the glory of his talent
    3 to stop everyone from earning glory
    4 everyone outdid him in glory and genius   4 _____

5 Haec studia in Latiō illō tempore vehementius
   colēbantur

   1 Then Latium eagerly opposed these subjects
   2 At that time, Latium wisely tried these pur-
      suits
   3 These studies were cultivated more strongly
      in Latium at that time
   4 Then in Latium, these interests were
      attempted at an earlier time   5 _____

6 Itaque Tarentīnī huic cīvitātem cēteraque
   praemia dōnāvērunt.

   1 And so, the Tarentines gave him citizenship
      and other rewards.
   2 However, the Tarentinian state took certain
      prizes from him.
   3 The Tarentines offered prizes for each citizen.
   4 Indeed, the Tarentinian state lost all its
      rewards.   6 _____

7 Archiam esse dignum amīcitiā atque laudātiōne

   1 that Archias was a worthy friend
   2 that the worthy friend of Archias was praised
   3 that they were worthy to be a friend of
      Archias
   4 that Archias was worthy of friendship and
      praise   7 _____

8 Mariō et Catulō cōnsulibus

   1 when Marius selected Catulus consul
   2 in the consulship of Marius and Catulus
   3 after Marius, Catulus was consul
   4 because Catulus became consul before Marius   8 _____

9 eōs cōnsulēs maximās rēs ad scrībendum
   prōvidēre posse
   1 that those consuls could provide the greatest
      resources for writing
   2 that these consuls were able to write about the
      most important matters
   3 that they brought important writing instru-
      ments to the consuls
   4 that both consuls were able to see great
      writers   9 _____

10 Archiās afficiēbātur summō honōre
    1 Archias was afflicted with a serious illness
    2 the highest office was taken from Archias
    3 they treated Archias without much honor
    4 Archias was treated with the highest honor   10 _____

PART IIIB

DIRECTIONS (**11–20**): *Do not write a translation of the following passages;
read them through carefully several times to ascertain their meaning. Base
your answers on the content of each passage only. Your answers do not have
to be complete sentences; a word or phrase may suffice. In the spaces provided,
write in English your answer to each question.* [10]

The Early Life of Augustus

Nātus est Augustus, M. Tulliō Cicerōne et C. Antōniō cōnsulibus, ante
diem IX Kalendās Octōbrēs ante prīmam lūcem sōlis. Parvō puerō
cognōmen Thūrīnus erat. Posteā Caesaris et deinde Augustī cognōmen
assumpsit. Quīdam hominēs putābant eum dēbēre appellārī Rōmulum, quod
vidērētur iterum cōnstituisse Rōmam. *Mūnātius Plancus* persuāsit hīs
hominibus ut Augustus vocārētur, quod Augustus esset sacrius et dignius
cognōmen.

Pater Augustī mortuus est ubi puer habēbat quattuor annōs. Nātus
duodecim annōs puer dīxit ōrātiōnem fūnēbrem prō mortuā *aviā*. Post

quīnque annōs, avunculus Iūlius Caesar in Hispāniam īvit et pugnābat contrā fīliōs Cn. Pompeī. Quamquam iter erat difficile, Augustus secūtus est suum avunculum. Iūlius Caesar laudāvit mōrēs et industriam adulēscentis.

Post mortem Iūlī Caesaris, Augustus quīnque bella cīvilia gessit. Societāte factā cum Antōniō et Lepidō, Augustus vīcit exercitūs Brūtī et Cassī. Post Augustī victōriam et mortem Brūtī, mīsit caput Brūtī Rōmam, ut esset sub statuā Caesaris.

Suetonius, Divus Augustus II, v–viii
(adapted)

Mūnātius Plancus — a Roman senator
aviā — from *avia,* grandmother

11 When was Augustus born?

_____

_____

12 What does the author tell us was one of the names Augustus held before he assumed the title of Augustus?

_____

_____

_____

_____

13 Why did some people think that Augustus should be named Romulus?

_____

_____

_____

14 What reason was given to persuade these people
    that he should be given the name Augustus?

    _____

    _____

    _____

    _____

15 What happened when Augustus was 4 years old?

    _____

    _____

    _____

    _____

16 When he was 12 years old, what did Augustus do
    that was so impressive?

    _____

    _____

    _____

    _____

17 When Augustus was 17 years old, where did his
    uncle Julius Caesar fight against Pompey's sons?

    _____

    _____

    _____

    _____

18 What did Julius Caesar find praiseworthy about
his nephew Augustus?

_____

_____

_____

_____

19 What did Augustus accomplish as a result of his
alliance with Antony and Lepidus?

_____

_____

_____

_____

20 After the death of Brutus, what did Augustus do?

_____

_____

_____

_____

PART IIIC

DIRECTIONS (**21–30**): *Read the following passage carefully, but do* not *write a translation. Below the passage, there are several questions or incomplete statements. For* each, *select the alternative that best answers the question or completes the statement* on the basis of the information given in the passage, *and write its* number *in the space provided.* [10]

In proeliō inter Antōnium et Augustum Cleopātra prīma sē dedit in fugam. Antōnius rēgīnam Cleopātram sequī cōnstituit et cum exercitū suō nōn mānsit. Imperātor, quī dēsertōrēs interfēcisse dēbuit, factus est dēsertor exercitūs suī. Mīlitēs Antōniī fortissimē pugnandō sine Antōniō dūrāvērunt. Sed illī mīlitēs, cum diū prō Antōniō absente pugnāvissent, tandem tamen Augustō, adversāriō Antōniī, sē dedērunt.

— Velleius Paterculus, *Historiae Rōmānae*, II, 85
(adapted)

21 Quid fēcit Cleopātra prīma?

  1 Ad Caesarem sē trādidit.
  2 Antōnium secūta est.
  3 Cum mīlitibus mānsit.
  4 Dē pugnā fūgit.   21 _____

22 Quō īvit Antōnius?

  1 cum suīs mīlitibus
  2 ad cōpiās patriae suae
  3 ad rēgīnam
  4 ad castra amīcōrum multōrum   22 _____

23 Imperātor discedēns dēseruit

    1 mīlitēs suōs
    2 rēgīnam Cleopātram
    3 cōpiās Augustī
    4 exercitum Cleopātrae   23 _____

24 Prīmō mīlitēs Antōniī, quamquam nūllum
    ducem habuērunt,

    1 ācriter pugnāvērunt
    2 auxilium exspectāvērunt
    3 hostēs vīcērunt
    4 Antōnium laudāvērunt   24 _____

25 Mīlitēs tandem sine duce relictī,

    1 ab hostibus interfectī sunt
    2 Augustō sē trādidērunt
    3 Rōmam redīvērunt
    4 ab Antōniō revocātī sunt   25 _____

Nāsīca, cum poētam Ennium vidēre voluisset, ab ancillā quaesīvit,
"Adestne domī Ennius?" Cum ancilla dīxisset Ennium domī nōn esse, Nāsīca
sēnsit illam dominī iussū dīxisse et Ennium intrā adesse.
Paucīs post diēbus cum Ennius apud Nāsīcam esset et eum ā iānuā
peteret, Nāsīca exclāmāvit sē domī nōn esse.
Tum Ennius inquit, "Quid est? Ego certē cognōscō tuam vōcem!"
Inquit Nāsīca, "Homō es impudēns. Ego cum tē peterem, ancillae tuae
crēdidī tē domī nōn esse. Tūne mihi et vōcī meae nōn crēdis ipse?"

                                        — Cicerō, *Dē Orātōre*, II, LXVIII, 276
                                                          (adapted)

Nāsīca — *Scīpiō Nāsīca, -ae*, m.

26 Cūr Nāsīca domum Ennī īvit?

    1 ad carmina scrībenda
    2 ut librōs emeret
    3 quod domum amāvit
    4 ut poētam vidēret   26 _____

27 Quid ancilla dīxit Nāsīcae?

1 Ennium eō tempore scrībere
2 Ennium cum amīcīs cēnāre
3 Ennium abesse
4 Ennium strēnuē labōrāre   27 _____

28 Quō audītō, Nāsīca putāvit

1 ancillam Ennium amāre
2 Ennium iubēre ancillam hōc modō respondēre
3 poētam domum mox reditūrum esse
4 sē diūtius exspectātūrum esse   28 _____

29 Quid Nāsīca dīxit Enniō, cum Ennius domum
    Nāsīcae vēnisset?

1 "Nāsīca nōn domī est."
2 "Ubi est tua ancilla?"
3 "Tē nōn audiō."
4 "Tū nōn es meus amīcus."   29 _____

30 Quibus verbīs optimē dēscrībitur haec fābula?

1 caveat emptor   3 ē plūribus ūnum
2 tempus fugit   4 quid prō quō   30 _____

PART IIID

DIRECTIONS (31–42): *Read the passage below carefully, but do not write a translation. Below the passage, there are several questions or incomplete statements. Choose 10 of these questions or statements, and, in the space provided, write the* number *of the word or expression that best answers the question or completes the statement.* [10]

Cicerō Atticō Sal.

Volō tē certiōrem facere mē factum esse patrem eōdem diē, quō L. Iūlius Caesar et M. Marcius Figulus dēlēctī sunt cōnsulēs. Mea Terentia et noster īnfāns puer salvī sunt.

Diū ā tē nōn audīvī. Scrīpsī anteā atque nārrāvī rēs meās tibi. Hōc
5 tempore in animō habeō Catilīnam, competītōrem nostrum, dēfendere. Spērō, sī līberātus erit, nōs meliōrēs amīcōs fore; sīn aliter acciderit, hūmāniter ferēmus.

Cupiō tē redīre quam prīmum ut in comitiīs mihi auxilium dēs. Nōn nūllī ex amīcīs tuīs potentibus mihi adversantur. Iānuāriō mēnse revenī Rōmam
10 rūrsus, sī placet tibi, ut cōnstituistī!

— Cicerō, *Epistulae Ad Atticum*, I, 2
(adapted)

31 To whom is this letter written?

1 Atticus   3 Caesar
2 Cicero   4 Figulus   31 _____

32 A synonym for the Latin word *volō* (line 1) is

1 *iubeō*   3 *cupiō*
2 *habeō*   4 *cōnstituō*   32 _____

33 What is the best translation of the Latin words *certiōrem facere* (line 1)?

1 to inform   3 to do
2 to leave   4 to warn   33 _____

34 To which name does the initial *L.* (line 1) refer?

    1 *Lūcullus*   3 *Līvius*

    2 *Lūcius*   4 *Lutātius*   34 _____

35 What is the relationship of Terentia to Cicero?

    1 daughter   3 sister

    2 wife   4 mother   35 _____

36 At this time, what are Cicero's intentions concerning his rival Catiline?

    1 defend Catiline

    2 embarrass Catiline

    3 destroy Catiline's reputation

    4 ignore Catiline   36 _____

37 The Latin word *meliōrēs* (line 6) is the comparative form of

    1 *magnus*   3 *multus*

    2 *parvus*   4 *bonus*   37 _____

38 In which tense and mood is the Latin verb *ferēmus* (line 7)?

    1 imperfect subjunctive

    2 future indicative

    3 present indicative

    4 pluperfect subjunctive   38 _____

39 The best translation for the Latin phrase *quam prīmum* (line 8) is

    1 first of all   3 recently

    2 as soon as possible   4 tomorrow   39 _____

40 Which rhetorical figure is illustrated in the Latin
expression *revenī Rōmam rūrsus* (lines 9 and 10)?

1 anaphora   3 alliteration
2 litotes   4 chiasmus   40 _____

41 When is Atticus expected to return to Rome?

1 summer   3 fall
2 spring   4 winter   41 _____

42 The two themes in this letter are

1 literary and scientific
2 economic and social
3 personal and political
4 historic and artistic   42 _____

PART IV

Answer the questions in Part IV according to the directions for Parts IVA,
IVB, IVC, and IVD. [30 credits]

PART IVA

DIRECTIONS (**43–52**): *In the space provided, write the* number *of the word
or expression that, when inserted in the blank, makes* each *sentence grammatically correct.* [10]

43 Fīlius senātōris cum _____ ad forum
ambulāvit.

1 amīcum   3 amīcī
2 amīcō   4 amīcōrum   43 _____

44 Marcus dīxit frātrem ad Ītaliam _____.

   1 venīre   3 veniet
   2 vēnit   4 veniat   44 _____

45 Puer _____ dōnum dedit.

   1 mātrem   3 mātrī
   2 ad mātrem   4 mātre   45 _____

46 Nōlīte _____ cibum!

   1 editis   3 edit
   2 edō   4 edere   46 _____

47 Iūlia est altior _____.

   1 fīliās   3 fīliā
   2 fīliam   4 fīliae   47 _____

48 Sī tempestās fuisset bona, nāvēs _____.

   1 nāvigāverant   3 nāvigābant
   2 nāvigābunt   4 nāvigāvissent   48 _____

49 Adulēscēns per _____ celeriter currēbat.

   1 viae   3 viīs
   2 viam   4 viā   49 _____

50 Mīlitēs castra _____ poterant.

   1 mōvisset   3 movēre
   2 movēbat   4 movēns   50 _____

51 Herculēs tam potēns erat ut leōnem facile _____ .

   1 interficeret   3 interficiet

   2 interficiendum   4 interficit   51 _____

52 Hīs rēbus _____ , cīvēs laetī erant.

   1 fēcissēmus   3 facere

   2 factīs   4 faciendum   52 _____

PART IVB

DIRECTIONS (**53–62**): *This part contains a passage in English in which words associated by derivation with Latin words are italicized. Below the passage, there are several questions or incomplete statements. For each, select the alternative that best answers the question or completes the statement, and write its* number *in the space provided.* [10]

The Crash

     For the first few hours, July 16 seemed a day like any other in the swirl of clouds and gas at the surface of planet Jupiter. Then, out of the planet's southern skies, a massive chunk of rock

5   and ice came hurtling through the Jovian heavens at 134,000 mph. The most spectacular celestial bombardment ever witnessed had begun. When the fragment collided with the planet's gaseous cover, a massive plume of gas

10 spewed from the impact site like a geyser, forming a brilliant fireball 1,000 miles high and 4,000 miles wide. Soon, astronomers on Earth saw the first clear pictures of the faraway cataclysm—and reached for the champagne.

15   The ill-fated projectile, which scientists labeled fragment A, was in itself an astrono-

          • Jovian

          • spectacular

          • celestial

          • projectile

          • fragment

mer's dream come true. But the fireworks that
followed over the next six days were enough to
have Galileo himself cheering from the
20   heavens.

U.S. News & World Report

53   The English word *Jovian* (line 5) is associated by
derivation with *Iovis,* the genitive form of the
Latin word

   1 *Iāniculum*   3 *Iānus*
   2 *Iuppiter*   4 *Iūlius*   53 _____

54   The English word *spectacular* (line 6) is associated by derivation with *spectō,* the Latin word
that means

   1 look at   3 be eager for
   2 wait for   4 come upon   54 _____

55   Which Latin word, paired with its English meaning, is associated by derivation with the English
word *celestial* (line 7)?

   1 *celebrō* — visit   3 *calidus* — hot
   2 *celer* — quick   4 *caelum* — sky   55 _____

56   Which Latin word, paired with its English meaning, is associated by derivation with the English
word *projectile* (line 15)?

   1 *iungō* — join   3 *iubeō* — order
   2 *iaceō* — lie   4 *iaciō* — throw   56 _____

57 Which Latin word, paired with its English meaning, is associated by derivation with the English word *fragment* (line 16)?

1 *frangō* — break   3 *fraudō* — deceive

2 *mēns* — mind   4 *mēnsa* — table   57 _____

DAVID MACAULAY
AUTHOR OF *CITY*
HOSTS PBS SPECIAL

What the Roman empire accomplished was astounding. Two thousand years before the invention of modern high-tech construction and communica-
5 tions equipment, computers, and mass transportation systems, the Romans linked North Africa, the Middle East, and most of Europe into a political and commercial empire that lasted for hun-
10 dreds of years.

In part, the Empire was maintained by Rome's powerful military. Yet the spread of Roman civilization across the vast empire was carried out
15 in large part by another force: the Roman city. The Romans built cities in their newly conquered lands to engage in commerce, to reward their soldiers with land and a place to live, and, as
20 they saw it, to civilize the barbaric peoples they conquered. For the most part, it worked. Many people far away from Rome took advantage of the possibilities afforded by their cities, and
25 many eventually became Roman citizens.

— David Macaulay

- invention

- computers

- commercial

- military

- possibilities
- eventually

58 The English words *invention* (line 3) and *eventually* (line 25) are associated by derivation with the Latin word

   1 *veniō*   3 *vendō*

   2 *videō*   4 *vincō*   58 _____

59 The English word *computers* (line 5) is associated by derivation with *putō*, the Latin word that means

   1 put   3 think

   2 strike   4 make   59 _____

60 The root of the English word *commercial* (line 9) is associated by derivation with the Latin word

   1 *mergō*   3 *committō*

   2 *mercātor*   4 *comparō*   60 _____

61 The English word *military* (line 12) is associated by derivation with the Latin word

   1 *mille*   3 *mīles*

   2 *lītus*   4 *littera*   61 _____

62 The English word *possibilities* (line 24) is associated by derivation with the Latin word

   1 *iter*   3 *poscō*

   2 *bilinguis*   4 *possum*   62 _____

PART IVC

DIRECTIONS (**63–67**): *For each sentence below, write, in the longer space provided, a Latin word with which the italicized word is associated by derivation. Any form of the appropriate Latin word, except prefixes and suffixes, will be acceptable. Then, write, in the shorter space provided, the number preceding the word or expression that best expresses the meaning of the italicized word.* [5]

63 The college student had been accused by his friends of *somnambulism*.

    1 cheating   3 sleepwalking
    2 arrogance   4 exaggeration

63 _____

64 The celebrity's *cupidity* was evident to the audience.

    1 greed   3 arrogance
    2 common sense 4 creativity

64 _____

65 The mural depicted a *rustic* scene.

    1 shocking   3 country
    2 dreary   4 colorless

65 _____

66 The athlete had a *tacit* agreement with her coach.

    1 unbreakable   3 financial
    2 illegal   4 unspoken

66 _____

67 The new drug produced *salutary* results.

1 dangerous   3 unknown
2 healthful   4 doubtful

67 _____   _____

PART IVD

DIRECTIONS (**68–72**): *In the space provided, write the* number *of the Latin expression that best answers the question or completes the statement.* [5]

68 If activities were arranged for early in the day, before noon, they would be completed

1 *ante merīdiem*   3 *ante bellum*
2 *post mortem*   4 *prō tempore*   68 _____

69 Camp counselors guide and direct the activities of young campers who are away from home. These counselors are exercising the authority known as

1 *in memoriam*   3 *in locō parentis*
2 *ad infinītum*   4 *ex librīs*   69 _____

70 Air travelers who had been advised of mechanical difficulties during their flight were relieved when they returned to

1 *vice versā*   3 *pater patriae*
2 *terra firma*   4 *ad nauseam*   70 _____

71 An artist exhibiting her best work would refer to her masterpiece as her

1 *addendum*   3 *memorandum*
2 *ultimātum*   4 *magnum opus*   71 _____

72 Which expression best describes the goal of Olympic athletes?

 1 *habeās corpus*
 2 *citius, altius, fortius*
 3 *rēs ipsa loquitur*
 4 *dē gustibus nōn disputandum est*   72 _____

PART V

DIRECTIONS (**73–102**): *Select 20 of the following statements or questions. In the space provided, write the* number *of the word or expression that best answers the question or completes the statement.*   [20 credits]

History and Public Life

73 The map below shows a region of the world known to the Romans.

What was this region called?

 1 *Gallia*   3 *Thrācia*
 2 *Bīthӯnia*   4 *Graecia*   73 _____

74 In which war was Aeneas a hero?

   1 Punic War   3 Trojan War
   2 Gallic War   4 Social War   74 _____

75 When a Roman senator gave a speech to the people, he addressed the citizens as

   1 *Patrēs Cōnscrīptī*   3 *Iūdicēs*
   2 *Quirītēs*   4 *Praetōrēs*   75 _____

76 The Roman battering ram was known as the

   1 *ariēs*   3 *vāllum*
   2 *fossa*   4 *scorpiō*   76 _____

77 The corrupt governor of Sicily who was prose-
   cuted by Cicero was

   1 Milo   3 Catiline
   2 Clodius   4 Verres   77 _____

78 The illustration below shows the Forum in Pompeii. The volcano that erupted and destroyed the city is in the background.

What is the name of this volcano?

1 Mt. Vesuvius   3 Mt. Etna

2 Mt. Olympus   4 Mt. Pelion   78 _____

79 Which sequence of the periods of Roman history is correct?

1 monarchy → republic → empire

2 monarchy → empire → republic

3 empire → republic → monarchy

4 republic → monarchy → empire   79 _____

80 The word *HELVETIA* appears on the stamp shown below.

Helvētia is the Roman name for

1 Spain   3 Belgium
2 Switzerland   4 Britain   80 _____

81 The abbreviation *SPQR* appears in the mosaic shown below.

What does this abbreviation stand for?

1 *Senātōrēs Plēbēs Quī Regunt*
2 *Senātus Populusque Rōmānus*
3 *Sextus Pūbliusque Rēgēs*
4 *Salūtant Populīque Redeunt*   81 _____

82 The Roman known for his courage in defending
a bridge against the Etruscans was

1 Regulus   3 Horatius
2 Marius   4 Fabricius   82 _____

Daily Life

83 A variety of masks are shown in the illustration
below.

These masks were intended to be worn by

1 students   3 gladiators
2 soldiers   4 actors   83 _____

84 The *stola* and *palla* were worn by

1 boys   3 women
2 public officials   4 priests   84 _____

85 The English equivalent of *pr. Īdūs Māiās is*

1 May 10   3 May 14
2 May 11   4 May 15   85 _____

86 In ancient Rome, the *secunda mēnsa* referred to a

1 military duty   3 right to vote
2 marriage arrangement   4 dessert   86 _____

87 *Dēnāriī, assēs*, and *sestertiī* were types of

1 coins   3 aqueducts
2 soldiers   4 slaves   87 _____

88 One of the ingredients used to make a modern-day pizza was unknown in the time of the ancient Romans. This ingredient was

1 cheese   3 flour
2 tomatoes   4 oil   88 _____

89 A copyright date of a book is shown in the illustration below.

Copyright © MCMLXXIII, by Harper & Row, Publishers, Inc. All rights reserved.

In what year was the book published?

(1) 1958   (3) 1973
(2) 1965   (4) 1983   89 _____

Myths and Legends

90 The couple in the illustration below received
Jupiter and Mercury with hospitality and were
immortalized by the gods as trees.

From Lester M. Prindle's "Mythology in Prints"

What were the names of this mythological couple?

1 Deucalion and Pyrrha
2 Jason and Medea
3 Pyramus and Thisbe
4 Baucis and Philemon   90 _____

91 The winged horse that was tamed by Bellerophon is shown in the illustration below.

What was the name of this winged horse?

1 Pegasus   3 Centaurus
2 Chimaera   4 Bucephalus   91 _____

92 Arachne boasted that her talent in weaving was superior to that of the goddess

1 Diana   3 Ceres
2 Juno   4 Minerva   92 _____

93 Who devised a method for cleaning the Augean stables?

1 Hercules   3 Polyphemus
2 Charon   4 Sisyphus   93 _____

94 Iris, from whom the English word "iridescent" is derived, is the name of the goddess of the

1 dawn   3 chase
2 rainbow   4 seasons   94 _____

95 Which mythological god and symbol are *not* correctly matched?

1 Juno — peacock   3 Jupiter — eagle
2 Venus — bluebird   4 Minerva — owl   95 _____

Literature

96 The illustration below depicts a statue of the author of the famous Latin work *Dē Bellō Gallicō*.

Who was this author?

1 Caesar   3 Cicero
2 Vergil   4 Suetonius   96 _____

97 Which Roman historian wrote the *Annālēs*?

    1 Catullus   3 Plautus

    2 Horatius   4 Tacitus   97 _____

98 Which Roman author is famous for writing letters?

    1 Pliny the Younger   3 Martial

    2 Augustus   4 Livy   98 _____

Architecture and Art

99 The illustration below shows a building where the Roman Senate met.

What is this building called?

    1 *Tulliānum*   3 *Basilica Aemilia*

    2 *Cūria*   4 *Rōstra*   99 _____

100 To commemorate their military victories, Titus and Septimius Severus were honored by the construction of

    1 libraries   3 bridges

    2 arches   4 aqueducts   100 _____

101 Where did most rich and influential people in
ancient Rome build their residences?

    1 Capitoline Hill   3 Palatine Hill

    2 Quirinal Hill   4 Aventine Hill   101 _____

102 The principal street in Rome, along which triumphal processions marched to the Forum, was
the

    1 *Via Aurēlia*   3 *Via Latīna*

    2 *Via Flāminia*   4 *Via Sacra*   102 _____

Answers   June 1996

Comprehensive Examination in Latin

PART I
(Allow a total of 5 credits for this part.)

PART II
(Allow a total of 5 credits, one-half credit for each of the following 10 italicized words.)

Redditae *mihi* tandem / sunt ā *Caesare* litterae / satis liberālēs et *ipse* / opīniōne *celerius* / ventūrus esse dīcitur. / Cui *utrum* / obviam prōcēdam / an *hīc* eum exspectem / cum cōnstituerō / *faciam* tē *certiōrem*. / Tabellāriōs mihi / quam *prīmum* remittās. / Valētūdinem cūrā *dīligenter*.

PART III

PART IIIA
(Allow a total of 10 credits, one credit for each of the following.)

(1) 1	**(3)** 2	**(5)** 3	**(7)** 4	**(9)** 1
(2) 4	**(4)** 2	**(6)** 1	**(8)** 2	**(10)** 4

PART IIIB
The answers to the questions in this part do not have to be complete sentences. A phrase or word may be sufficient for a completely correct one-credit response. Disregard errors in English. Allow no partial credit. Not all of the acceptable answers have been included.

(Allow a total of 10 credits, one credit for each of the following.)

(11) during the consulship of Cicero and Antonius; September 23; before dawn; nine days before the Kalends of October

(12) Thurinus; Caesar

(13) Augustus seemed to have founded Rome again.

(14) Augustus was a (more) sacred (deserving, worthy) name.

(15) His father died.

(16) He delivered the funeral oration for his grandmother.

(17) in Spain

(18) Caesar praised Augustus' character (morals, customs, habits, industry, hard work, diligence).

(19) He conquered the armies of Brutus and Cassius.

(20) He sent the head of Brutus to Rome to be under (at the foot of) Caesar's statue.

PART IIIC
(Allow a total of 10 credits, one credit for each of the following.)

(21) 4	(23) 1	(25) 2	(27) 3	(29) 1
(22) 3	(24) 1	(26) 4	(28) 2	(30) 4

PART IIID
(Allow a total of 10 credits, one credit for each of 10 of the following.)

(31) 1	(33) 1	(35) 2	(37) 4	(39) 2	(41) 4
(32) 3	(34) 2	(36) 1	(38) 2	(40) 3	(42) 3

PART IV

PART IVA
(Allow a total of 10 credits, one credit for each of the following.)

(43) 2	(45) 3	(47) 3	(49) 2	(51) 1
(44) 1	(46) 4	(48) 4	(50) 3	(52) 2

PART IVB
(Allow a total of 10 credits, one credit for each of the following.)

(53) 2	(55) 4	(57) 1	(59) 3	(61) 3
(54) 1	(56) 4	(58) 1	(60) 2	(62) 4

PART IVC
(Allow credit for any correctly spelled form of the Latin word. Allow no credit for prefixes or suffixes. Not all of the acceptable answers have been included.)

(Allow a total of 5 credits, one-half credit for each correct answer in each column.)

Column 1	Column 2
(63) somnus, ambulō	(63) 3
(64) cupidus, cupiō, cupiditās	(64) 1
(65) rūs, rūsticus	(65) 3
(66) taceō, tacitus	(66) 4
(67) salūs, salvus, salūtāris	(67) 2

PART IVD
(Allow a total of 5 credits, one credit for each of the following.)

(68) 1	(69) 3	(70) 2	(71) 4	(72) 2

PART V
(Allow a total of 10 credits, one credit for each of 20 of the following.)

(73) 1	(78) 1	(83) 4	(88) 2	(93) 1	(98) 1
(74) 3	(79) 1	(84) 3	(89) 3	(94) 2	(99) 2
(75) 2	(80) 2	(85) 3	(90) 4	(95) 2	(100) 2
(76) 1	(81) 2	(86) 4	(91) 1	(96) 1	(101) 3
(77) 4	(82) 3	(87) 1	(92) 4	(97) 4	(102) 4

Examination   June 1997

Comprehensive Latin

PART I

Part I is administered at the school's convenience at some time before the written test is given. You are asked to read aloud a passage of Latin for the teacher to judge on the basis of your proficiency in the spoken language. [5 credits]

PART II

DIRECTIONS: *Your teacher will read aloud a short passage in Latin. Listen carefully to this first reading. Then your teacher will read the passage in short phrases with a pause after each phrase. After each pause, write, in Latin, the phrase read by your teacher. Do* not *write a translation of the passage.*

There will be no penalty for improper use of macrons or capitalization. After you have completed writing the passage in Latin, your teacher will read the entire passage one more time so that you may check your work. [5 credits]

The passage that the teacher reads will be found in **Answers, Part II**, *at the end of this examination.*

PART III

Answer the questions in Part III according to the directions for Parts IIIA, IIIB, IIIC, and IIID.   [40 credits]

PART IIIA

DIRECTIONS (**1–10**): *Do* not *write a translation of the following passage; read it through carefully several times to determine its meaning. Then, in the space provided, write the* number *of the choice that best translates each* underlined expression *as it is used in the passage.* [10]

The Dog: A Faithful Friend

Ex multīs animālibus quae nōbīs nōta sunt, <u>fidēlissimum hominī ante</u>
<u>omnia alia est canis.</u> Ōlim quīdam canis, <u>ipse graviter vulnerātus</u>, dominum
(1)
percussum dēfendit contrā hominēs scelestōs. <u>Nē post mortem dominī</u>
(2)
<u>quidem corpus relīquit</u>, sed avēs et aliās ferās reppulit. In aliā fābulā nōtā,
(3)
<u>canis agnōvit in multitūdine virum</u> quī suum dominum ante necāverat. Dentēs
(4)
ostendit et tantā ferōcitāte lātrāvit <u>ut scelestus territus malum factum</u>
<u>cōnfitērētur.</u> In aliō exemplō, cum vir, Lycius nōmine, interfectus esset, canis
(5)
fidēlis eius nōluit cibum capere, et <u>tandem canis trīstis ipse fame cōnsumptus</u>
(6)
<u>est.</u> Alius canis, appellātus Hyrcānus, <u>sē iniēcit in flammās fūnereās Lyciī</u>
(7)
mortuī.

Sed nōtissimum exemplum fidēlitātis canīnae erat ille maximus et pius
canis cuiusdam cīvis. <u>Dum cīvis in carcere est</u>, ille canis cotīdiē hunc vīsitābat.
(8)
Deinde, cum cīvis interfectus est et corpus in viam ēiectum est, <u>canis cibum</u>
<u>ad dominum mortuum attulit.</u> Dēnique, <u>corpore cīvis in Tiberim iniectō</u>, īdem
(9)   (10)
canis natāvit in aquā et cadāver sustinēre cōnātus est, ne submergērētur.

Magna multitūdō hominum in rīpā stābat et multitūdō hoc spectāculum
fidēlitātis admīrāta est.   — C. Plinius Secundus, *Naturālis Historiae*, VIII.40.142–145
(adapted)

---

1 **fidēlissimum hominī ante omnia alia est canis**

  1 before every faithful human being there is a
    dog
  2 the dog is very faithful to the other human
    being in every way
  3 the most faithful to a human being before all
    others is the dog
  4 before everyone, the dog is most faithful to the
    other human being

1 _____

2 ipse graviter vulnerātus

    1 wounding the same man grievously
    2 he wounded himself gravely
    3 although he severely wounded him
    4 he himself having been seriously wounded   2 _____

3 Nē post mortem dominī quidem corpus relīquit

    1 Since he did not abandon a certain body after
       the master's death
    2 So that the master would not abandon his body
       after death
    3 Not even after his master's death did he aban-
       don the body
    4 And he did not abandon his master's body as he
       was dying   3 _____

4 canis agnōvit in multitūdine virum

    1 the dog recognized the man in a crowd
    2 that a dog will recognize a man in a multitude
    3 a dog feared many men in the large gathering
    4 that the dog may fear a man in a group   4 _____

5 ut scelestus territus malum factum cōnfitērētur

    1 as the most evil man on Earth admitted this
       murder
    2 so that the bad man confessed to the crime of
       murder of a foreigner
    3 in order that a wicked man might scare a con-
       fessed criminal
    4 that the evil man, terrified, confessed his crime   5 _____

6 tandem canis trīstis ipse fame cōnsumptus est

  1 while the dog himself had consumed the sad family
  2 finally, the sad dog himself was consumed by hunger
  3 the sad dog with the same reputation had consumed so much
  4 then the dog was consumed because of the same sad rumor   6 _____

7 sē iniēcit in flammās fūnereās Lyciī mortuī

  1 was hurled by the hot flames of the dead Lycius' funeral
  2 threw himself into the funeral flames of the dead Lycius
  3 the funeral flames cast him toward the dead Lycius
  4 laid himself down in the funeral flames in place of the dead Lycius   7 _____

8 Dum cīvis in carcere est

  1 While the citizen was in jail
  2 Because the citizen had been in a carriage
  3 When a citizen turned him into meat
  4 Whether he was missing the citizen   8 _____

9 canis cibum ad dominum mortuum attulit

  1 the dead master's food attracted the dog
  2 the food brought death to the dog and his master
  3 the dog brought food to his dead master
  4 the master's dead dog was quickly carried away   9 _____

10 corpore cīvis in Tiberim iniectō

    1 the body was thrown near the Tiber by a citizen

    2 the citizen hurled his body into the Tiber

    3 to make the citizen drag the body out of the Tiber

    4 after the citizen's body had been thrown into the Tiber 10 _____

PART IIIB

DIRECTIONS (11–20): *Do* not *write a translation of the following passages; read them through carefully several times to ascertain their meaning. Base your answers on the content of each passage only. Your answers do* not *have to be complete sentences; a word or phrase may suffice. In the spaces provided, write in English your answer to* each *question.* [10]

Death of a Consul

Trēs hōrās ferōciter undique pugnātum est. Prope cōnsulem tamen pugna violentior ācriorque erat. In pugnā fortissimī mīlitēs eum sequēbantur, et cōnsul ipse suīs mīlitibus in perīculō auxilium celeriter ferēbat. Hostēs eum facile cognōvērunt. Dum cōnsulem summā vī oppugnant, mīlitēs Rōmānī cōnsulem dēfendēbant. Tandem dux hostium, Dūcārius nōmine, cōnsulem et faciē et vestīmentīs et armīs cognōvit. Maximā cum īrā, "Hic," inquit, "est vir quī meās legiōnēs necāvit et urbem agrōsque vāstāvit. Nunc ego eum interficiam." Dūcārius in mediōs Rōmānōs impetum fēcit et cōnsulem necāvit.

Cōnsule necātō, multī Rōmānī fugere temptāvērunt sed et montēs et flūmina Rōmānōs mīlitēs ā fugā prōhibuērunt. Itaque magna pars cōpiārum interfecta est. Paucī mīlitēs, quī etiam tum vīvēbant, ab hostibus captī sunt.

— Līvius, *Ab Urbe Conditā*, XXII, vi
(adapted)

11 How long did the battle last?

_____

12 Where was the fighting rather fierce?

_____

_____

13 What did the consul do during the battle?

_____

_____

_____

_____

14 While the enemy was attacking the consul, what
    did the Roman soldiers do?

_____

_____

_____

_____

15 State *one* way in which Ducarius was able to rec-
    ognize the consul.

_____

_____

_____

_____

16 What is *one* action, which the consul had taken
    previously, that enraged Ducarius?

_____

_____

_____

_____

17 Who killed the consul?

_____

_____

_____

_____

18 What did many Romans try to do after the consul
   had been killed?

   _____

   _____

   _____

   _____

19 In addition to the enemy, name *one* obstacle
   which hindered the Roman soldiers.

   _____

   _____

   _____

   _____

20 What happened to the few soldiers who remained
   alive?

   _____

   _____

   _____

   _____

PART IIIC

DIRECTIONS (**21–30**): *Read the following passage carefully, but do* not
*write a translation. Below the passage, there are several questions or incom-
plete statements. For* each, *select the alternative that best answers the question
or completes the statement* on the basis of the information given in the passage, *and write its* number *in the space provided.* [10]

A Loving Wife

Mausōlus fuit, ut ait Marcus Tullius Cicerō, rēx terrae Cariae. Mausōlus in
mātrimōnium Artemisiam dūxit. Artemisia Mausōlum suum virum amāvisse
dicitur super amōris omnēs fābulās. Is Mausōlus inter lacrimās et manūs

uxōris ē vītā excessit. Artemisia maximō cum dolōre *cinerēs* cum *unguentīs* mixtōs in urnam posuit. Ad cōnservandam memoriam virī mortuī, Artemisia sepulchrum maximum aedificāvit. Hoc sepulchrum inter septem omnium terrārum spectācula numerābātur.

— Aulus Gellius, *Noctēs Atticae*, XVIII
(adapted)

cinerēs — from *cinis, cineris*, m. ash
unguentīs — from *unguentum, ī*, n. ointment, perfume

21 Marcus Tullius Cicerō dīxit Mausōlum esse

 1 ducem patriae Cariae 3 sine pecūniā
 2 laetum mercātōrem 4 bonum scriptōrem 21 _____

22 Quis erat Artemisia?

 1 amīca rēgīnae 3 optima māter
 2 uxor Mausōlī 4 bona dea 22 _____

23 Quālis erat amor Artemisiae?

 1 semper falsus
 2 similis Cicerōnis amōrī
 3 perīculōsus et superbus
 4 maximus amor in fābulīs 23 _____

24 Cum Mausōlus ē vītā excessisset, Artemisia

 1 domō cucurrit
 2 cinerēs in urnam dēposuit
 3 suōs līberōs convocāvit
 4 quoque mortua est 24 _____

25 Artemisia magnum sepulchrum aedificāvit ut

 1 amīcōs habēret
 2 librōs virī servāret
 3 memoria virī cōnservārētur
 4 iter faceret 25 _____

Caesar on the March

Caesar in bellō et in equō omnibus praestābat. Nōn sōlum equō sed etiam pedibus iter faciēbat. Sī vel sōl lūcēbat vel tempestās nōn bona erat, Caesar capite nūdō prōgrediēbātur. Longissima itinera incrēdibilī celeritāte cōnfēcit et multa mīlia passuum in singulōs diēs ambulāvit. Saepe Caesar pervēnit ante nūntiōs quōs praemīserat.

— Suetonius, *Dīvus Iūlius*, I.57
(adapted)

26 Caesar omnēs superābat

   1 in rēbus sacrīs   3 in rēbus mīlitāribus
   2 in arēnā   4 in urbe   26 _____

27 Saepe Caesar cōnstituit

   1 ambulāre   3 ā servīs portārī
   2 sōlus pugnāre   4 laudārī   27 _____

28 Caesar prōcēdēns in caput imposuit

   1 tunicam   3 galeam
   2 corōnam   4 nihil   28 _____

29 Quōmodo Caesar maxima itinera perfēcit?

   1 tardissimē   3 quam celerrimē
   2 currū   4 nāve longā   29 _____

30 Cum Caesar nūntiōs praemīsisset, nūntiī tamen

   1 īre nōluērunt
   2 post Caesarem pervēnērunt
   3 prope flūmen morāti sunt
   4 in agmine mānsērunt   30 _____

PART IIID

DIRECTIONS (**31–42**): *Read the passage below carefully, but do* not *write a translation. Below the passage, there are several questions or incomplete statements. Choose 10 of these questions or statements, and, in the space provided, write the* number *of the word or expression that best answers the question or completes the statement.* [10]

The Early History of the Flute

Minerva dīcitur *tībiam* prīmam ex osse cervī fēcisse et tum ad Montem Olympum īvisse ut mūsicam faceret. Iūnō et Venus eam rīdēbant quod Minerva et *caesia* erat et *buccās* īnflābat. Itaque dea Minerva in silvam ad fontem fūgit. Ibi dea, mūsicam faciēns, in aquā sē cōnspexit et vīdit sē
5   meritō rīsam esse. Deinde tībiam dēiēcit. "Sī quis," Minerva inquit, "tībiam invēnerit, gravī cum poenā vexābitur."

Marsyās, ūnus ē satyrīs, tībiam invēnit et dīligenter sonum dulcem facere incēpit. Marsyās prōvocāvit Apollinem ad certāmen. Apollō citharā, Marsyās tībiā lūdēbat. In hōc certāmine iūdicēs erant Mūsae quae Apollinem victōrem
10   nōmināvērunt. Apollō autem subitō īrātus fiēbat et Marsyam superbum graviter pūnīvit.

—Hyginus, *Fābulae*, CLXV
(adapted)

tībiam — from *tībia, ae*, f. flute
caesia — from *caesius, a, um*, bluish gray
buccās — from *bucca, ae*, f. cheek

31   According to this story, Minerva made the first flute from the

1   words of the gods   3   petals of a flower
2   bone of a deer   4   song of a bird   31 _____

32   The English word *ossify* is associated by derivation with the Latin word *osse* (line 1) and the suffix -*fy*, which is a form of the Latin verb

1   *faciō*   3   *fugiō*
2   *ferō*   4   *frangō*   32 _____

33 The Latin word *eam* (line 2) refers to

1 Juno   3 Olympus
2 Minerva   4 Venus   33 _____

34 Juno and Venus laughed when they

1 fled to the forest to escape the horrible music
2 asked Minerva to throw away the flute
3 reached Mount Olympus safely
4 saw Minerva's change in appearance while she
   played the flute   34 _____

35 What was Minerva's reaction when she saw her
reflection in the fountain's water?

1 She saw that she was deservedly laughed at.
2 She praised her own image.
3 She admired the musical instrument she was
   playing.
4 She realized that she was beautiful.   35 _____

36 What did Minerva do after she threw down the
flute?

1 She ran to Mount Olympus for help.
2 She decided to invent another instrument.
3 She inflicted a curse upon anyone who found
   the flute.
4 She returned to Juno and Venus.   36 _____

37 The opposite of the Latin word *gravī* (line 6) is

1 *dūrō*   3 *celerī*
2 *levī*   4 *nōbilī*   37 _____

38 In which tense and mood is the Latin verb
    vexābitur (line 6)?

    1 future indicative
    2 perfect subjunctive
    3 imperfect indicative
    4 pluperfect subjunctive   38 _____

39 A satyr, referred to in line 7, is a creature who is
    half man and half

    1 bird   3 lion
    2 bull   4 goat   39 _____

40 The superlative form of the Latin word *dīligenter*
    (line 7) is

    1 *dīligēns*   3 *dīligentissimē*
    2 *dīligentior*   4 *dīligentēs*   40 _____

41 Which English word is *not* associated by deriva-
    tion with the Latin word *sonum* (line 7)?

    1 mason   3 sonic
    2 resonant   4 sonorous   41 _____

42 According to legend, what was the role of the
    Muses?

    1 to prepare food for the gods
    2 to calm the winds
    3 to preside over the arts and the sciences
    4 to be present at the death of a hero   42 _____

PART IV

   Answer the questions in Part IV according to the directions for Parts IVA,
IVB, IVC, and IVD. [30 credits]

PART IVA

DIRECTIONS (**43–52**): *In the space provided, write the* number *of the word or expression that, when inserted in the blank, makes* each *sentence grammatically correct.* [10]

43 Spectā, _____, equōs magnōs in Circō Maximō!

1 Marce	3 Marcō
2 Marcus	4 Marcum

43 _____

44 Dux scīvit mīlitēs impetum _____.

1 faciet	3 factō
2 facere	4 fēcī

44 _____

45 Bonī servī _____ laudātī sunt.

1 dominus	3 dominōs
2 dominum	4 ā dominō

45 _____

46 Puella laeta ante _____ stābat.

1 portam	3 portā
2 portae	4 porta

46 _____

47 Multī hominēs magnam fāmam _____ cupiunt.

1 habent	3 habēre
2 habērent	4 habuerint

47 _____

48 Catilīna _____ multōs annōs mānsit.

1 Rōmā	3 Rōmae
2 Rōma	4 Rōmam

48 _____

49 Fugitīvus celeriter currēbat nē _____

   1 cēpisse   3 capī

   2 capiēbat   4 caperētur   49 _____

50 Illa est fēmina _____ vīdī.

   1 quōs   3 quibus

   2 quam   4 quārum   50 _____

51 Erant tantae stellae in caelō, ut nōs eās
pernumerāre nōn

   1 possēmus   3 possunt

   2 posse   4 poterātis   51 _____

52 Captīvus sine _____ vīvit.

   1 spē   3 spēs

   2 speī   4 spērum   52 _____

PART IVB

DIRECTIONS (**53–62**): *This part contains a passage in English in which words associated by derivation with Latin words are italicized. Below the passage, there are several questions or incomplete statements. For each, select the alternative that best answers the question or completes the statement, and write its number in the space provided.* [10]

Pompeii, Perilously Popular

     Last year nearly 1.6 million people—up
from 1.3 million people the year before—
trooped through the haunting ruins of the
Roman city that a hail of pumice and a *tempest*   • tempest
5 of fiery volcanic ashes smothered during an
unexpected eruption of nearby Mount   • unexpected
Vesuvius in A.D. 79. At least 2,000 of
Pompeii's population, variously *estimated* at   • estimated
between 12,000 and 20,000, died.

10   What is visible includes the Forum—the   • visible, includes
center of the city's public and commercial life.
— *New York Times*

53 The English word *tempest* (line 4) is associated
by derivation with *tempestās,* the Latin word that
means

1 storm   3 temple
2 witness   4 fear   53 _____

54 Which Latin word, paired with its English meaning, is associated by derivation with the English
word *unexpected* (line 6)?

1 *spērō* — hope   3 *sociō* — associate
2 *salūtō* — greet   4 *spectō* — watch   54 _____

55 The English word *estimated* (line 8) is associated
by derivation with the Latin word

1 *aestuō*   3 *ēsuriō*
2 *aestimō*   4 *ēducō*   55 _____

56 The English word *visible* (line 10) is associated
by derivation with the Latin word

1 *vincō*   3 *videō*
2 *vīvō*   4 *violō*   56 _____

57 Which Latin word, paired with its English meaning, is associated by derivation with the English
word *includes* (line 10)?

1 *claudō* — close   3 *colō* — dwell
2 *laudō* — praise   4 *locō* — place   57 _____

California Sea Otters

Biologists admire and often delight in the resourcefulness of sea otters. But they worry over otters' inability to cope with the world they are reclaiming. Tankers endlessly pass
5 back and forth along the coast; and many conservationists predict that a spill is inevitable. The *Exxon Valdez* spill killed as many as 5,000 Alaska otters, more than double California's entire otter population. California
10 is now building a five-million-dollar otter rehabilitation center at Santa Cruz. After a spill, oiled otters will be brought there for cleaning. But California Fish and Game biologist Jack Ames argues that it is far more effec-
15 tive to prevent spills than to try to rehabilitate oiled otters afterward. "*Exxon Valdez* proved that," he says, noting that despite valiant efforts, only a few of the Alaska otters were saved.
20 If California sea otters were reproducing more successfully, their advocates would be less concerned about oil spills.

* admire

* conservationists, predict
* inevitable

* prevent

—*National Geographic*

58 The English word *admire* (line 1) is associated by derivation with *mīror,* the Latin word that means

1 delay   3 warn
2 wonder   4 pity   58 _____

59 The English word *conservationists* (line 6) is associated by derivation with *servō,* the Latin word that means

1 wander   3 seek
2 summon   4 guard   59 _____

60 The English word *predict* (line 6) is associated by derivation with the fourth principal part of the Latin word

1 *dīcō*   3 *dō*

2 *dēligō*   4 *dēleō*   60 _____

61 Which Latin word, paired with its English meaning, is associated by derivation with the English word *inevitable* (line 7)?

1 *ēvertō* — overturn   3 *vīta* — life

2 *ēvādō* — go forth   4 *vītō* — avoid   61 _____

62 The English word *prevent* (line 15) is associated by derivation with *veniō*, the Latin word that means

1 blow   3 come

2 speak   4 sell   62 _____

PART IVC

DIRECTIONS (**63–67**): *For each sentence below, write, in the longer space provided, a Latin word with which the italicized word is associated by derivation. Any form of the appropriate Latin word, except prefixes and suffixes, will be acceptable. Then, write, in the shorter space provided, the number preceding the word or expression that best expresses the meaning of the italicized word.* [5]

63 My friend had a *doleful* expression on his face.

1 sad   3 confused

2 pleasant   4 trusting

63 _____   _____

64 An *animated* discussion took place at the political debate.

    1 disturbing   3 preliminary
    2 lengthy   4 lively

64 _____   _____

65 The witness attempted to *clarify* her statement.

    1 shorten   3 change
    2 explain   4 defend

65 _____   _____

66 The young woman displayed her *ire*.

    1 sense of humor   3 anger
    2 ability   4 fear

66 _____   _____

67 The Department of Motor Vehicles will *revoke* his license.

    1 recall   3 review
    2 renew   4 revise

67 _____   _____

PART IVD

Directions (**68–72**): *In the space provided, write the* number *of the Latin expression that best answers the question or completes the statement.* [5]

68 *extract*

   1 give up   3 stabilize
   2 meet   4 drag   68 _____

69 *opponent*

   1 punish   3 press
   2 put   4 permit   69 _____

70 *resident*

   1 swim   3 sit
   2 shine   4 sleep   70 _____

71 *document*

   1 teach   3 grant
   2 think   4 send   71 _____

72 *reverse*

   1 annoy   3 turn
   2 feed   4 frighten   72 _____

PART V

DIRECTIONS (**73–102**): *Select* 20 *of the following statements or questions. In the space provided, write the* number *of the word or expression that best answers the question or completes the statement.*   [20 credits]

History and Public Life

73 The map below shows a Roman city.

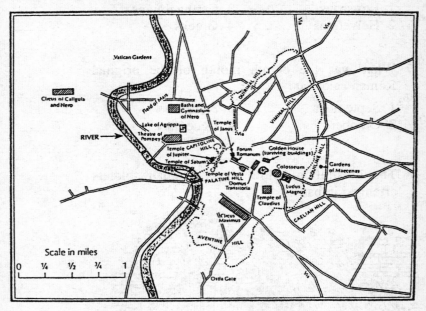

What is the name of the river in this city?

1 Rubicon   3 Po

2 Rhine   4 Tiber   73 _____

74 The rule of Romulus and the story of the Sabine women are both associated with the earliest period of Roman history. This period is called the

1 Hellenistic Age   3 Republic

2 Monarchy   4 Empire   74 _____

75 Hannibal's rampage through the Italian country-side was conducted during the

1 Samnite Wars   3 Punic Wars
2 Social War   4 Trojan War   75 _____

76 Mucius Scaevola sacrificed his hand to demonstrate Roman courage to the

1 Etruscans   3 Carthaginians
2 Helvetians   4 Greeks   76 _____

77 What was the eighth month of the original Roman calendar?

1 September   3 November
2 October   4 December   77 _____

78 The illustration below shows Roman soldiers arranged in battle.

What is this formation called?

1 *pīlum*   3 *novissimum agmen*
2 *lōrica*   4 *testūdō*   78 _____

79 The first emperor of Rome to receive the title
Augustus was

1 Antony   3 Pompey
2 Octavian   4 Crassus   79 _____

80 Spartacus is famous in Roman history because he

1 led a slave revolt in Italy
2 rid the Mediterranean Sea of pirates
3 raised an army to fight the Egyptians
4 defeated the Parthians   80 _____

81 A candidate for public office was easily recog-
nized on a Roman street because he wore

1 a specially whitened toga
2 a medallion on a chain
3 a purple tunic
4 golden sandals   81 _____

82 What was the name of the "public welfare program" intended to satisfy the Roman mob?

1 *secunda mēnsa*   3 *pānem et circēnsēs*
2 *Larēs et Penātēs*   4 *magnum opus*   82 _____

Daily Life

83 The illustration below shows a Roman family relaxing in a home.

What is this area called?

1 *culīna*   3 *trīclīnium*
2 *peristȳlium*   4 *cubiculum*   83 _____

84 What does the M. in the name M. Agrippa stand for?

1 Marius   3 Marcus
2 Marcellus   4 Metella   84 _____

85 Which family member had absolute authority over the household?

1 *avunculus*   3 *paterfamiliās*
2 *avia*   4 *nepōs*   85 _____

86 The illustration below shows a device used by ancient Romans to do mathematical calculations.

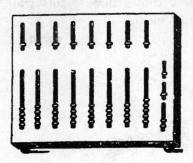

What is this device called?

1 *amphora*   3 *candēlābrum*

2 *bulla*   4 *abacus*   86 _____

87 On which day would the Roman date *a.d. IV Īd. Iūn.* fall?

1 June 9   3 June 13

2 June 10   4 June 15   87 _____

88 Triumphal processions through the *Forum Rōmānum* took place on the

1 *Via Sacra*   3 *Via Latīna*

2 *Via Appia*   4 *Via Flāminia*   88 _____

Myths and Legends

89 The illustration below shows three giants who were the workmen of Vulcan.

What are these one-eyed creatures called?

1 Gorgons	3 cyclops
2 centaurs	4 Harpies

89 _____

90 The town of Delphi in Greece was best known for its

1 volcano	3 music
2 baths	4 oracle

90 _____

91 Although she is always referred to as "Helen of Troy," Helen was actually Queen of

1 Carthage	3 Sparta
2 Alexandria	4 Rome

91 _____

92 Orpheus, the son of Apollo, was a renowned
    musician who traveled to the underworld to try to
    reclaim his wife. Her name was

    1 Eurydice   3 Pandora
    2 Penelope   4 Maia   92 _____

93 The deity illustrated below was the goddess of
    grain, who is associated with the change of the
    seasons.

    The Romans called this goddess

    1 Ceres   3 Venus
    2 Diana   4 Minerva   93 _____

94 According to Roman mythology, the Roman god
    of the sea also created the horse. His name was

    1 Vulcan   3 Mercury
    2 Neptune   4 Jupiter   94 _____

95 The beauty contest that caused the Trojan War
    was called the Judgment of

    1 Paris   3 Pan
    2 Midas   4 Minos   95 _____

Literature

96 Cicero's closest friend and the recipient of many
of his letters was

    1 Manlius   3 Regulus
    2 Clodius   4 Atticus   96 _____

97 The *Iliad* is to Homer as the *Aeneid* is to

    1 Plato   3 Vergil
    2 Cato   4 Lucretius   97 _____

98 The authors Plautus and Terence are known for
their

    1 philosophical essays   3 epigrams
    2 epics   4 comedies   98 _____

99 The Temple of Jupiter Stator was the place where
Cicero delivered his first oration against

    1 Pompey   3 Caligula
    2 Jugurtha   4 Catiline   99 _____

Architecture and Art

100 The illustration below shows the round temple
that contained the sacred fire of Rome.

This building is called the Temple of

    1 Saturn   3 Concord
    2 Vesta   4 Juno   100 _____

101 The illustration below shows a neoclassical building in a modern city.

What kind of capitals do the columns of this building have?

1 Ionic   3 Doric
2 Corinthian   4 Gothic   101 _____

102 The Parthenon is on the Acropolis pictured below.

In which city is this acropolis located?

1 Rome   3 Thebes
2 Athens   4 Ostia   102 _____

Answers   June 1997

Comprehensive Examination in Latin

PART I
(Allow a total of 5 credits for this part.)

PART II
(Allow a total of 5 credits, one-half credit for each of the following 10 italicized words.)

Tū *quod* mē hortāris ut *animō* sim magnō et *spem* habeam *recuperandae* salūtis, id *velim* sit eius *modī*, ut rectē spērāre possīmus. *Nunc* miser quandō tuās *iam* litterās accipiam? Quis ad mē perferet? Quās ego exspectāssem Brundisī, sī esset licitum per nautās quī *tempestātem* praetermittere *nōluērunt*.

PART III
PART IIIA
(Allow a total of 10 credits, one credit for each of the following.)

(1) 3	**(3)** 3	**(5)** 4	**(7)** 2	**(9)** 3
(2) 4	**(4)** 1	**(6)** 2	**(8)** 1	**(10)** 4

PART IIIB
The answers to the questions in this part do not have to be complete sentences. A phrase or word may be sufficient for a completely correct one-credit response. Disregard errors in English. Allow no partial credit. Not all of the acceptable answers have been included.

(Allow a total of 10 credits, one credit for each of the following.)

(11) three hours
(12) near the consul
(13) brought help (to his soldiers in danger)
(14) defended the consul
(15) face, clothing, weapons
(16) killed the legions (of Ducarius), destroyed the city, destroyed the fields
(17) Ducarius, leader of the enemy
(18) to flee
(19) mountains, rivers
(20) They were captured (by the enemy).

PART IIIC
(Allow a total of 10 credits, one credit for each of the following.)

(21) 1	**(23)** 4	**(25)** 3	**(27)** 1	**(29)** 3
(22) 2	**(24)** 2	**(26)** 3	**(28)** 4	**(30)** 2

PART IIID
(Allow a total of 10 credits, one credit for each of 10 of the following.)

(31) 2	**(33)** 2	**(35)** 1	**(37)** 2	**(39)** 4	**(41)** 1
(32) 1	**(34)** 4	**(36)** 3	**(38)** 1	**(40)** 3	**(42)** 3

PART IV

PART IVA
(Allow a total of 10 credits, one credit for each of the following.)

(43) 1	**(45)** 4	**(47)** 3	**(49)** 4	**(51)** 1
(44) 2	**(46)** 1	**(48)** 3	**(50)** 2	**(52)** 1

PART IVB
(Allow a total of 10 credits, one credit for each of the following.)

(53) 1	**(55)** 2	**(57)** 1	**(59)** 4	**(61)** 4
(54) 4	**(56)** 3	**(58)** 2	**(60)** 1	**(62)** 3

PART IVC
(Allow credit for any correctly spelled form of the Latin word. Allow no credit for prefixes or suffixes. Not all of the acceptable answers have been included.)

(Allow a total of 5 credits, one-half credit for each correct answer in each column.)

Column 1	Column 2
(63) dolor, doleō	**(63)** 1
(64) animus, anima, animō, animal	**(64)** 4
(65) clārus, clārō, faciō	**(65)** 2
(66) īra, īrātus, īrācundia, īrascor	**(66)** 3
(67) vocō, vōx, revocō	**(67)** 1

PART IVD
(Allow a total of 5 credits, one credit for each of the following.)

(68) 4	**(69)** 2	**(70)** 3	**(71)** 1	**(72)** 3

PART V
(Allow a total of 20 credits, one credit for each of 20 of the following.)

(73) 4	**(78)** 4	**(83)** 2	**(88)** 1	**(93)** 1	**(98)** 4
(74) 2	**(79)** 2	**(84)** 3	**(89)** 3	**(94)** 2	**(99)** 4
(75) 3	**(80)** 1	**(85)** 3	**(90)** 4	**(95)** 1	**(100)** 2
(76) 1	**(81)** 1	**(86)** 4	**(91)** 3	**(96)** 4	**(101)** 1
(77) 2	**(82)** 3	**(87)** 2	**(92)** 1	**(97)** 3	**(102)** 2

Notes

Notes

Notes

Notes

Barron's Regents Exams and Answers

Latin

June 1998 Examination

Includes:

- A full-length New York State Regents Examination
- Complete Answers

This Regents Supplement is supplied free of charge to insure that you get the latest exam when you buy Barron's Regents Exams and Answers.

Barron's Educational Series, Inc.

Examination June 1998

Comprehensive Examination in Latin

PART I

Part I is administered at the school's convenience at some time before the written test is given. You are asked to read aloud a passage of Latin for the teacher to judge on the basis of your proficiency in the spoken language. [5 credits]

PART II

Directions: Your teacher will read aloud a short passage in Latin. Listen carefully to this first reading. Then your teacher will read the passage in short phrases with a pause after each phrase. After each pause, write, in Latin, the phrase read by your teacher. Do *not* write a translation of the passage.

There will be no penalty for improper use of macrons, punctuation, or capitalization. After you have completed writing the passage in Latin, your teacher will read the entire passage one more time so that you may check your work. [5]

PART III

Answer the questions in Part III according to the directions
for Parts IIIA, IIIB, IIIC, and IIID.

PART IIIA

Directions (1–10): Do *not* write a translation of the following passage; read it through carefully several times to ascertain its meaning.
Then, in the spaces provided, write the *number* of the alternative
that best translates *each* underlined expression *as it is used in the
passage.* [10]

Brothers Who Changed Allegiance

Erant apud Caesarem in numerō equitum Allobrogēs duō

frātrēs, Roucillus et Egus, fīliī Adbucillī, <u>quī prīncipātum in</u>

<u>cīvitāte multōs annōs tenuerat</u>. Roucillus et Egus erant
　(1)

hominēs magnā virtūte, <u>quōrum opere optimō fortissimōque</u>

<u>Caesar in omnibus Gallicīs bellīs ūsus erat</u>. <u>Hī frātrēs propter</u>
　(2)

<u>suam virtūtem nōn sōlum cum Caesare in honōre habēbantur,</u>
　(3)

sed etiam cum exercitū cārī habēbantur.

Sed mox Roucillus et Egus arrogantiam et stultitiam

dēmonstrābant. <u>Suōs mīlitēs dēspiciēbant et pecūniam ex</u>
　(4)

<u>equitibus cēpērunt</u>. Equitēs ad Caesarem appropinquāvērunt

et <u>dē suīs iniūriīs Caesarī dīcēbant</u>. Frātribus convocātīs,
　(5)

<u>Caesar illōs sēcrētō pūnīvit</u>. Haec rēs tamen magnam
　(6)

offēnsiōnem et contemptiōnem ad omnēs tulit. *Pudōre* adductī, frātrēs Roucillus et Egus discēdere ā Caesare et novam

fortūnam invenīre et <u>novās amīcitiās petere cōnstituērunt</u>.
(7)

<u>Quod frātrēs nōbilī familiā nātī erant</u> et in honōre apud
(8)

Caesarem ōlim fuerant, Pompeius eōs celeriter recēpit et

<u>Pompeius eōs circumdūxit et eīs dēmōnstrāvit omnia sua</u>
(9)

<u>praesidia</u>. Nam ante id tempus neque mīles neque eques ā

Caesare ad Pompeium trānsīverat, <u>cum paene cotīdiē mīlitēs</u>

<u>ā Pompeiō ad Caesarem perfugerent</u>.
(10)

— Caesar, Dē Bellō Cīvilī, III, 59–61
(adapted)

pudōre — from *pudor*, sense of shame

1 quī prīncipātum in cīvitāte multōs annōs tenuerat

    1 whose leader controlled the government for many years

    2 who had held the leadership in the state for many years

    3 by whom many states had been controlled over the years

    4 who had planned to lead many people of the state for years   1 _____

2 quōrum opere optimō fortissimōque Caesar in omnibus Gallicīs bellīs ūsus erat

    1 whose excellent and very brave work Caesar had used in all the Gallic wars

    2 all of whom called upon Caesar to fight bravely in the wars with the Gauls

    3 who worked with courage to stop Caesar in all the wars with the Gauls

    4 who fought bravely against noble Caesar during all the Gallic wars   2 _____

3 Hī frātrēs propter suam virtūtem nōn sōlum cum Caesare in honōre habēbantur

  1 The brothers alone honored Caesar because of his courage
  2 Only those brave brothers were without Caesar's honor
  3 Caesar gave honors only to those courageous brothers
  4 These brothers because of their courage not only were held in honor with Caesar   3 _____

4 Suōs mīlitēs dēspiciēbant et pecūniam ex equitibus cēpērunt.

  1 They looked down upon their own soldiers and took money from the horsemen.
  2 The soldiers despaired and also lost their money.
  3 They began to desert their soldiers and to refuse to pay them fairly.
  4 The soldiers wrote about the robbery of the cavalry's money.   4 _____

5 dē suīs iniūriīs Caesarī dīcēbant

  1 they led Caesar to those injured
  2 they blamed themselves for Caesar's wrongs
  3 they spoke to Caesar about their injustices
  4 they removed Caesar from these dangers   5 _____

6 Caesar illōs sēcrētō pūnīvit

  1 Caesar found out those secrets
  2 Caesar punished them secretly
  3 They told Caesar some secrets
  4 They came to Caesar in secrecy   6 _____

7 novās amīcitiās petere cōnstituērunt

   1 were able to please their new friends
   2 went out to help new friends
   3 refused to encourage new friendships
   4 decided to seek new friendships   7 ____

8 Quod frātrēs nōbilī familiā nātī erant

   1 That these brothers sailed with an illustrious family
   2 Since the brothers had told of a celebrated family
   3 Because the brothers had been born of a well-known family
   4 That they found the brothers in a famous household   8 ____

9 Pompeius eōs circumdūxit et eīs dēmōnstrāvit omnia sua praesidia

   1 Pompey led them around and showed them all his defenses
   2 Pompey's forces surrounded them and took everything from them
   3 Pompey led everyone to the fortress and then dismissed all of his troops
   4 Pompey's troops were addressed and were shown the whole fortress   9 ____

10 cum paene cotīdiē mīlitēs ā Pompeiō ad Caesarem perfugerent

   1 because daily the soldiers came to Pompey from Caesar
   2 since Caesar's soldiers fought with Pompey's army daily
   3 although soldiers daily heard from Pompey and Caesar
   4 when almost daily the soldiers were fleeing from Pompey to Caesar   10 ____

PART IIIB

Directions (11–20): Do *not* write a translation of the following passage; read it through carefully several times to ascertain its meaning. Base your answers on the contents of passage *only*. Your answers do *not* have to be complete sentences; a word or phrase may suffice. In the spaces provided, write in English your answer to *each* question. [10]

How to Host a Successful Banquet

M. Varrō, scriptor, librum scrīpsit in quō loquitur dē optimō *convīvārum* numerō et dē cēnae partibus.

Varrō scrībit numerum convīvārum esse ā tribus ad novem. Cum convīvae sunt paucissimī, nōn dēbent esse pauciōrēs quam trēs. Cum convīvae sunt plūrimī, nōn dēbent esse plūrēs quam novem. Novem est numerus Mūsārum. "Nam convīvās multōs habēre mihi nōn placet," inquit, "quod magnus est clāmor."

Necesse est optimum *convīvium* habēre quattuor rēs: amīcōs hominēs, locum bonum, tempus idōneum et cibum sūmptuōsum.

Colloquium igitur eō tempore dēbet esse leve et nōn grave. Convīvae dē rēbus in forō atque in negōtiīs dīcere nōn dēbent. Oportet dominum convīviī esse amīcum et hospitālem.

In convīviō bonī librī recitārī dēbent, quod mentem stimulant. Tandem secundae mēnsae cum dulcibus et frūctibus efferuntur.

— Aulus Gellius, *Noctēs, Atticae*, XI, 1–7
(adapted)

convīvārum — from *convīva*, dinner guest

convīvium — banquet, dinner

11 Who was Marcus Varro?

_____

_____

12 According to Marcus Varro, what is the smallest
    number of guests that should attend a banquet?

_____

13 What is the number of Muses?

_____

14 Why is it *not* a good idea to have a large number of
    guests at a banquet?

_____

_____

15–16 List *two* of the four things necessary for a very
        good banquet.

_____

_____

17 What type of conversation should take place at the
    time of the banquet?

_____

_____

18 What is *one* quality of the ideal master of the
    banquet?

_____

_____

19 Why should good books be recited at the banquet?

_____

_____

20 Name *one* thing that is brought out at the end of the banquet.

_____

_____

PART IIIC

Directions (21–30): Read the following passages carefully, but do *not* write a translation. Below each passage, these are several questions or incomplete statements. For *each*, select the alternative that best answers the question or completes the statement *on the basis on the information given in the passage*, and write its *number* in the space provided. [10]

The Tragedy of Laocoon

Lāocoōn erat Troiānus *sacerdōs* deī Apollinis. Lāocoōn contrā voluntātem Apollinis in mātrimōnium fēminam dūxit atque duōs filiōs habuit. Post multōs annōs Lāocoōn cum filiīs ad mare appropinquāvit ut deō sacrificium faceret. Apollō ab īnsulā proximā per flūctūs maris duōs serpentēs mīsit ut filiōs Lāocoontis necāret. Cum Lāocoōn suīs filiīs moritūrīs auxilium daret, Lāocoōn ipse tum ā serpentibus eīsdem necātus est. Cīvēs Troiānī, quī spectābant, putāvērunt Lāocoontem et filiōs interfectōs esse quod Lāocoōn anteā *hastam* in equum Troiānum iēcisset.

— Hyginus, *Fabulae*, CXXXV
(adapted)

sacerdōs — priest
hastam — from *hasta*, spear

21 Quid ēgit Lāocoōn contrā voluntātem Apollinis?

    1 Pācem fēcit.
    2 Uxōrem et fīliōs habuit.
    3 Domō nāvigāvit.
    4 Mūrum aedificāvit.   21 ____

22 Lāocoōn ad mare īvit ut

    1 nāvēs spectāret   3 deum honōrāret
    2 piscēs caperet   4 amīcōs laudāret   22 ____

23 Quid duō serpentēs fēcērunt?

    1 Ad montem sē mōvērunt.
    2 Sub arbore dormīvērunt.
    3 Fīliōs Lāocoontis petīvērunt.
    4 Suās formās mūtāvērunt.   23 ____

24 Lāocoōn, ferēns auxilium ad filiōs, etiam

    1 fugere potuit
    2 celeriter nāvem ascendit
    3 ab uxōre vocātus est
    4 interfectus est   24 ____

25 Quid Lāocoōn anteā fēcerat?

    1 Hastam in equum iēcerat.
    2 Multa mīlia passuum cucurrerat.
    3 Lūnam spectāverat.
    4 Ignem exstīnxerat.   25 ____

Imperial Monuments

Imperātōrēs Rōmānī magnōrum Rōmānōrum laudandōrum causā multās rēs aedificāvērunt. *Arcus*, signum victōriae, prope templum Saturnī in Forō Rōmānō ab imperātōre Tiberiō aedificātus est. Hic arcus factus est quod signa mīlitāria, quae in pugnā āmissa erant, ā Rōmānīs recepta sunt. Igitur cīvēs Rōmānī erant laetī. Templum Fortūnae cōnstructum est in hortīs, quōs Iūlius Caesar, dictātor, populō Rōmānō dederat. Erat aliud parvum templum, quod prō gente Iuliā consecrātum est. Pulchra statua dīvō Augustō extrā urbem Rōmam in oppidō propinquō posita est.

— Tacitus, *Annālēs*, II, 41
(adapted)

Arcus — arch

26 Ubi monumentum victōriae ab Tiberiō aedificātum erat?

1 trāns flūmen   3 extrā urbem
2 in Forō Rōmānō   4 in hortīs pūblicīs   26 _____

27 Rōmānī arcum aedificāvērunt quod

1 āmissās rēs mīlitārēs reportāvērunt
2 hostēs advēnērunt
3 magnum timōrem habuērunt
4 ducēs discessērunt   27 _____

28 Quās rēs Iūlius Caesar cīvibus Rōmānīs dederat?

1 nāvēs   3 hortōs
2 gemmās   4 equōs   28 _____

29 Parvum templum factum est in nōmine

1 antīquōrum nautārum
2 familiae Iūliae
3 gladiātōris Rōmānī
4 omnium animālium   29 _____

30 Rōmānī magnum opus artis in honōre Augustī
   posuērunt

   1 in mediā urbe
   2 in magnā silvā in Britanniā
   3 in summō colle in Graeciā
   4 in oppidō prope Rōmam   30 _____

PART IIID

Directions (31–42): Read the passage below carefully, but do *not*
write a translation. Below the passage, there are several questions
or incomplete statements. Choose *10* of these questions or statements, and in the space provided, write the *number* of the word or
expression that best answers the question or completes the statement.   [10]

Hannibal — Enemy of the Romans

   Hannibal, Hamilcaris fīlius, Carthāginiēnsis erat. Nēmō dubitat
populum Rōmānum omnēs gentēs virtūte superāvisse.
Dīcendum est Hannibalem superāvisse cēterōs imperātōrēs
sapientiā et populum Rōmānum fortitūdine antecessisse
5 tōtās nātiōnēs. Nam cum Hannibal pugnāvit ācriter
in Ītaliā, semper victor discessit. Sī Hannibal *invidiā* cīvium
suōrum nōn vulnerātus esset Rōmānōs superāre potuisset.
   Hannibal, similis patrī, *ōdium* ad Rōmānōs tenuit. Quidem,
cum Hannibal ex suā patriā expulsus esset, semper cum Rōmānīs
10 in animō bellum gessit.
                    — Nepōs, *Liber dē exellentibus ducibus exterārum gentium*, XXIII, i–ii
                                                              (adapted)

invidiā — from *invidia*, envy

ōdium — hatred

31 Which English word is derived from the Latin word
    dubitat (line 1)?

    1 duct   3 ubiquitous
    2 bitter   4 dubious   31 _____

32 Which Latin word means the opposite of *omnēs*
    (line 2)?

    1 *nūllās*   3 *magnās*
    2 *bonās*   4 *lātās*   32 _____

33 The best translation of the Latin words *dīcendum
    est* (line 3) is

    1 about to speak   3 they will say
    2 it must be said   4 to have spoken   33 _____

34 Which Latin word is most similar in meaning to
    superāvisse (line 3)?

    1 *vīcisse*   3 *mānsisse*
    2 *cucurrisse*   4 *vocāvisse*   34 _____

35 In lines 3 through 5, which comparison does the
    author make?

    1 Hannibal's honesty to the Romans' deceit
    2 Hannibal's wisdom to the Romans' bravery
    3 Hannibal's treachery to the Romans' integrity
    4 Hannibal's foolishness to the Romans' cleverness   35 _____

36 What is the superlative form of the Latin word
    ācriter (line 5)?

    1 *ācris*   3 *ācerrimē*
    2 *ācrior*   4 *ācriōrēs*   36 _____

37 What is the best translation of *semper victor discessit* (line 6)?

  1 he always left as the conqueror
  2 he often discussed victory
  3 he often lived among them
  4 he always praised the winners   37 _____

38 In which case are the Latin words *cīvium suōrum* (lines 6 and 7)?

  1 nominative   3 genitive
  2 vocative   4 ablative   38 _____

39 In lines 6 and 7, what opinion does the author express?

  1 Rome will finally conquer Carthage.
  2 Hannibal could have conquered Rome.
  3 The war will soon be over.
  4 Many nations could use a leader with Hannibal's abilities.   39 _____

40 The word *patriā* (line 9) refers to

  1 Carthage   3 Sparta
  2 Athens   4 Ostia   40 _____

41 How does this passage conclude?

  1 Hannibal returns to the leadership of Carthage.
  2 Hannibal is wounded on the battlefield.
  3 Hannibal delivers a speech to his troops.
  4 Hannibal wages war with the Romans in his mind.   41 _____

42 During which wars did Hannibal fight with Rome?

  1 Peloponnesian   3 Gallic
  2 Trojan   4 Punic   42 _____

PART IV

**Answer the questions in Part IV according to the directions
for Parts IVA, IVB, IVC, and IVD.**

PART IVA

Directions (43–52): In the space provided, write the *number* of the
word or expression that, when inserted in the blank, makes *each*
sentence grammatically correct.   [10]

43   Meus frāter est fortior quam _____.

   1 tuō frātrī   3 tuum frātrem
   2 tuī frātris   4 tuus frāter   43 _____

44   Putō Annam mox _____.

   1 veniēbātis   3 ventūram esse
   2 vēnisset   4 vēnerat   44 _____

45   Marcus, _____ pūniēbātur, lacrimābat.

   1 quārum   3 quī
   2 cuius   4 quam   45 _____

46   Puellae currunt ut equōs _____.

   1 videant   3 vidēte
   2 vidēre   4 videntem   46 _____

47   Discipulī, _____librōs!

   1 legentis   3 lege
   2 lectī esse   4 legite   47 _____

48   Sī servī optimē cibum parārent, ā dominō _____.

   1 laudāvisse   3 laudātur
   2 laudārentur   4 laudārī   48 _____

49　Magna vīlla prope _____ erat.

　　1 montem　　　　　　3 monte
　　2 montī　　　　　　　4 mōns　　　　　　　　49 ____

50　Lūdī in circō _____ spectābantur.

　　1 magnus senātor
　　2 magnum senātōrem
　　3 ā magnīs senātōribus
　　4 magnōs senātōrēs　　　　　　　　　　50 ____

51　Adulēscentēs in forō _____ possunt.

　　1 ambulandum　　　　3 ambulāns
　　2 ambulāre　　　　　　4 ambulāte　　　　　51 ____

52　Nūntiō _____, dux erat laetissimus.

　　1 andīvērunt　　　　　3 audientem
　　2 audītō　　　　　　　4 audīre　　　　　　　52 ____

_____

PART IVB

Directions (53–62): This part contains a passage in English in which words associated by derivation with Latin words are shown to the right of the passage. Below the passage, there are several questions or incomplete statements. For *each,* select the alternative that best answers the question or completes the statement, and write its *number* in the space provided.　[10]

Events crowd in on our lives today, from all　　• events
over the world. Mostly they come in the form of
5- to 15-second sound-bites, devoid of analysis.
Their immediacy overshadows inquiry into the　　• inquiry
5　larger implications of events and concern for the
forces unfolding through time that make them

happen. What constitutes significant news gets
subtly reshaped in this process—toward the
meaningless, specific details of violence, and
10   away from the underlying, unifying complexi-
ties of these random acts, in order to get on with
the next sound-bite. We can all nominate our
favorite villains for the abyss into which the
consciousness of American history has fallen
15   —television, school textbooks, multiple-choice
tests, you name it. But the real trends are more
diffuse and harder to overcome. A sense of time
working its way gets lost beneath the increasing
immediacy and boundless entanglements of
20   modern life.

— *Smithsonian*

- significant
- process

- unifying
- acts
- nominate

- consciousness

- sense

- immediacy

53   The English word *events* (line 1) is associated by derivation with *ēveniō*, the Latin word that means

    1 make   3 come out
    2 calm down   4 finish   53 _____

54   The English word *inquiry* (line 4) is associated by
derivation with *quaerō*, the Latin word that means

    1 ask   3 read
    2 help   4 approach   54 _____

55   The English word *significant* (line 7) is associated
by derivation with the Latin words

    1 *simul* and *fidō*   3 *silentium* and *ferō*
    2 *silva* and *finiō*   4 *signum* and *faciō*   55 _____

56   The English word *process* (line 8) is associated by
derivation with *prōcēdō*, the Latin word that means

    1 see ahead   3 go forward
    2 fall behind   4 run through   56 _____

57 The English word *unifying* (line 10) is associated by derivation with the Latin word

    1 *ūnus*   3 *undique*
    2 *unda*   4 *ūtilis*   57 _____

58 The English word *acts* (line 11) is associated by derivation with *āctus*, the fourth principal part of the latin word

    1 *addūcō*   3 *accipiō*
    2 *abripiō*   4 *agō*   58 _____

59 Which Latin word, paired with its English meaning, is associated by derivation with the English word *nominate* (line 12)?

    1 *numerus* — number   3 *novem* — nine
    2 *nōmen* — name   4 *nātūra* — nature   59 _____

60 The English word *consciousness* (line 14) is associated by derivation with *sciō*, the Latin word that means

    1 know   3 trade
    2 allow   4 write   60 _____

61 Which Latin word, paired with its English meaning, is associated by derivation with the English word *sense* (line 17)?

    1 *sequor* — follow   3 *sentiō* — feel
    2 *sedeō* — sit   4 *servō* — save   61 _____

62 The English word *immediacy* (line 19) is associated by derivation with *medius*, the Latin word that means

    1 mind   3 memory
    2 middle   4 measure   62 _____

PART IVC

Directions (63–67): For *each* sentence below, write in the longer space provided, a Latin word with which the italicized word is associated by derivation. Any form of the appropriate Latin word, *except* prefixes and suffixes, will be acceptable. Then, write, in the shorter space provided, the *number* preceding the word or expression that best expresses the meaning of the italicized word.   [5]

63 The members of the committee were noted for their *amiability*.

   1 experience   3 impatience
   2 friendliness   4 sluggishness

63 _____   _____

64 In this area of the park you can expect to find *pedestrians*.

   1 flocks of birds   3 people who walk
   2 statues of heroes   4 children on bicycles

64 _____   _____

65 Many changes will occur in the next *millennium*.

   1 political campaign   3 labor contract
   2 experimental design 4 thousand years

65 _____   _____

66 The rainfall *accelerated* the plant's growth.

   1 stabilized   3 permitted
   2 hastened   4 slowed

66 _____   _____

67 The athlete was a *magnanimous* person.

    1 conceited   3 hostile

    2 big-hearted   4 soft-spoken

67 _____   _____

PART IVD

Directions (68–72): For *each* Latin abbreviation used in English, write in the space provided the *number* of the English translation, chosen from the list below, that most nearly has the same meaning.   [5]

Latin Abbreviation	English Translation	
68 *p.m.*	1 for example	68 _____
69 *stat.*	2 against	69 _____
70 *vs.*	3 immediately	70 _____
71 *e.g.*	4 afternoon	71 _____
72 *et al.*	5 the same	72 _____
	6 and others	
	7 note well	

PART V

Directions (73–102): Select *20* of the following statements or questions. In the space provided, write the *number* of the word or expression that best answers the question or completes the statement. [20]

History and Public Life

73 On the map below, numbers have been placed in certain geographic areas.

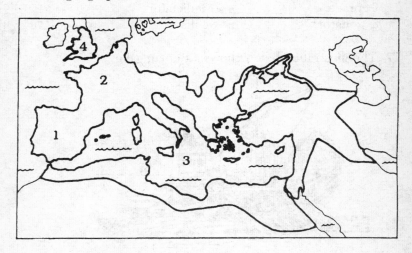

Which number represents what the Romans called *Mare Nostrum*?

(1) 1   (3) 3
(2) 2   (4) 4   73 _____

_____

74 Who was the founder and first king of Rome?

1 *Servius Tullius*   3 *Tarquinius Superbus*
2 *Numa Pompilius*   4 *Rōmulus*   74 _____

75 What is Caesar reported to have said when he crossed the Rubicon River?

  1 *"Carpe diem."*
  2 *"Ālea iacta est."*
  3 *"Errāre hūmānum est."*
  4 *"In hōc signō vincēs."*   75 ____

76 Cincinnatus was a farmer called from his plow to lead the Roman army and serve as a

  1 praetor   3 dictator
  2 senator   4 king   76 ____

77 The illustration below shows a Roman galley.

This Roman galley was called a
  1 *catapulta*   3 *vīlla*
  2 *gladius*   4 *trirēmis*   77 ____

78   The illustration below shows a *larārium* located in a Roman house.

What did the Romans customarily do at the *larārium*?
1 honored the gods
2 entertained their children
3 cooked dinner
4 kept their accounts   78 _____

79   The commercial and political center of ancient Rome was the

1 *Īnsula Tiberīna*   3 *Forum Rōmānum*
2 *Mōns Palātīnus*   4 *Campus Martius*   79 _____

80 Cicero was the first man in his family to attain the consulship. Therefore, he was known as

    1 *pater patriae*
    2 *amīcus populī Rōmānī*
    3 *magister equitum*
    4 *novus homō*　　　　　　　　　　　80 _____

81 The head of the Roman state religion was called the

    1 *quaestor*　　　　　3 *cēnsor*
    2 *pontifex maximus*　4 *lictor*　　　　　81 _____

82 Two well-known Romans had the same name. One is famous as Rome's first consul, while the other is infamous as one of Caesar's assassins. Their mutual name is

    1 Brutus　　　　　3 Seneca
    2 Scipio　　　　　4 Pliny　　　　　　82 _____

Daily Life

83 The illustration below shows a *quadrīga*, a four-horse chariot.

Where would this four-house chariot have competed?

1 *Basilica Aemilia*   3 *Cūria Hostīlia*
2 *Cloāca Maxima*   4 *Circus Maximus*   83 _____

84 In Roman times, October 31 would have been written

1 *Prīd. Id Oct.*   3 *Nōn. Oct.*
2 *a.d. VI Kal. Nov.*   4. *Prīd. Kal. Nov.*   84 _____

85 In a Roman home, the master's study was called the

1 *hypocaustum*   3 *taberna*
2 *tablīnum*   4 *palaestra*   85 _____

86 *Palla, stola,* and *petasus* refer to

1 weapons   3 articles of clothing
2 writing implements   4 children's toys   86 _____

87 Romans spend many hours at their baths. These baths were called

    1 *castra*   3 *loca*

    2 *thermae*   4 *portae*   87 _____

88 In the name *Marcus Tullius Cicerō*, *Tullius* is the

    1 *nōmen*   3 *praenōmen*

    2 *cognōmen*   4 *agnōmen*   88 _____

Myths and Legends

89 The illustration below shows the punishment of the reckless youth who drove the Sun chariot too close to Earth.

What was the name of the youth?

    1 Hercules   3 Midas

    2 Bellerophon   4 Phaëthon   89 _____

90 According to mythology, Medusa had the power to

   1 predict the future
   2 heal the sick
   3 turn those who looked upon her to stone
   4 give immortality to humans   90 _____

91 The bow and arrow are symbols for the Roman goddess of the hunt. Her name was

   1 Minerva   3 Diana
   2 Ceres   4 Juno   91 _____

92 The island on which the Minotaur lived was called

   1 Sardinia   3 Corsica
   2 Delos   4 Crete   92 _____

93 Which ancient story's theme is similar to that of William Shakespeare's *Romeo and Juliet*?

   1 Pyramus and Thisbe
   2 Dido and Aeneas
   3 Theseus and Ariadne
   4 Jason and Medea   93 _____

94 After many years, Ulysses returned to his faithful wife. Her name was

   1 Calypso   3 Penelope
   2 Circe   4 Proserpina   94 _____

95 The illustration below shows an eagle, a symbol of strength and power.

In mythology, which god was represented by the eagle?

1 Jupiter   3 Pluto
2 Neptune   4 Saturn   95 ____

Literature

96 Who is considered Rome's most famous orator and was also a master of prose?

1 Tibullus   3 Lucretius
2 Cicero   4 Tacitus   96 ____

97 Who was the great teacher of rhetoric on the island of Rhodes whose pupils were Caesar and Cicero?

1 Demosthenes   3 Titus Livius
2 Socrates   4 Apollonius Molo   97 ____

98 Which type of literature did Catullus, Horace, and Ovid write?

1 history   3 poetry
2 biography   4 comedy   98 ____

99 Which literary device is used in the expression *"nōn feram, nōn patiar, nōn sinam"*?

1 chiasmus   3 simile
2 anaphora   4 personification   99 ____

Architecture and Art

100 The picture below shows a woman looking at an artistic work.

Which form of art was used to create this work?

1 sculpture   3 printing
2 mosaic   4 frieze   100 ____

101 Which structures were forbidden within the city wall?

1 tombs   3 shops
2 homes   4 law courts   101 ____

102 A traveler in Britain can still see remains of the great wall built by the Roman Emperor

1 Trajan   3 Hadrian
2 Nero   4 Octavian   102 ____

Answers
June 1998

Comprehensive Examination in Latin

PART I

(Allow a total of 5 credits for this part.)

PART II

(Allow a total of 5 credits, one-half credit for each of the following 10 italicized words.)

Per *haec* tempora, Marcus Cicerō, quī *omnia* incrāmenta sua sibi dēbuit, vir novitātis nōbilissimae et ut *vītā* clārus, ita ingeniō *maximus*, quīque effēcit nē, *quōrum* arma vīcerāmus, eōrum ingeniō vincerēmur, cōnsul Catilinae et aliōrum virōrum, cōniūrātiōnem *singulārī* virtūte, cōnstantiā, vigiliā cūrāque aperuit. Catilīna *metū* cōnsulāris imperī urbe pulsus est; *aliī* virī nōminis clārī *auctōre* senātū, iussū *cōnsulis* in carcere necātī sunt.

PART IIIA

Allow a total of 10 credits, one credit for each of the following:

| (1) 2 | (3) 4 | (5) 3 | (7) 4 | (9) 1 |
| (2) 1 | (4) 1 | (6) 2 | (8) 3 | (10) 4 |

PART IIIB

The answers to the questions in this part do not have to be complete sentences. A phrase or word may be sufficient for a completely correct one-credit response. Disregard errors in English. Allow no partial credit. Not all of the acceptable answers have been included.

Allow a total of 10 credits, one credit for each of the following:

(11) author, writer

(12) three

(13) nine

(14) It is noisy.

(15–16) (friendly) people, (a good) place, (suitable) time, (sumptuous, expensive, delicious) food

(17) light, not serious, not weighty, not political, not about matters in the forum, not about business

(18) friendly, friendliness, hospitable, hospitality

(19) They stimulate the mind.

(20) dessert, fruit, sweets, second table

PART IIIC

Allow a total of 10 credits, one credit for each of the following:

(21) 2	(26) 2
(22) 3	(27) 1
(23) 3	(28) 3
(24) 4	(29) 2
(25) 1	(30) 4

PART IIID

Allow a total of 10 credits, one credit for each of 10 of the following:

(31) 4	(35) 2	(39) 2
(32) 1	(36) 3	(40) 1
(33) 2	(37) 1	(41) 4
(34) 1	(38) 3	(42) 4

PART IVA

Allow a total of 10 credits, one credit for each of the following:

(43) 4	(48) 2
(44) 3	(49) 1
(45) 3	(50) 3
(46) 1	(51) 2
(47) 4	(52) 2

PART IVB

Allow a total of 10 credits, one credit for each of the following:

(53) 3	(58) 4
(54) 1	(59) 2
(55) 4	(60) 1
(56) 3	(61) 3
(57) 1	(62) 2

PART IVC

(Allow credit for any correctly spelled form of the Latin word. Allow no credit for prefixes or suffixes. Not all of the acceptable answers have been included

Allow a total of 5 credits, one-half credit for each correct answer in column:

Column I	Column II
(63) amō, amīcus, amīcitia, amor	(63) 2
(64) pēs, pedes, pedester	(64) 3
(65) mīlle, mīlia, annus	(65) 4
(66) celer, celeriter, celeritās, celerō	(66) 2
(67) magnus, magnitūdo, animus, anima	(67) 2

PART IVD

Allow a total of 5 credits, one credit for each of the following:

(68) 4   (69) 3   (70) 2   (71) 1   (72) 6

PART V

Allow a total of 20 credits, one credit for each of 20 of the following:

(73) 3	(78) 1	(83) 4	(88) 1	(93) 1	(98) 3
(74) 4	(79) 3	(84) 4	(89) 4	(94) 3	(99) 2
(75) 2	(80) 4	(85) 2	(90) 3	(95) 1	(100) 2
(76) 3	(81) 2	(86) 3	(91) 3	(96) 2	(101) 1
(77) 4	(82) 1	(87) 2	(92) 4	(97) 4	(102) 3